THE SAVAGE AND MODERN SELF

ROBBIE RICHARDSON

The Savage and Modern Self

North American Indians in Eighteenth-Century British Literature and Culture

UNIVERSITY OF TORONTO PRESS
Toronto Buffalo London

© University of Toronto Press 2018
Toronto Buffalo London
utorontopress.com
Printed in the U.S.A.

ISBN 978-1-4875-0344-4 (cloth)

Library and Archives Canada Cataloguing in Publication

Richardson, Robbie, 1979–, author
The savage and modern self : North American Indians in eighteenth-century British literature and culture / Robbie Richardson.

Includes bibliographical references and index.
ISBN 978-1-4875-0344-4 (hardcover)

1. Indians in literature.   2. English literature – 18th century – History and criticism.   3. National characteristics, British, in literature.   I. Title.

PR448.I536R53 2018   820.9'35299709033   C2017-907895-X

This book has been published with the help of a grant from the Federation for the Humanities and Social Sciences, through the Awards to Scholarly Publications Program, using funds provided by the Social Sciences and Humanities Research Council of Canada.

University of Toronto Press acknowledges the financial assistance to its publishing program of the Canada Council for the Arts and the Ontario Arts Council, an agency of the Government of Ontario.

Canada Council **Conseil des Arts**
for the Arts **du Canada**

ONTARIO ARTS COUNCIL
CONSEIL DES ARTS DE L'ONTARIO
an Ontario government agency
un organisme du gouvernement de l'Ontario

Funded by the   Financé par le
Government   gouvernement
of Canada   du Canada

Canadä

Contents

Illustrations

Acknowledgments

Writing this book has been a long process, and I have many people and organizations to thank for helping me. My PhD supervisor Peter Walmsley provided generous guidance for my academic work, but also, perhaps more importantly, has given me a model for the kind of academic I will continually strive to be. My committee at McMaster University, Daniel Coleman and Eugenia Zuroski, were excellent readers and influential scholars for my work, and my external examiner, Laura Stevens, helped give shape to the project going forward to book form. Ruth Phillips is a scholarly hero who supervised my postdoctoral fellowship and ushered me into the world of material culture studies. The anonymous peer reviewers all gave excellent direction, as did Cheryl Suzack for the manuscript review committee, and the book would not exist in this form were it not for their feedback. My editor Richard Ratzlaff at University of Toronto Press has been very supportive and patient in seeing this project to completion.

I am very lucky to work with wonderful colleagues at the University of Kent. Declan Kavanagh is a brilliant friend and ASECS partner in crime, Jennie Batchelor and Donna Landry are excellent mentors and academic role models, and David Herd has been an awe-inspiring and supportive Head of School. My former colleague Paddy Bullard helped introduce me to the British academic world, for which I am grateful. Many others continue to inspire me with their brilliant work and hospitality. I am also extremely grateful to the students at Kent, whose intellectual curiosity and positivity make them a privilege to teach.

I am thankful to staff at the British Library, the John Carter Brown Library, the Lewis Walpole Library and Yale Centre for British Art, Rare Books at McMaster University, the British Museum, National Portrait

Gallery, Smithsonian Institution, the Wellcome Library, Derby Museum and Art Gallery, and The National Museums, Liverpool, for the images. I received financial support from the North Shore Micmac District Council, Indspire (formerly the National Aboriginal Achievement Foundation), and the Social Sciences and Humanities Research Council of Canada while writing this book, both during my PhD at McMaster and as a postdoctoral fellow at the Institute for Comparative Studies in Literature, Art and Culture at Carleton University. I could not have pursued this work without their assistance.

Chapter 3 appeared in an earlier form as "The Site of the Struggle: Colonialism, Violence, and the Captive Body" in *Native Americans and Anglo-American Culture, 1750-1850: The Indian Atlantic*, edited by Tim Fulford and Kevin Hutchings and published by Cambridge University Press, and chapter 4 was also published in a different form as "Consuming Indians: *Tsonnonthouan*, Colonialism, and the Commodification of Culture" in *Eighteenth-Century Fiction*.

I could have hardly imagined when I began studying Native people in eighteenth-century British literature that I myself, a Mi'kmaq from Canada, would wind up living in Britain. My own transatlantic movement occurred during the writing of this book, and I am grateful to friends on both sides of the ocean. My mother Wendy Richardson and her partner Jim Ball, and my siblings Scott Patles-Richardson and Deborah Richardson and their families, are always a source of love and encouragement. My father James Richardson has given me his restless and adventurous spirit. Mark Coté and Jennifer Pybus, as well as Sabina and Nico, have provided grounding and continuity in the move across the world. My cat Mary, a stray from the streets of Winnipeg, joined me here and ended her days in London, and she is dearly missed. The Walker family have welcomed me to this country and taught me the exotic ways of Yorkshire. I would not have been able to complete this work without the love and support of Francesca Walker, who has been my companion and partner in exploring crumbling cemeteries, derelict castles, and haunted country piles. Finally, this book is dedicated to my grandparents Walter and Audrey Becker and to the late George and Marie Richardson, all anchors to vast and unwieldy generations. Wela'lin.

THE SAVAGE AND MODERN SELF

Introduction

This book examines representations of North American "Indians" in eighteenth-century British literature and draws attention to their use by writers of the period to negotiate elements of early modernity and shape new formations of subjectivity. As a literary figure that both affirmed imperial fantasies of benevolent conquest through transcultural brotherhood or willing conversion to Christianity, and disrupted that vision with signs of brutal violence or natural moral superiority, the Indian was distinctly multivalent. This literary study argues that the unique depiction of the Indian as a non-European subject of both affinity and disavowal, across a variety of genres and cultural expressions, critiqued and helped articulate evolving practices and ideas such as consumerism, colonialism, "Britishness," and, ultimately, the "modern self" over the course of the century. While Indians were often viewed in Enlightenment stadial history as existing in a "savage state," lacking the comforts of civilization, this study argues that the hybrid Indian-Briton who emerges in the cultural imagination at the end of the eighteenth century in works such as Robert Bage's *Hermsprong; or, Man as He is Not* (1796), whose new identity is defined by an appropriation of the Indian, exemplifies modern British subjectivity.[1] The modern, in other words, does not set itself against the "savage" North American in the imaginative works which this study covers, but instead finds definition in imagined scenes of cultural contact.

There are countless studies that look to the construction of the "white man's Indian" in Western culture, particularly in the North American context,[2] and yet eighteenth-century British literature is largely overlooked for its depictions of Indians.[3] Representations in the period exist somewhere between European epistemologies and epochs, outside of the wonder of early modern first contact and the cultural origins of the colonial American nation and subject.[4] Previous scholars have often dismissed "Indians' cameo appearances in literature" during the century as relatively sparse, "nondescript ... [and] of limited significance," or "at most subordinate to the main currents of eighteenth-century thought," but this book places these representations alongside important articulations of identity and cultural critique.[5] At the same time, for the most part I avoid discussions of the emergence of colonial North American national cultures, and of texts that were printed exclusively outside of Britain. While the field of Early American literature has in recent years become invaluable for its integration of Indigenous voices into its canon and increasingly global outlook, my work attempts to conceive of the Indian outside of the paradigm of North American settler states.[6] Thus the early Puritan captivity narratives, which have been long read as originary moments in American literary history, but whose appearance and impact in Britain is limited, do not receive the attention one would perhaps expect in looking at representations of Indians in the period.[7] Transatlantic influence undeniably shaped British texts, and this is a fundamental aspect of this study's methodology and understanding of eighteenth-century culture, but its focus is on the effects within Britain rather than on emerging colonial narratives of self-definition.

In many studies that look at representations of Indians, both negative and positive depictions are seen to reinforce white cultural dominance.[8] For Anishinaabe writer Gerald Vizenor, the Indian, or *indian* as he would later write, is a mark of the absence of Native people, part of a narrative generated by colonial discourse offering "consolations in the dominant culture." As he points out,

> The word Indian ... is a colonial enactment, not a loan word, and the dominance is sustained by the simulation that has superseded the real tribal names. The Indian was an occidental invention that became a bankable simulation; the word has no referent in tribal languages or cultures.[9]

The Indian is a fiction with a powerful hold on both white and Native people still, and for Vizenor it always represents a sense of European cultural superiority. I believe, however, it is important to trace various permutations of this fiction in the eighteenth century as a way of understanding not only the nature of the consolations this discursive construction provided to British culture, but also the ways in which it was deployed to disrupt British culture or otherwise critique it. This construction is at times informed by actual encounters with Indigenous people, mediated through the accounts of explorers, traders, missionaries, and others, and in some cases is reflective of some Native cultural values and experiences.[10] However, my purpose here is not to either prove or disprove British understandings; rather, it is to examine the function of this discourse in eighteenth-century British culture and society. At the heart of this work is the attempt to understand the relationship between the shifting attitudes in Britain to Indians over the course of the century and the concurrent transformation of aspects of modernity.

I focus particularly on the time period between the Acts of Union of 1707 and the years after the American Revolutionary War and during the French Revolution, up to the 1790s. These bookends mark the beginning of a "British" identity through the merging of Scotland with England and Wales into Great Britain, and the troubling threat to its existence posed by a transatlantic civil war and radical French ideas. In works such as Alexander Pope's "Windsor-Forest" (1713) and *The Spectator* no. 50 (1711), Indians are used to imaginatively validate a new British identity and empire following the Acts of Union and the Treaty of Utrecht, while in the later period, writers depicted the Indian as a masculine subject capable of reconciling sentiment and fortitude in British men, as in Henry Mackenzie's *Man of the World* (1773). In between, representations of Indians would draw attention to the violence at the heart of colonialism, no matter how benevolent in intent, point out the dangers in consumerism and commodified culture, and influence the shape of personal identity in imagined scenes of transculturation. I examine plays, poetry, novels, captivity narratives, and periodicals, as well as visual and material culture, all of which primarily, often exclusively, appeared in Britain. These texts were selected because they depict sites of encounter between Indians and Europeans, and it is in these "contact zones" where new cultural forms and contexts are generated.[11] This broad selection over genres and media is intended to show the consistent position of the Indian as a cultural force across a variety of representations, though the novel would come to be more dominant beginning in the 1750s as both a market commodity and a vehicle for exploring subjectivity.

The concept of "modernity" which I utilize throughout this book is not meant to evoke a uniform and inevitable shift to an easily defined historical period, but does follow many other scholars in drawing attention to cultural and political changes in the century which broadly produced the sense of "newness" that exemplifies what Fredric Jameson describes as the "modern feeling."[12] These include the beginnings of the nation-state and national identity, the expansion of empire as both a geographic area and mental exercise, interest in fashion and taste, the rise of print culture and industry, an overall economic shift to banking, credit, and debt, and the commodification of cultural production. But perhaps more importantly, modernity as understood and deployed in this book is not the grand "objective" forces of technological advancement "whose 'origins' and characteristics can be identified with certainty," but rather, as Kathleen Wilson suggests in an echo of Foucault, is "a set of relations that are constantly being made and unmade, contested and reconfigured, that nonetheless produces among its contemporaneous witnesses the conviction of historical *difference*."[13] And fundamental to this sense of difference is of course feelings of optimism, fear, and ambivalence. The modernity of the eighteenth century was by no means a cause for universal celebration, and writers used Indians to navigate their responses.[14]

The methodology of this work is informed by Foucault's genealogy, operating "on a field of entangled and confused parchments, on documents that have been scratched over and recopied many times."[15] It does not pretend, of course, to have the breadth of a complete genealogy of the Indian in the eighteenth century, but it does draw on a variety of genres and texts written from the beginning to the end of the century. And like Foucault, this book seeks to "identify the accidents, the minute deviations – or conversely, the complete reversals – the errors, the false appraisals, and the faulty calculations that give birth to those things that continue to exist and have value for us; it is to discover that truth or being does not lie at the root of what we know and what we are, but [in] the exteriority of accidents."[16] The purpose of genealogy "is not to discover the roots of our identity, but to commit itself to its dissipation."[17] The discursive construction of the Indian is complex and connected to the emergence of new cultural practices in Britain, and from an Indigenous perspective, it is important to see the relation between the Indian as a productive field of negotiation for European writing and the simultaneous ejection of Native people from modernity. Postcolonial theorists have been working for some time on the task of deconstructing the hegemonic European subject who dominated the nineteenth and twentieth century, uncovering the ways in which Western modernity was shaped and challenged by those who were oppressed by it. Yet much of this scholarship, as Cherokee scholar Jace Weaver notes, is "oddly detached when discussing indigenous peoples and their lives."[18] For Native scholars, the "post-" in "postcolonial," as Chickasaw scholar Jodi A. Byrd suggests, "represents a condition of futurity that has not yet been achieved" by Native people in North America.[19] In my work I draw from both postcolonial and Indigenous-centred perspectives to work on decentring the hegemony of Western modernity.[20] Indians were ostensibly peripheral to the rise of British global cultural and economic domination, but as I show in this book, imaginative and real encounters with Native people were crucial to European self-imagining in the eighteenth century.

This book is additionally informed by recent work that looks at the transatlantic nature of eighteenth-century culture, and the interconnectedness of the people who comprised the Atlantic world. This field of study, as Laura Stevens notes, has enabled a shift in scholarship "from paradigms of isolated development to models of interrelatedness and multidirectional flow."[21] Native people were an integral part of transatlantic culture, as Weaver draws attention to in his formulation of the "Red Atlantic," and this work also hopes to show the centrality of "Native resources, ideas, and peoples themselves" to "Atlantic cultural exchange."[22] Yet this book differs from many transatlantic histories in that it is focused on the British reception and discursive construction of the Indian, and on the influence of Atlantic cultures solely in the United Kingdom. In this sense, it can be classified as what historian David Armitage calls "cis-Atlantic," which "studies particular places as unique locations within an Atlantic world and seeks to define that uniqueness as the result of the interaction between local particularity and a wider web of connections."[23] Even though many, if not most, of the authors in this study never crossed the Atlantic or met an Indian in person, they nonetheless were influenced by and participated in this broader cultural formation.

The chapters that follow are organized chronologically, which has served as a basic organizing principle in attempting to tackle such a generically diffuse body of texts. This also allows, however, for a developmental look at British depictions of Indians across the century and the changing shape of these representations as more information about Native North American people became available. The exception to this chronology is the final chapter on material culture, which looks to British collections of Indigenous objects across the whole period.

The first chapter, "Indians and the Construction of Britishness in the Early Eighteenth Century," explores the evolving trope of the Indian from one of generalized exoticism, as in John Dryden's plays and poetry, to the more specific construction it would become beginning in works such as John Dennis's play *Liberty Asserted* (1704). While earlier depictions tended to confuse or conflate the people of India with those from America (which still occasionally happened later in the century), the image of North American Indians became more solidified in the first decade of the century and increasingly became a site of identification. Moreover, and more importantly, the trope of the Indian was indispensable to the notion of the liberty of the British subject following the Glorious Revolution of 1688 and validated the self-imagining of predominantly Whiggish Britons as cosmopolitan and benevolent imperial masters in the scramble for world supremacy. The 1710 visit by the "Four Indian Kings," representatives of the Iroquois, was a culturally significant event that led to a body of art and literature that reflected on the meaning of Britishness following the Acts of Union of 1707, most famously in the form of a satirical letter in the *Spectator*. At the same time, the story of Inkle and Yarico, about an English trader betraying an innocent Indian maiden for profit, tempered this optimism with sentiment and was a reminder of the danger of merchant greed. In other words, from very early on the Indian became a kind of other-self, both mirror and projection, and also an enabling trope for the imagination of Britain as a benevolent force in the European scramble for world supremacy. As I will show in this book, that the Indian is connected to the most current developments in the British cultural imagination, rather than represents a retreat to the primitive past, often speaks to the potentials and perils of modernity.

Chapter 2, "The Indian as Cultural Critic: Shaping the British Self," first discusses examples of Indian characters in literary texts providing critiques of British culture and identity, and second examines British characters who "go native" in some form but whose transformation is unsuccessful. I argue that Indians critique a form of identity described by Dror Wahrman as the *ancien régime*, typified by fluid boundaries of subject categories, and present a kind of subjectivity that would later characterize the "modern self." The first section looks at the popular imposter narrative *An apology for the life of Bampfylde-Moore Carew* (1749), a periodical essay from 1742 that re-imagines Joseph Addison's letter from the Indian king in the *Spectator*, and John Cleland's play *Tombo-Chiqui, or, the American Savage* (1758), suggesting that in each case the Indian presents specific criticisms of British culture that provide alternative forms of political structure or individual conduct. Part two examines the captivity narrative and portrait of Peter Williamson, whose dubious claims to have been captured by Indians brought him fame upon his return to Scotland; Sir William Johnson, who married the Mohawk woman Molly Brant and was satirized in Charles Johnstone's novel *Chrysal; or, The Adventures of a Guinea* (1760); and the damaged soldier Lieutenant Obadiah Lismahago in Tobias Smollett's *The Expedition of Humphry Clinker* (1771). While they are unsuccessful or mocked in their transcultural forays, which somewhat contradicts the notion of the *ancien régime* as a period of fluid subjectivity and identity play, these men demonstrate the unique status of the Indian as both other and potential self in the eighteenth century.

The third chapter, "Captivity Narratives and Colonialism," looks at texts written by British soldiers and colonists who claimed to have been captured by Indians during the Seven Years' War and explores their representations and disavowals of transculturation. While these narratives have long been dismissed as propaganda against Indians and the French or as brutal spectacles of violence, this chapter argues that their failed efforts to assert cultural difference ultimately produce abject British subjects. The violence depicted in these texts, usually described in gruesome detail, creates an image of the Indian as a merciless savage incapable of kindness, while the suffering captive offers a site of sympathetic identification for the reader attuned to sentimental literature. However, the captives are implicated in their own miseries by their participation in both the colonial apparatus and in Indian culture, and are ultimately rejected by and alienated from metropolitan culture at the end of their ordeals. These narratives lack the religious frameworks of redemption found in the earlier Puritan captivity narratives, and for readers to identify with the captives they must at the same time reflect on the consequences and costs of empire. Thus the stereotype of the "ignoble savage," at times more beast than human, in these texts serves to undercut colonial discourse and not simply denigrate Native people.

The next chapter, "Novel Indians: *Tsonnonthouan* and the Commodification of Culture," primarily uses the anonymous novel *Memoirs of the Life and Adventures of Tsonnonthouan* (1763) to examine mid-century anxieties over the commodification of culture, or the conflation between commerce and writing, and the effects of colonialism and capitalism on the British subject. Moreover, this novel speaks to the fear among

Britons that their efforts at civilizing the Indians were actually producing the opposite effect. The Indian is subject to the degenerative forces of British culture, but at the same time is in this novel and other texts a surrogate for the Briton facing new, unique developments in culture and individual experience. Just as the Indian must negotiate the potentially destructive effects of colonialism, the Briton is also threatened by the crassness of fashion, consumerism, and an expanding overseas empire.

Chapter 5, "Becoming Indians: Sentiment and the Hybrid British Subject," examines the appropriation of Indian subjectivities in British texts around the period of the American Revolutionary War. This is a paradoxical development, given that the British press almost uniformly loathed Indians at the time, and identity categories were distinctly hardened as compared to just a few years earlier,[24] but this chapter argues that writers used the Indian in part as a site for the imaginative reunification of the fractured transatlantic British subject in the wake of Britain's loss of the American colonies, as a means for redefining the bounds of family and kinship, and as a corrective to the emotional excesses of sentimental masculinity. It looks at novels such as Bage's *Hermsprong* (1796), the anonymous *The Female American* (1767), Mackenzie's *The Man of the World* (1773), John O'Keeffe's play *The Basket-Maker* (1789–90), and various iterations of William Richardson's short story "The Indians, A Tale" (1774), and examines their uses of the hybrid Indian-Briton. The appropriation of Indigenous culture is well documented in the American and Canadian context, and can be understood largely as a kind of indigenization of the colonial subject to grant settler populations ownership and mastery over the land they have occupied.[25] This same phenomenon in British texts has a different cultural and ideological function, and is used by writers to present a reformed and modern version of subjectivity.

The final chapter, "Native North American Material Culture in the British Imaginary," looks at the ways in which Indigenous material culture shaped literary representations of Indians, and argues that these objects, like the literary Indian, were also sites of disavowal and appropriation. This chapter presents a parallel narrative to the representation of Indians in literary texts by examining the relationship between British people in the eighteenth century and the North American cultural objects that they privately collected or viewed in museums, cabinets of curiosities, coffeehouses, and other venues. More specifically, it looks at the body of Native material culture that arrived in large amounts throughout the century and the ways in which these materials shaped British perceptions of Native people and their own sense of identity. From the British Museum to coffeehouses to private auctions, there were numerous sites where Britons encountered Indigenous objects, and there has been little scholarship on the ways in which this material, imbued with Native skill, knowledge, and memory, was perceived by British people and interacted with other forms of representation in print and visual culture. These objects allowed for an aesthetic and sensory experience whose materiality gave a greater immediacy and personal connection to both other cultures and the colonial project. Objects such as wampum, calumets, and tomahawks were regularly written into fictional texts and came to be recognized by their physical appearance and symbolic functions; furthermore, they became metonymic for Indians, whose perceived fetishistic relationship to their own material culture both reflected on and critiqued the emerging British consumer culture. Many of the objects brought to Britain as examples of the brutality of "savage" warfare, particularly tomahawks and scalping knives, were in fact manufactured in Sheffield and Birmingham. Texts from the period are strangely silent about this phenomenon, which is a reminder of how cultural objects in collections, as Susan Stewart suggests, "are naturalized by the erasure of labor and the erasure of context of production."[26] Yet these British-made curiosities and savage weapons are perhaps the finest evidence of the interconnectedness of the British self and the construction of the Indian.

The writing of the "savage self" is not uniform or universal, but represents one of the strands of eighteenth-century thought connected to the broader pre-history of British global domination. There continued to be throughout the century a divided view of Indians, but this does not disprove the significance Indians played in subject formation; indeed, it shows the difficulty Britons faced when encountering alterity and seeing within it a disturbing and compelling sameness, a reflection of their failures and fantasies. Laura Brown notes that there is "an irony characteristic of the implication of modernity with alterity."[27] She explains that in what she describes as "the fable of the 'native prince'," in which the supposed royalty from "primitive" populations visited the metropolis in fact and fiction, cultural difference is ignored in favour of "a sentimental identification between the native and the European."[28] This is, according to Brown, an irony characteristic of modernity itself because of "its yoking of exploitation and liberation, brutality and progress, fears and hopes."[29] By viewing the relationship between modernity and otherness as one of both appropriation and disavowal, we can see the significance of the figure of the Indian as an enabling discourse, beyond the scattered visits by "Indian princes" throughout the century. Indeed, the Indian, a nightmarish savage and a pitied friend, embodies the yoking of polarities more than any other cultural group in the British imagination during the period.

1 Indians and the Construction of Britishness in the Early Eighteenth Century

I have, since [the Indian kings'] departure, employed a friend to make many enquiries of their landlord the upholsterer, relating to their manners and conversation, as also concerning the remarks which they made in this country: for, next to the forming a right notion of such strangers, I should be desirous of learning what ideas they have conceived of us.

– Joseph Addison, *The Spectator* no. 50 (1711)

The arrival of three Mohawks and one Mahican man representing the Iroquois confederacy in Britain in 1710 was, for many British people, a key sign of the expanding global importance of their ambitious nation. Indians had been in England before, but never had there been such widespread visual and textual commemoration as on these visits.[1] Queen Anne commissioned official portraits, and numerous texts described the history of the people from whom these emissaries were sent, the goals of their mission, and their activities while in England. In his satirical letter from *Spectator* no. 50, Joseph Addison imagines the reactions of one of these "Indian kings" to life in London. As Addison explains in the epigraph above, the desire for such a letter is not only to understand the exotic visitor and his people by witnessing his interior life, but also to offer a new perspective on British culture that only the Indian can provide. The perceived lack of social graces and guile of the "king" is set off against the artifice of a new sense of "British" identity following the Acts of Union of 1707. This example of cultural curiosity and a desire to inhabit the gaze of another subjectivity suggests that representations of Indians in eighteenth-century texts are never far from articulations of emerging modernity. This chapter will trace the beginnings of these representations in the preceding centuries, tied to the modernizing forces of exploration and trade, and look to the more singular signification of the Indian, as compared to other non-European people, which would begin to take shape. The Indian emerges from a number of fundamental questions around Britain's place in the world as a powerful yet benevolent force and the individual Briton's identity in the face of expansionism and a cosmopolitan public sphere. These representations not only reflected such concerns during and following the "opening of modernity" from 1688 to 1707 but also shaped them.[2] Indeed, the very discourses and self-imaginings partly enabled by Indians in this period, of gentle conquest and financial reward, would come to be unraveled by less noble savages later in the century.

"The Indians of our age": Native Peoples in Britain to the Time of Dryden

Representations of Native people in England began in the early stages of the European colonization of the Americas in the sixteenth and seventeenth centuries, and travel collections such as Richard Hakluyt's *Principal Navigations, Voyages, and Discoveries of the English Nation* (1589), in addition to earlier translations of Spanish accounts, were read with great interest and influenced the literature of the period, including, most famously perhaps, Shakespeare's *The Tempest* (1610). The travels of Martin Frobisher, Francis Drake, and Walter Raleigh, which were featured in Hakluyt and printed in their own editions, also provided information on the peoples of the Americas. Encounters from this period, though diverse and provisional in many ways, frequently involve trade and episodes of brutal violence and cruelty.[3] In some cases, as when John Davis had his four-piece orchestral ensemble play for Inuit people in canoes, who banged their drums while he and his crew were employed in "making signes of joy, and dauncing," the encounters possess a sense of the wondrous and new.[4] Some of the manners and customs writing prior to the Restoration, such as Thomas Hariot's beautifully illustrated *A briefe and true report of the new found land of Virginia* (1590), provided a template for the later rise in comparative ethnography.[5] Outside of ethnographic and voyage literature, however, there was little textual representation of Native peoples with any degree of specificity.[6] Instead, North American Indians in English drama, poetry, and prose were often grouped with the peoples of India, Africa, and other locales under a general rubric of exoticism.[7] Thus in William D'Avenant's court

XVIII.

Theirdanſes vvhich they vſeatt their hyghe feaſtes.

AT a Certayne tyme of the yere they make a great, and ſolemne feaſte whe runto their neighbours of the townes adioninge re-payre from all parts, euery man attyred in the moſt ſtrange faſhion they can deuiſe hauinge certayne marks on the backs to declare of what place they bee. The place where they meet is a broade playne, about the which are planted in the grownde certayne poſts carued with heads like to the faces of Nonnes couered with theyr vayles. Then beeing ſett in order they dance, ſinge, and vſe the ſtrangeſt ge-ſtures that they can poſſiblye deuiſe. Three of the fayreſt Virgins, of the companie are in the myddſt, which imbraſſinge one ano-ther doe as yt wear turne abowt in their dancinge. All this is donne after the ſunne is ſett for auoydinge of heate. When they are weerye of dancinge. they goe oute of the circle, and come in vntill their dances be ended, and they goe to make merrye as is expreſſed in the 16. figure.

Figure 1.1 From Thomas Hariot, A briefe and true report of the new found land of Virginia. Engraving by Theodor de Bry after John White, 1590. British Library. Used with permission.

masque *The Temple of Love* (1635), the wonders of the "Eastern world" are represented in part by "a naked Indian on a whitish elephant," who is wearing the "tire and bases of several-coloured feathers, represent-ing the Indian monarchy."[8] While the elephant is evocative of both the East and Africa, the feather-clad, naked "Indian" indicates a confla-tion of potential colonial subjects. This metaphoric understanding of non-European people in part demonstrates the characteristics of early modern, pre-Enlightenment epistemologies, but is also indicative of the as-yet unrealized fantasies of empire among the British court.[9]

By the mid-seventeenth century, there were still relatively few rep-resentations of Indians in fictional literature. In some appearances, they became idealized people representing man before the Fall; Mil-ton writes in *Paradise Lost* (1667) that the "first naked Glorie" of Adam and Eve was like "of late / *Columbus* found th' *American* so girt / with featherd Cincture, naked else and wilde / Among the Trees and Iles and woodie Shores" (IX.1115–18). The Indian was innocent and free, a figure that, for Milton and later John Locke, represented the pre-societal state of humanity.[10] By far the majority of Indians' appearances in print, however, came through a large body of missionary texts, beginning roughly in the 1640s, calling for the conversion of the "heathens," also often called the "poor Indians," to Christianity.[11] Thus, while some of the English admired the unclothed innocence of the Indians, they were alarmed at their religion, which many Britons perceived as literal devil-worship. Embedded within this literature of proselytization was a sense of pity for Indians who had been brutalized by the Spanish conquest, which was widely known in Britain thanks to English translations of sixteenth-century Spanish priest Bartolomé de las Casas's writing in *The Spanish Colonie* (1583) and *The Tears of the Indians* (1656).[12] This sense of pity would prove significant in forming the ideological apparatus of British colonialism and in rallying those missionaries and colonists working for the widespread conversion of the Indians.[13]

It is during this period that the phrase "noble savage," often associated with the French and, more specifically, Jean-Jacques Rousseau's *Discourse on the Origin of Inequality Among Men* (1754),[14] was first used in a British text. In John Dryden's *The Conquest of Granada* (1672), the defiant hero Almanzar, raised by Moors but of Spanish royal descent, proclaims, "I am as free as Nature first made man / 'Ere the base Laws of servitude began / When wild in woods the noble Savage ran."[15] The noble savage is, in the phrase's first usage, one who bears no allegiance to any sovereign and is isolated; as Almanzar states in the same passage, "I alone am king of me." Yet it is also a universalized state, not necessarily particular to any national or ethnic group. The phrase itself would not acquire any further purchase during the eighteenth century, but the concept that it is now understood to evoke appeared frequently.

In several of his works, Dryden more specifically depicted Indians from North and South America in ways that would anticipate the dominant tropes of the eighteenth century. "Religio Laici" (1682) recites the argument of the Deists on universal salvation:

'Tis said the sound of a Messiah's Birth
Is gone through all the habitable earth:
But still that text must be confin'd alone
To what was then inhabited, and known:
And what Provision could from thence accrue
To Indian souls, and worlds discover'd new?[16]

To this argument, which is convincing enough to "startle reason [and] stagger frail belief," Dryden responds with the claim that "boundless wisdom, boundless mercy, may / Find ev'n for those bewilder'd souls, a way."[17] In other words, even the unsaved Indian souls will find their way to heaven thanks to a merciful God. As Stevens suggests, Dryden's response to the Deists was "insufficient" because "[t]o believe that heathens could be saved implied that they were better off than Christians."[18] Yet it points to the ways in which the figure of the Indian was used by multiple religious denominations in England to critique the shortcomings of other sects, and Dryden is responding to the frequent Deist use of Indians as evidence of the innateness of human morality, without revealed religion.[19] Indeed, Indians served a profound theological problem for orthodox Protestants, as the pre-Catholic Dryden indicates, since only a cruel God would punish souls who were merely ignorant, and had not willfully rejected the Gospel. The figure of the Indian continued to fuel the arguments of more radical groups such as the Deists and the Quakers throughout the eighteenth century, since the unimpeachable virtue of these uninformed souls was for them a proof of the "inner light" of all God's creation.[20] Dryden and others tried, perhaps unsuccessfully, to negotiate between this view and the conservative theology they wished to defend.

In addition to his evocation of the theological dilemma posed by Indians to Anglican orthodoxy, Dryden set two of his major plays in the New World: *The Indian Queen* (1664), co-authored with his brother-in-law Sir Robert Howard, and its sequel, *The Indian Emperor, or the Conquest of Mexico by the Spaniards* (1665). Exotic settings were a common feature of Restoration drama but, in these works, the more recent Spanish colonization of the New World is evoked both implicitly and explicitly as a means of imagining Britain's own fantasies of global conquest. Though it is set in Mexico before the arrival of the Spanish, *The Indian Queen* is framed by European conquest; in the prologue, an Indian girl and boy are awakened by the presence of foreign invaders. At first the boy laments, "our soft rest must cease, / And fly together with our country's peace! / No more must we sleep under plantain shade, / Which neither heat could pierce, nor cold invade" (ll. 1–4). Upon inspecting these new arrivals, however, the girl, Quevira, proclaims, "If these be they, we welcome then our doom! / Their looks are such, that mercy flows from thence, / More gentle than our native innocence" (ll. 13–16). She puts herself at their mercy, declaring to her friend and to the invading audience, "By their protection, let us beg to live; / They came not here to conquer, but forgive.– / If so, your goodness may your power express, / And we shall judge both best by our success" (ll. 19–22). The Aztec children are ostensibly welcoming the invading Incas, but their language turns the scene into a dramatization of first contact with the English theatregoers. By constructing the play itself as a moment of colonial encounter, Dryden invites the audience to imagine themselves as benevolent masters, morally superior to the Spanish conquistadors in their goal of salvation rather than material gain. The epilogue continues with this analogy, with Montezuma wryly addressing the audience:

You have seen all that this old world can do,
We, therefore, try the fortune of the new,
And hope it is below your aim to hit
At untaught nature with your practised wit:
Our naked Indians, then, when wits appear,
Would as soon chuse to have the Spaniards here.   (ll. 5–10)

He adds that, considering the cost of the production, it would be "a true voyage to the Indies lost" if the audience and critics dislike the performance. Though it is obviously with tongue in cheek, the analogy of the contact zone places the people in the theatre in a dominant position over the production of the "new world," and suggests that both venues require English sensitivity and compassion to 'profit' from the experience.

In *The Indian Emperor*, Dryden more explicitly deploys colonial tropes. Picking up twenty years after the ending of *The Indian Queen*, its sequel depicts the destruction of Mexico at the hands of Cortez. The prologue, whose speaker is not described or named, warns the audience that "[t]he scenes are old, the habits are the same / We wore last year, before the Spaniards came. / Now, if you stay, the blood, that shall be shed / From this poor play, be all upon your head" (ll. 5–8). The use of "now" distinguishes this production from the previous experience of the pre-European New World, in which the bloodshed among the Indians did not implicate Christians. The violence of *The Indian Emperor*, by contrast, is meant to make the audience reflect on the tragic implications of Spanish colonialism. Dryden is evoking the Black Legend of cruel Spanish conquest, and as a priest and several Spanish soldiers are torturing Montezuma in the final act, the priest declares that because the Indian Emperor refuses "our true God," and also "hid his Gold, from Christian hands," the soldiers must kill him and "merit heaven thereby." This points to the perversion and cruelty of Spanish religion, and, as Stevens suggests, the "inefficiency" of their colonial practices.[21] The condemnation of the Spanish colonizers implicitly elevates the perceived humanity and nurturing role of English colonialism, and Indians become pawns in the affective economy of pity and ambition.

Dryden, one of the most dominant and influential authors of his day, indicates in his writing how the colonization of the Americas became a pattern of thought in English literature, pervasive enough to be moulded into metaphors for the enjoyment of a theatrical production. In the prologue to *The Conquest of Granada*, which ostensibly has nothing to do with the Native people of America, Dryden complains of playwrights who "bring old iron and glass upon the stage, / To barter with the Indians of our age" (ll. 27–8). Again, the stage is set as a space of colonial encounter, though here the "Indians" are stand-ins for the critics and the "vulgar" crowds who enjoy translated French farce and works of "dull sense," while the colonizing traders are the writers, or "mongrel wits," who are prolific in producing "trash." While Dryden lacks the ethnographic specificity that would come in later representations of Native people in the eighteenth century, he sets the stage, as it were, for the emergence of some of the tropes that would define Indians. The dynamic of the contact zone in Dryden is decidedly one-sided, and his Indians are subject to the desiring and pitying gaze of the English Christian. In some works, this dynamic remained throughout the century following Dryden's death, particularly in the large body of missionary writings on North America. There was, however, a significant change in the air with the rapid pursuit of an overseas empire starting in the 1680s and the increasing incursions of British settlers onto Native land.

A True History of the Captivity and Restoration of Mrs. Mary Rowlandson, published in England in 1682, depicted a very different dynamic of cultural contact than that of Dryden, as Rowlandson and her children are captured by Indians, who appear as "cruel and barbarous Salvages," on the frontier of Massachusetts. The fact that editions of this narrative appeared in both Massachusetts and London during the same year suggests it struck a chord with the Anglo transatlantic sensibility.[22] The suffering English female body is symbolic of the costs of empire but also of the resiliency of the English subject empowered by God's divine providence. Yet the true impact of this text in England may be overstated, since Britons had in fact already been reading captivity accounts by or about their countrymen and other Christians being held among non-Europeans for at least one hundred years.[23] Furthermore, though Rowlandson's narrative was certainly immensely popular in the colonies and has remained in print since its initial appearance, it was not reprinted in Britain after its first publication until 1900.[24] It was read alongside relatively more nuanced French texts, such as Lahontan's *New Voyages to North America* (1703) and its depiction of the philosophical Huron Adario, as well as English works that romanticized and pitied Indians; for example, the same year Rowlandson's narrative appeared with great success in London, a document entitled *A true account of the dying words of Ockanickon, an Indian King* was published and, unlike the Puritan narrative, was re-printed the following year. This text, which was sent to England by a Quaker living in New Jersey by the name of John Cripps, depicts the last words of Lenape (later named the Delaware by the British) chief Ockanickon, upon whose death "many Tears were shed both by the Indians and English." This sympathetic picture of Ockanickon, who wishes that the "Indians and the Christians" should live together peacefully, suggests that Indians are not simply the godless savages of Rowlandson's text, and the old chief is buried alongside Quakers, "according to his desire."[25] In her *Oroonoko* (1688), Aphra Behn writes that the natives of Surinam are "like our first parents before the Fall," and they represent "an absolute idea of the first state of innocence, before man knew how to sin."[26] Though the narrator claims that the Indians "understand no vice, or cunning, but when they are taught by the white men," she also asserts that "it were not difficult to establish any unknown or extravagant religion among them."[27] Her bemoaning of England's loss of "those mountains of gold" to the Dutch connects the ideological function of innocent and superstitious Indians to the imperial fantasies of untold wealth in the South American jungle. Yet, tellingly, within Behn's representation of these Edenic people there is ambivalence, and upon a second visit the Indians appear less innocent than gullible, with hideous, mutilated bodies and menacing signs of aggression.[28] Clearly the figure of the Indian, often undifferentiated between North and South America, was not a singular construction.

Liberty Asserted and Benevolent Brotherhood

This lack of specificity began to change throughout the opening decade of the century, and the first play written about Native North American people in English during the eighteenth century, critic John Dennis's popular *Liberty Asserted* (1704), is set in Canada among the Iroquois "Angie," or Mohawk people.[29] The play came out during the War of the Spanish Succession, and is perhaps more about the author's aversion to the French than it is about the Iroquois. Even before this time of heightened tension, Dennis had long despised the French; in an account of a short stay in France as a young man, he begins with the declaration, "I will give you a true and natural portrait of the French, and I will commence by telling you that I mortally hate them."[30] After the appearance of *Liberty Asserted*, Dennis, who according to Theophilus Cibber "certainly over-rated his importance," feared he had so offended Louis XIV with the play that the king would demand that Dennis be surrendered to France as part of the Treaty of Utrecht. He is said to have once fled the shores of Sussex back to London in "his Gown and Slippers" after visiting a friend and seeing a ship he took to be privateers out to capture him,[31] and he later implored his old patron the Duke of Marlborough to prevent him from being offered up to his bitter enemies.[32] The Duke assured him that this would not happen, as he himself had been a much greater enemy to the French than Dennis, and, he asserted, he "[was] not afraid of being sacrificed."

The preface of the play is mostly spent condemning the French and espousing Whig political principles, notwithstanding Dennis's claim that it is "an English and not a Party Play" (v). He writes that "[i]f we were but as true to Liberty, as the French are to Tyranny, they would soon be as despicable in their Circumstances as they are now in their Principles" (iv). Given the uniqueness of the setting, relatively little space in the preface is dedicated to contextualizing the exotic North American locale and its Native people. Dennis gives a short explanatory note "for the Sake of those who have never read either Hennepin or La Hontan" (viii); the French may be slaves to tyranny, but they are still ethnographic authorities. He explains that the French possess a large part of Canada while the English dominate New York and New England, and "as the English and French divide the country, they divide the Natives." Thus, "the five Warlike Nations of the Iroquois are our Confederates," while the Hurons, who number less, "are Friends to the French" (viii). This was true at the time and, however unintentionally, Dennis does tap into colonial realities, but the introduction is not overly concerned with historical context.

While the preface is anti-French, the play itself promotes a vision of the unity of all humanity, under the tutelage of the merciful and free English. The image of benevolent conquest as the hallmark of

British colonialism and heroism existed prior to this play, as in Sir William Temple's *Of Heroic Virtue* (1692), in which he proclaims that "[t]he designs and effects of [non-benevolent] conquests are but the slaughter and ruin of mankind, the ravaging of countries, and defacing the world: those of wise and just governments are preserving and increasing the lives and generations of men, securing their possessions, encouraging their endeavours, and by peace and riches improving and adorning the several scenes of the world."[33] The placement of this vision of colonial improvement among the Iroquois and Hurons in Canada is a significant first. While texts about missionary efforts were already widely available, the military conquest of North America in the early part of the eighteenth century was not yet in the broader public consciousness; most information about North America came, as Dennis suggests in his preface, from French sources. There simply was not yet a large number of soldiers crossing the Atlantic, as there would be beginning in the 1750s, and the colonists who were in the Americas were peripheral to most Britons. In addition, Britain had not yet achieved a defining military victory in North America,[34] and depended instead on the decidedly less heroic plantation system for wealth extraction. While some writers fantasized about a conquest akin to the Spanish sacking of Mexico and Peru, conquest in America was more often seen as conquering rival European powers and their patterns of colonization rather than the Indigenous people themselves. Indeed, at this stage, British colonialism was seen as more heroic if it was validated by the consent of the Indians.[35]

The play centres on the profound friendship between the English general Beaufort and Ulamar, the general of the Iroquois Five Nations. Ulamar was actually born a Huron, but he and his mother Sakia were taken when he was an infant and adopted into Angian society. Ulamar was taught European modes of conduct by Beaufort from a young age but also loves his adopted people, while Sakia loathes all Iroquois as her born enemies and hides Ulamar's paternity from him. Through the course of the play we discover that his father is a French general named Miramont, who turns out to be the noble Governor Frontenac, and Sakia bitterly laments the hostilities between the Iroquois-English alliance and the Huron-French forces. She also agonizes over Ulamar's love of the Angian princess Irene, because it would mean a marriage into the very centre of Angian society. Irene serves as a mediator for the homosocial relationship between Beaufort and Ulamar, since they both love her but each "cannot bear the Thought" of losing the other (19). When Irene's father, the Angian chief Zephario, offers his daughter to Beaufort, the Englishman insists she go to Ulamar, since that is what she desires and he "could die for Ulamar or her." Impressed by the friendship between the two men and by Beaufort's selflessness, the chief declares, "The English always were a Gallant Nation, / And Foes to Force, and Friends to Liberty. / They who without the Mind possess the Body, / Possess by Force, and *Ravish, not Enjoy*: / He who can Absolutely rule himself, / And can leave others free is truly Noble" (25). The project of English colonialism is depicted, in rhetoric that is still resonant, as the spreading of liberty and freedom among the invaded population. The imagined sexualized body of the Americas, which Sir Walter Raleigh famously boasted "hath yet her *maidenhead*," is metonymically evoked in Irene.[36] However, unlike earlier colonial heroes such as Raleigh, Beaufort decides not to "ravish" Irene and allows her to be with her true love, with the knowledge that he could legitimately possess her if he desires. Richard Frohock, using Peter Hulme's description of the Inkle and Yarico narrative, notes that Dennis displaces actual colonial struggle for land and resources for "the fictions of romantic encounter," and he "completely eclipses imperialist ambition behind the fictions of benevolent action and intent."[37]

The various "fictions" of the play are similar to the strategies of representation in subsequent ethnographic and travel accounts, which assert European hegemony while at the same time claiming innocence and passivity. Mary Louise Pratt labels this kind of rhetorical technique as "anti-conquest," because "these strategies of innocence are constituted in relation to older imperial rhetorics of conquest associated with the absolutist era."[38] While Pratt is speaking more specifically to the rise of "objective" natural science in imperialist discourse, Dennis also situates his benevolent conquest in relation to previous discourses of imperialism. Beaufort laments the earlier manifestations of colonialism, declaring, "Oh Europe, Europe! How hast thou been dull / To thy undoing? How thy heedless Magistrates / Have suffer'd poor unthinking Sots, to unlearn, / Their native Customs, and their native Tongues, / To speak your Jargon, and assume your ways" (34). Indeed, the text often adopts an explicitly anti-colonial position, condemning the modes of aggressive expansion that demand conquered people "imitate" their masters, "[t]ho' aukwardly our Asses ape your Dogs." This critique becomes specifically against the French as it is further articulated in the play, and Ulamar condemns them for their introduction of "cursed Luxury"

among the Hurons, "[w]hich makes them needy, venal, base, perfidi-
ous / Black Traytors to their Country, Friends to you" (34). Beaufort
adds, "For you win Provinces, as Hell gains Souls; / 'Tis by corrupting
them you make them yours: / They might defie your malice were they
faithful: / But first you enslave them to their own base Passions; / And
afterwards to yours." It was already well-known that this was almost
precisely what English traders sought to do in the colonies through
the introduction of alcohol and other trade goods, and this ambivalent
articulation of anti-colonial sentiment both justifies and masks England's own colonial enterprise. Beaufort's insistence on the innate value
of Indigenous cultures, as well as Ulamar's claim that "every brave
Man's Country is the Universe" (17), suggests that Dennis is offering
a transnational, cosmopolitan vision of masculine subjectivity, one
that would become embodied by the Indian later in the century. Here
we can see the homosocial bonds between patriotic men as the "anti-
conquest" which Pratt describes. The play ends with Beaufort's invitation to the French, after defeating their forces, to join "[w]ith us
Asserting Godlike Liberty" (68).

Following the Glorious Revolution of 1688, many Britons, particularly Whigs such as Dennis, saw a "new age of liberty" that made the
British a shining example for the world, providing what David Hume
would later describe as "the most entire system of liberty that ever
was known amongst mankind."[39] The notion of the empire as a force
for spreading this new liberty became an important part of imperial
rhetoric during the eighteenth century, as we shall see in the case of
the Indian kings, and Native North American people were important symbols in this discourse. Ulamar praises Beaufort in the end as
a "[t]ruly worthy Son, / Of Great Britania thro' the World renown'd,
/ For propping falling Liberty, / Supporting sinking Nations,"
and adds that the British are more interested in "rescuing one poor
wretch" than in "subverting and destroying Empires, / And making Millions wretched" (67). Ulamar himself embodies this liberty,
though he learned his virtues through Beaufort, and *Liberty Asserted*
is the first successful play to bring representations of Native people to
the stages of London in the eighteenth century and proclaim them to
be as enamored with liberty as the English. Many more Indians
would appear in literature following the actual appearance of
"Agnie" people in London six years later, and the imaginative texts
produced around this visit used Indians to explore a new cultural
and political landscape.

The Four Indian Kings

In April of 1710, the representatives of the Iroquois confederacy, widely known as the Four Indian Kings, arrived in Portsmouth en route to visit Queen Anne in London.[40] They were part of the slow but steady stream of Native people from the Americas to visit England since at least 1498. Various peoples were brought from their homelands during this period, oftentimes coercively, to be put on public display,[41] and they often, as in the case of the four Inuit people Martin Frobisher brought to England on separate voyages in 1576 and 1577, died shortly after arrival. Thus Trinculo remarks in *The Tempest* (1610) that the crowds in England "will not give a doit to relieve a lame beggar, / [yet] they will lay out ten to see a dead Indian" (II.ii.30–1). The diplomatic mission from the Iroquois in 1710, however, had a far greater impact than any previous visitation, and was represented very differently. These four men were depicted, and treated, as "Indian kings," which presented a contrasting vision of Native societies and governance from the stateless, natural existence that had been largely accepted prior to this visit. The notion of kingship also emphasized Native peoples' potential similarity with British society, making them exotic but recognizable people with whom Britons could culturally identify. This is reflected in the physical descriptions of them as generally "well form'd" and appreciative of "*English* Beef" and "our fine pale Ales before the best *French* Wines," and particularly in the portraits commissioned, which combine English heraldic symbolism and Native iconography in ways that emphasize singular traits over cultural stereotypes.[42] Their tattoos, for example, as well as their clan animals are differentiated in each painting. These men, in fact, were not "kings," since there was no such thing in the Iroquois confederacy, nor were they in any way equivalent to such a position.[43] It does appear, however, that they were nonetheless experienced warriors, and well respected among their people.

This visit cast a remarkable shadow across the century, leaving a cultural memory that shaped subsequent visits by other non-Europeans. Part of what distinguishes this embassy among others is that it came in the midst of a massive proliferation in print culture, and thus there was a large body of literature produced that was inspired by the "kings," including "fourteen broadsides, twelve or more chapbooks, numerous ballads and other publications."[44] Laura Brown points out that there was a "dramatic shift" in the size of the print industry from the sixteenth and seventeenth centuries to the eighteenth century, seen not only in the increase in printed material, but in the size of individual printing houses and number of people employed by them. She notes that this industry was not only a major contributor to important cultural changes during the period, but was, with its relentless technical innovations, free enterprising spirit, and dedication to profit, itself "a showcase for the broader cultural implications of modernity."[45] The volume and breadth of the popular literature which discussed the kings, from the *Spectator* to decidedly less elite ballads, suggest a new access to cultural events and democratization of the public sphere. The Indian kings provided one of the first media events of the century.

There were other significant developments and events in British political history surrounding this visit; the War of the Spanish Succession was in its latter stages, and Queen Anne had only days before the kings' visit switched from the expensive Whig policy of heroically helping out Britain's continental allies to the so-called blue-water Tory strategy of focusing on the nation's own naval and colonial endeavours. This move was beneficial for the Tories, who could present the Indian kings as symbols for this new strategy in the war, and maximize the publicity their visit would generate.[46] Thus, while the mission was no doubt in part widely covered as part of an actual interest in the kings, this press also served a political objective.

By the time of the Indian kings' visit, the sense of national identity in Britain was undergoing important transformations; the Acts of Union of 1707, which brought together Scotland with England and Wales into the Kingdom of Great Britain, created a new, layered sense of 'Britishness,' and, as Mel Kersey suggests, many writers "addressed the disparities between post- and pre-Union cultures" in an attempt to "reconcile older, 'purer' cultural identities with the mixed identity of Britishness."[47] Addison's essay in *Spectator* no. 50 (27 April 1711), mentioned in the beginning of this chapter, uses the visit of the Indian kings as the premise for exploring this dynamic. He claims he has managed to obtain the papers of "King *Sa Ga Yean Qua Rash Tow*," chronicling his impressions of the visit to "the Isle of *Great Britain*," from the upholsterer who was the landlord for part of the kings' stay; upon reading this essay, Swift lamented that he had given the idea for this satire to Steele (though it was in fact Addison who wrote this piece), and regretted doing so because he "intended to have written a book on that subject" but "[Addison] has spent it all in one paper."[48] Clearly the possibility of reflecting on British culture through the figure of an

Indian was an alluring prospect for the wits of the day. Michel de Montaigne had already done so in France over a century earlier, with his "Of Cannibals" (1580), but certainly Addison's piece is the first of its kind in eighteenth-century English writing.

Addison begins his essay with the epigraph, "Nunquam aliud Natura, aliud Sapienta dicit," or "Never does nature say one thing and wisdom another." He attempts to represent the natural, unadorned simplicity of the Indian king in relation to the artifice of British life, and is particularly interested in satirizing fashion, partisan politics, and the irreligiousness and hypocrisy of many English people. Another contemporary source from the Iroquois visit describes the "natural Eloquence and Simplicity, peculiar to that Sort of People, who, tho' unpolish'd by Art and Letters, have a large Share of good Sense and natural Reason."[49] The rational savage was largely constructed by French authors at the time, particularly Lahontan, but was developed in British texts throughout the century, in part from Locke in his argument for the possibility of natural reason existing outside a "civilized environment."[50] The king's observations begin with his description of St Paul's Cathedral, in which he speculates how "this prodigious Pile was fashioned into the Shape it now bears":

> It was probably at first an huge mis-shapen Rock that grew upon the Top of the Hill, which the Natives of the Country (after having cut it into a kind of regular Figure) bored and hollowed with incredible Pains and Industry, 'till they had wrought in it all those beautiful Vaults and Caverns into which it is divided at this Day. As soon as this Rock was thus curiously scooped to their Liking, a prodigious Number of Hands must have been employed in chipping the Outside of it, which is now as smooth as the Surface of a Pebble; and is in several Places hewn out into Pillars that stand like the Trunks of so many Trees bound about the Top with Garlands of Leaves. (189–90)

The king perceives the church as an organic whole, and his brethren similarly assume it was created by the God to whom it is dedicated. Addison, who along with Steele was interested in disseminating a uniquely British culture of politeness, is through the king's eyes creating a vision of Britain that seamlessly connects artifice and natural unity. The cathedral, as a stand-in for the nation, was constructed by many hands, and now appears in the eyes of the Indian king to be polished and eternal. Addison effectively combines the fantasy of pre-Union cultural purity with the post-Union self-fashioning in the metaphor of the church, and to do so in this publication was indeed significant; as Kersey suggests, "[f]or those Britons who could read, the public's reception and discussion of the *Spectator* enacted a daily performance of identity."[51] At the same time, the king observes other aspects of British culture that are too artificial, such as those parishioners in the church who, instead of worshiping God, are "bowing and curtisying to one another" (190). The divide between Whigs and Tories is an unnecessary and unnatural division, and the king is warned that the Tories are apt to hate him for being a foreigner, while the Whigs would attack him for being a king. Ultimately it is the cathedral itself that escapes the satire of the king and provides a unifying metaphor for Britain, which seems to reinforce Linda Colley's argument for the importance of Protestantism in British nation building.[52] At the end of the essay, however, Addison does not sound a note of self-assured nationalism, but rather one of cultural relativism, writing, "I cannot likewise forbear observing, That we are all guilty in some Measure of the same narrow way of Thinking, which we meet with in this Abstract of the *Indian* Journal[,] when we fancy the Customs, Dress, and Manners of other Countries are ridiculous and extravagant, if they do not resemble those of our own" (192).

While *Spectator* no. 50 uses the Indian kings to fortify a version of British identity, the visitors also offered an alternative and transgressive way of being. In 1712, two years following the visit, a group of British noblemen identified as "Mohocks" allegedly terrorized the streets of London, and Steele reports in *The Spectator* no. 324 that "[a]greeable to their Name, the avowed design of the Institution is Mischief."[53] The memory of the Indian kings provoked some rakish members of the gentry to explore the possibilities in other subjectivities, using the imaginary Indian costume in a way that has some resonance with, and even anticipates, the Boston Tea Party in 1773. John Gay wrote his play *The Mohocks* in the same years as the scare, and he emphasizes the ease of disguise in shifting identity for the libertines behind the gang. While ballads such as "The Mohocks Revel" (1712) declared that these British men decried "Crowns and Scepters" and were "'[g]ainst Monarchy," both the historical tale and *The Mohocks* itself point to the distinct class element of identity in the eighteenth century more broadly. In the play, the Mohocks give each other names such as "Cannibal" and "Molock," and are able to switch in and out of their identities. They promise that "[n]o laws shall restrain / Our libertine reign, / We'll riot, drink on, and be free" (ll. 25–8), and, indeed, they have terrorized the population of London to such a degree that the constables who are meant to be tracking them down surrender meekly when confronted by them. The rogues then switch clothes with the hapless night watchmen, and are able to convince others that the watchmen are, in fact, the Mohocks. Though they are found out in the end, and maintain that their game of making others pass as them is simply "an innocent frolick," this play demonstrates the ability of "gentlemen" to transform themselves in ways that the non-elite classes cannot. This transformation is ultimately a menace to British society, as seen by the large amount of negative and paranoid press that the Mohocks received. While there was a more fluid sense of the boundaries of identity at this time,[54] the performance of an Indian or "savage" subjectivity, as chapters 2 and 5 will suggest, was not a desirable act until much later in the century. In a decidedly different note from Addison's call for toleration at the end of his imagined letter, Steele adds in his essay on the British Mohocks in the *Spectator* that "the Manners of *Indian* Savages are no becoming Accomplishments to an *English* fine Gentleman" (424). While the rational Indian may offer important critiques and insights into British identity, the notion at this time of appropriating their way of life meant degeneration into savagery, not an elevation of reason and sentiment.

If, on the one hand, the Indian kings allowed for a reflection on what it meant to be British internally, they also embodied the expanding borders of mercantile capitalism and British influence abroad. Hinderaker describes them as crucial and enduring symbols for the "imaginative construction of the first British empire," and much of the print surrounding their visit points out the potential benefits Britain could obtain from a friendship with the Iroquois. Thus the author of the publication *The four kings of Canada. Being a succinct account of the four Indian princes lately arriv'd from North America* (1710) points out in his final chapter "how easie, as well as advantageous, it wou'd be to *Great Britain* to establish powerful Colonies" in the "fertile" homeland of the Indians (45). In "Windsor-Forest" (1713), Pope famously evokes the visit of the kings in his fantasy of a new imperial era following the Treaty of Utrecht, when he writes of a time when "ships of uncouth form shall stem the tyde, / And feather'd people croud my wealthy side, / And naked youths and painted chiefs admire / Our speech, our colour, and our strange attire!" (ll. 401–4). The broader purpose of the king's visit, which was either not well-known or deemed unimportant among the printing houses, in fact stemmed from a military failure in the colonies, and the Iroquois men were sent to revive the efforts of colonial governors and administrators to invade and "conquer" the French colony.[55] It was presented, however, as a plea for help from the Indian kings to rescue their people from French Catholic forces. Following their attendance at a performance of *Macbeth*, in which, according to one account, the "mobocracy" in the theatre demanded that the kings sit on the stage facing the crowd during the play, the lead actor presented an epilogue to the Indian kings that welcomed those who "[n]ow seek protection on Britannia's shore." It continues, "O Princes, who have with amazement seen / So good, so gracious and so great a Queen; / Who from her royal mouth have heard your doom / Secur'd against the threats of France and Rome."[56] The kings allowed the British to imagine themselves as a benevolent colonial force, as in Dennis's earlier play, and the Iroquois request for more churches and clergy in their settlements enforced this belief. Mohawk historians have confirmed that there was a desire for more Christian missionaries, but have suggested that this was not as much to preach and convert in any orthodox sense as to ward off witchcraft.[57]

The kings were not universally well received. Among those who disapproved of the Indian kings being treated as if they were European royalty were some of the Whigs who resented the political advantage the "blue water" Tories gained through the visit. Daniel Defoe was one of these unhappy Whigs, who also strongly identified with his fellow Protestant dissenters in the colonies who he read were being scalped and slaughtered in large numbers.[58] He would later describe Mohawks as "the most Desperate, and most Cruel of the Natives of *North-America*," and he claims it is a "particular Barbarity singular to them" that when they take prisoners, "either of the *English* or other Natives, they always *Scalp'd them*."[59] He reminds his readers that this is the same "small Nation of *Savages* in the Woods ... from whence our four pretended *Indian* Kings came lately of their own Fools Errand."[60] It is not surprising that Defoe's *The Life and Surprising Adventures of Robinson Crusoe* (1719), often described as the first British novel in the modern sense, should be in large part about an Englishman claiming a piece of the New World and subjugating and re-naming an Indian man. It is tempting, though perhaps untenable, to link Crusoe's pathological hatred of the cannibalistic "savages" with Defoe's own antipathy towards the Indian kings, fueled by their celebration among the British public.

The embassy of the Indian kings was in many ways a carefully orchestrated event to achieve an immediate political effect, which was the renewal of the campaign against the French in North America. As a broader cultural phenomenon, it allowed British writers to consider the shape of identity and nationhood by imagining its own modernity in another culture's eyes. Throughout the eighteenth century there are echoes of the visit by the Indian kings, often in unexpected places. The landlord for their stay, mentioned in Addison's essay as providing the king's journal, was the upholsterer Thomas Arne. In a piece in *The Tatler* no. 171, Steele reports that the Indians were so grateful for their landlord's kindness in caring for one of them when he fell ill, and for Arne's comfortable furniture, that they rename him "Cadaroque" (281). This is presumably derived from Katarakouy, the location of the strongest fort in their homeland and site of modern day Kingston, and is meant to be an honour to Arne. At the time of the Iroquois visit, Arne, or rather Cadaroque, had an infant son, who presumably grew up around the family memory and, likely, framed mezzotints of the Indian kings. In 1740, this son, Thomas Augustine Arne, would help compose "Rule, Britannia!," the "first mature cultural expression of Britain's new imperial identity."[61] Thus the quintessential anthem of British patriotism and self-confidence was composed in the shadow and memory of the Indian kings.

Thomas Tickell's "On the Prospect of Peace" (1712), published two years after the visit by the Indian kings, combines Dennis's fantasy of liberating conquered people through British colonialism with the reality of the visit by the Iroquois. Tickell writes of Queen Anne that "[h]er Labours are to plead th'Almighty's Cause, / Her Pride to teach th' untam'd Barbarian Laws: / Who conquers, wins by brutal Strength the Prize; / But 'tis a Godlike Work to civilize" (8). He continues,

> Did not the Painted Kings of India greet
> Our Queen, and yield their Sceptres at Her Feet!
> Chiefs who full Bowls of hostile Blood had quaff'd
> Fam'd for the Javelin, and invenom'd Shaft,
> Whose haughty Brows made Savages adore,
> Nor bow'd to less than Stars, or Sun before.
> Her pitying Smile accepts their suppliant Claim,
> And adds Four Monarchs to the Christian Name.   (8–9)

Despite his confusion over where the "Indians" who visited London came from, Tickell sees in them the possibility for a righteous

Figure 1.2 Portraits of Four Indian Kings of Canada: The Four Indian Kings. Artist: Bernard Lens after Bernard Lens III, 1710. Mezzotint, Yale Center for British Art, Paul Mellon Collection. Used with permission.

and profitable empire built on British moral superiority and trade. He imagines that "[f]earless our Merchant now may fetch his Gain, / And roam securely o'er the boundless Main" (9), while at the same time "savage Indians swear by ANNA's Name" (15). In this vision of expansion, British merchants can spread their trade virtually unchecked, but this unfettered access to foreign goods and markets brought with it a contrasting anxiety that such gain could also entail corruption and ruin.

Colonial Contacts and Betrayals: *Inkle and Yarico*

Another key paradigm of cultural contact was established through the story of Pocahontas, which famously projects the fantasy of the desirability of the European male onto the "Indian princess," a trope which has appeared in countless texts since that time. It also became a crucial story in American national history beginning in the nineteenth century, as it provided an early coherent origin.[62] Aphra Behn's *The Widow Ranter* (1690) evokes a similar tale, in which the Virginian Indian queen Semernia falls in love with English colonist Francis Bacon. In the end he kills her accidentally while fighting off other Indians, and subsequently takes his own life by swallowing poison. This tale suggests, as Margo Hendricks notes, that "miscegenation is both desirable *and* dangerous."[63] Indeed, while the Pocahontas story was circulated beginning quite early in the century in Robert Beverley's *The History and Present State of Virginia* (1705), it was eclipsed by the much more ambivalent story of Inkle and Yarico, one of the most popular narratives of the eighteenth century, in which miscegenation becomes a metaphor for the immorality of imperialism.[64] Whereas Dennis's play masks colonial struggle with romantic encounter, this tale uncovers it with the same strategy, and the promise of commercial modernity is tempered by the danger of instrumental reason.

The story of Inkle and Yarico first appears in Richard Ligon's *A True and Exact History of the Island of Barbadoes* (1657, 1673), though Ligon only briefly mentions his encounter with an "Indian maid" from the mainland who falls in love "upon the first sight" of a young Englishman being pursued by her people, and saves him from harm.[65] She nurses him in a cave, and they eventually find his ship and board it. Upon their arrival in Barbados, he "forgot the kindness of the poor maid, that had ventured her life for his safety, and sold her for a slave, who was as free born as he: And so poor Yarico, for her love, lost her liberty." John Oldmixon repeats this version in his *The British Empire in*

America (1708), with the added commentary that the man's behaviour was "hardly credible in an *Englishman*," but more suitable in a Spaniard or a Frenchman (16). Oldmixon elaborates on the original, noting that Yarico was "so true a Savage" that she refused to wear clothes, and that she would later have a child with a white servant. However, it is in Richard Steele's piece in *The Spectator* no. 11 (13 March 1711), printed a little over one month before the piece on the Indian kings, that the story of Inkle and Yarico is more fully developed.

Steele's version of the story is an expansion of Ligon's tale, and is told by a woman named Arietta in response to a fop's classical misogynist tale about the inconstancy of women. The story begins with the character Thomas Inkle of London, a young man who sails to the Indies "to improve his Fortune by Trade and Merchandize" (42). Inkle's father made sure to instil in his son "an early Love of Gain, by making him a perfect Master of Numbers, and consequently giving him a quick View of Loss and Advantage, and preventing the natural Impulses of his Passions, by Prepossession towards his Interests" (42). Steele's version elaborates the context of mercantile capitalism and blind self-interest which is implicit in the previous versions, and his use of a female narrator offers a potential critique of reckless male colonialism as it plays out, as Nicole Horejsi notes, "on the body of a woman."[66] More specifically, the originary betrayal of colonialism occurs on the body of an Indian woman, so often allegorized as the figure of America. Indeed, after Yarico discovers and rescues the exhausted Inkle, she brings "a great many spoils" to his cave so that it is "richly adorned," mirroring the flow of goods from the colonies to Britain.

Though she is described as a "naked American," Yarico nonetheless "every Day came to him in a different Dress, of the most beautiful Shells, Bugles, and Bredes" (43). Brown observes that in eighteenth-century imperialist discourse, "female adornment becomes the main emblem of commodity fetishism," and women are associated with mercantile capitalism and its attractions and ambiguities because "[their] marginality allows them to serve, in the writings of celebrants and satirists alike, as a perfect proxy or scapegoat."[67] Thus in Pope's *The Rape of the Lock* (1712, 1714), the English desire for imported goods is gendered as feminine; Pope's Clarissa notes that women are "deck'd with all that Land and Sea afford" (V: 11), and earlier Belinda's dressing table is said to hold "[t]he various Off'rings of the World" (I: 130). This "glitt'ring Spoil" includes "India's glowing Gems" and Arabian perfumes, as well as combs made from elephant ivory and tortoise shell

(I: 132–6). In Steele's text, Yarico's adornment in exotic goods causes her to transform into a valuable commodity for the merchant Inkle, who decides to sell her when he arrives in the Barbados and the planters set up a "[m]arket of the *Indians* and Slaves, as with us of Horses and Oxen" (43). Steele explains,

> Mr. *Thomas Inkle*, now coming into *English* Territories, began seriously to reflect upon his Loss of Time, and to weigh with himself how many Days Interest of his Money he had lost during his Stay with *Yarico*. This Thought made the young Man very pensive, and careful what Account he should be able to give his Friends of his Voyage. Upon which Considerations, the prudent and frugal young Man sold *Yarico* to a *Barbadian* Merchant; notwithstanding that the poor Girl, to incline him to commiserate her Condition, told him that she was with Child by him; But he only made use of that Information, to rise in his Demands upon the Purchaser. (43–4)

The cold calculation of the British merchant, epitomized a few years later in Defoe's *Robinson Crusoe*, is in *Inkle and Yarico* responsible for the moral bankruptcy of British colonialism. Hulme speculates that Yarico, "caught between the devil of cannibalism and the deep blue sea of the trading soul, is less of a 'savage' than a transposition of the difficult position of the English aristocracy, caught between the savagery of the lower orders and the growing threat from the merchant classes."[68] She is, as Indians would often become in eighteenth-century texts, a stand-in for a form of British subjectivity facing a potential threat or drastic change to its existence. The anti-colonial critique of the tale, which would by the end of the century be used as a condemnation of slavery by abolitionists, here articulates an anxiety over the emergence of the middle class. However, the widespread popularity of this story throughout the century suggests that it represented more than just the dangers of the merchant class, and also addressed the deep misgivings many in Britain felt over the expansion of trade and empire. New desires could corrupt the soul. Of course, this is not to suggest that Steele opposed colonialism; indeed, he himself owned a plantation in Barbados, inherited from his wife.[69] Moreover, the displacement of slavery from black bodies to an Indian body obscures the reality of the transatlantic slave trade. Nonetheless, Mr. Spectator shows that the commercial economy must also involve a sentimental economy, and after Arrieta finishes the story he "left the Room with Tears in [his] Eyes" as a tribute to its teller. The Indian is the ideal vehicle to carry sympathy between British readers.

An illuminating contrast to the story of Yarico's betrayal is the ballad "The Four Indian Kings," based on the Iroquois visit and printed throughout the century and into the Victorian period. In this short poem, one of the kings falls in love with an English woman he sees in St James's Park. He proclaims that "[t]he young ladies of this nation, / They are more than mortal sure."[70] This particular young woman, he bemoans, "is far above me, / Although I am an Indian king." He sends a messenger to deliver a ring to her, and to declare his interest while he waits "burning / Wrapt in scorching flames of love" (217). The woman tells the messenger that she cannot be with the king, even if he were "king of many nations" and she "born of mean relations," because "[h]e's a Heathen by profession, / I a Christian bred and born" (218). The messenger assures her that the kings are all fond of Britain and open to receiving "the light of grace," and she replies to him that if the king considers changing his faith, she will entertain his proposition. The earliest broadside ends at this point, on the brink of conversion and miscegenation, though in later editions, such as "The Three Indian King's Garland" from 1765, the king becomes a Christian and they marry in the presence of Queen Anne. Both this ballad and *The Spectator* narrative turn contact zones between British and Indigenous peoples into spaces of romantic encounter and sentimental drama, making them "classically Freudian," as Hulme suggests of Yarico and Inkle.[71] More specifically, these stories turn fantasies of economic conquest and religious conversion into sentiment, suggesting that the Indian, in this early stage of empire, was an important site of personal identification for the British subject and an ideal partner to help shape imperial desires.

Conclusion

For British people following the Glorious Revolution and in the first decades of the eighteenth century, there was a growing sense of what we now call "modernity"; Fredric Jameson describes the "modern feeling" as "the conviction that we ourselves are somehow new, that a new age is beginning, that everything is possible and nothing can ever be the same again."[72] The rise of empire and the nation, the birth of consumer culture, the discourse of liberty and rights, and personal identity have all been traced to this period by scholars of the eighteenth century and, perhaps more than any other non-European people, representations of Indians from the Americas were placed in dialogue with these "modern" British discourses. Thus the ambivalence over the narratives

involving Native peoples, from the deeply betrayed Yarico to the sup-
pliant Iroquois, speaks to the ambivalence over modernity itself. And
Indians were decidedly linked to modernity, though often in complex
and contradictory ways.[73] In *The Tatler* no. 278 (1711), one essay notes
that those who study classical history and knowledge are engaging in
"frivolous Enquiries, and impertinent Studies," and that "[t]hese por-
ing Bookworms will run you a long Detail of every injured Prince and
State that sued to the *Roman* Senate for Protection, but know nothing of
the Four *Indian* Kings that were lately here" (438). The kings' visit epito-
mizes the new and the modern, in contrast to the antiquarian impulse
to find meaning in the ancient and increasingly irrelevant past. Similarly, the tale of Inkle and Yarico in *The Spectator* is told by Arietta in
response to the fop's classical tale of the Ephesian Matron, offering a
fundamentally new perspective in the face of a story that is "not quite
Two thousand Years old" (41).[74] As the following chapters will show,
the importance of the figure of the Indian throughout the century is
more often connected to the current developments in British culture
rather than a desire or nostalgia for the primitive past.

The period subsequent to 1710 witnessed an even greater proliferation in printed materials, and the simultaneous rise in both the novel
and a vast body of ethnographic and historical writings on Native
North American peoples suggests, on the surface, that the former provided the interiority and individualism equated with modern subject-
hood, while the latter supplied the "Other" with which to define that
Self. On closer reading, however, the two are entangled, forming a kind
of "ethnography of the Self" which sought to re-define Britishness and
the boundaries of identity. This is particularly evident in some of the
non-canonical British novels of the eighteenth century, including the
anonymously penned *Memoirs of the Life and Adventures of Tsonnonthouan* (1763) and *The Female American* (1767) by "Unka Eliza Winkfield."
In captivity narratives produced during the mid-eighteenth century,
the Indian threatens to split the unified British self by revealing its own
artifice; if the "savage" of the captivity narrative is able to re-write the
British body into an Indian body (i.e., "going native" in some form),
then identity itself is called into question. The Indian, in other words,
both makes and unmakes the modern self. During the 1770s, this threat
of fracture with the colonies becomes a desire to appropriate the Indian
into British subjectivity in the form of the hybrid Indian-Briton who
generally represents a corrective to the effeminate gentry or overly sentimental man of feeling.

In 1776, the year of the American Declaration of Independence and also the year which Wahrman quite precisely dates as the birth of the modern self, noted chronicler and journal writer James Boswell, perhaps the quintessential example of a man in possession of the interiority requisite for selfhood, met in London with Mohawk leader Thayendanegea (or Joseph Brant, as he is more commonly known) for an interview to appear in *The London Magazine*.[75] Boswell begins his article with the historical note that "[i]t is well known that the chief of the Mohock Indians visited England in the reign of Queen Anne," and adds that Brant is the grandson to that chief.[76] The kings, now reduced to one, yet again come up at a pivotal time. Boswell reflects that Brant "has not the ferocious dignity of a savage leader," and "to those who study human nature, he affords a very convincing proof of the tameness which education can produce upon the wildest race." During the time of Queen Anne, by contrast, the "wild American chief" represented a "very rude and uncivilized nation," and "somewhat more than half a century has made a very great change upon the Mohock nation." It does not occur to Boswell, nor could it have, that his own self-confidence in who he is, and his comfortable privileging of British ways of knowing the world, could in some way be connected to those Iroquois men. For Brant, dressed in the "ordinary European habit" while at the same time bearing his tomahawk, upon which "is carved the first letter of his Christian name, … and his Mohock appellation," it was impossible not to see the conjoined nature of English and Mohawk selves.

2 The Indian as Cultural Critic: Shaping the British Self

In short, you are Men in nothing, but so far as you resemble us, whom you call savages.

– John Cleland, *Tombo-Chiqui* (1758)

On 16 February 1738, Theophilus Cibber, son of then poet laureate and noted Pope antagonist Colley Cibber, appeared onstage at Drury Lane as a "poor untutor'd Savage" who was meant to function, as the prologue he delivered proclaimed, as "[a] Glass too true, in which we all may see, / Not what we are, but what we ought to be."[1] The younger Cibber was widely known for his extravagant and debauched lifestyle, and was almost universally loathed and seen as a dissipated rake; his call for the audience to find moral guidance in his character no doubt brought a level of ambiguity or absurdity to the role that is absent in the written text. And even though the play was shouted off the stage and never performed again,[2] we see here the desire to look to the Indian as a model for appropriate behaviour, deeply connected to modes of individual conduct and a perceived core of selfhood existing outside of the trappings of commercial society and fashion. Later in the century, the scandalous John Cleland would unsuccessfully revive this play, and his eponymous Indian in *Tombo-Chiqui* would similarly proclaim the above epigraph to his British hosts, in an even more stark declaration of the superiority of natural man.

This chapter will examine the role that representations of Indians played in shaping personal identity during the mid-eighteenth century. It will first look at fictional Indians providing critiques of British culture, as in the example above, that prefigure cultural shifts in Britain that would happen later in the century. It will then examine the ambivalent representations of Britons such as Sir William Johnson and Peter Williamson who attempt, in one way or another, to become Indians. Taken together, these sections explore the imagined and "real" contact zones between British and Indian selves and their effects on British subjectivity. The Indian as represented in these texts provides an alternative self, and both critiques and shapes newer forms of individual and collective conceptions of Britishness. While the figure of the Indian does in many ways provide an otherness with which to contrast British people, it also opens a space of cultural imagination which exploits the fantasy of Indian freedom and integrity. British people themselves become othered in these texts, alienated from their history, yet they are unable to access the stable cultural practices of the people they sought to both eliminate and appropriate.

The first section will look at the 1749 and 1750 editions of *An apology for the life of Bampfylde-Moore Carew*, a widely popular work which novelizes the life of the eponymous impostor and so-called gypsy,[3] who is transported to North America for his transgressions and seeks out rational Indians to liberate him from white colonial laws. In doing so he transforms from an essentially "characterless" individual to, at least temporarily, a stable subject.[4] The second text is a periodical article that first appeared in the *Universal Spectator* for 30 January and 6 February 1742, and was also excerpted in the *London Magazine* that year. Ostensibly a continuation of Joseph Addison's well-known letter from an Indian king in the *Spectator* no. 50, the essay records the observations of an Indian encountering some of the cultural events and fashionable activities of mid-century London that typify fluidity and play. Finally, I will turn to John Cleland's play *Tombo-Chiqui, or, the American Savage*, printed in 1758 though never performed. Like the earlier play *Art and Nature* (1738) by James Miller, which saw the young Cibber perform the part of the American "savage" Julio, Cleland's play is an adaptation of Louis François Delisle De La Drevetière's wildly successful French play *Arlequin Sauvage* (1721).[5] This text, like the *Universal Spectator* piece, uses the trope of a North American Indian critiquing British society at home by virtue of their innate lack of pretense, but it also contains a romantic sub-plot between an English woman and an Indian man that expresses surprisingly little anxiety over the prospect of miscegenation in London.

The second part of the chapter will look at eighteenth-century Britons most well-known for their time among Indians and the ambivalence in Britain surrounding their transculturations on the peripheries of empire. It will first examine the popular Indian captivity narrative of Scottish entrepreneur and author Peter Williamson and the subsequent and surprising circulation of an image of him dressed as an Indian, despite his text's assertion of the unspeakable violence and savagery of his captors. The chapter will next turn to Superintendent of Indian Affairs Sir William Johnson, who actually had a Native family with Joseph Brant's sister Molly Brant while among the Mohawks, and his satirical literary representation in Charles Johnstone's novel *Chrysal; or, The Adventures of a Guinea* (1760). Finally the chapter will consider Tobias Smollet's fictional captive soldier Lieutenant Obadiah Lismahago from *The Expedition of Humphry Clinker* (1771), perhaps the most well-known of all these hybrid subjects among literary critics. These men speak to one of the important myths in North American, and particularly American, culture: the white man adopted into a Native society and accepted fully as a member of that group. This hybrid figure, embodied in James Fenimore Cooper's *The Last of the Mohicans* (1826) and Kevin Costner's *Dances With Wolves* (1990), often works on an ideological level to displace Indigenous people and strengthen settler claims to land ownership. While such adoptions did indeed happen in practice, there is little evidence of their producing the kinds of heroic subjects documented in the mythology around "going Indian." Philip Deloria's *Playing Indian* traces the related phenomenon of cultural appropriation, from the Boston Tea Party to New Age sweatlodges, and the ways in which Indigenous cultures have been both effaced from and written into American national history.[6] In early and mid-eighteenth-century Britain, cultural appropriation and hybridity did not operate in the same way and, indeed, despite the fluidity of personal identity in the period which this chapter will discuss, it can be said that hybrid identities did not exist at all in the forms more familiar in subsequent times until near the end of the century. While there was less certainty about the differences between races and cultures, particularly in comparison with later proto-scientific discourses,[7] there were nonetheless demarcated, sometimes superficial, cultural distinctions that were not as frequently transgressed.[8] This section will look at transcultural exchange and influence during the eighteenth century and the ways in which these representations prefigured and challenged the kinds of cross-cultural fellowship and romanticization that began to emerge in North America around the time of the Revolutionary War, which will be discussed in the fifth chapter. The figures discussed in this part of the chapter embody the period's ambivalence over a Briton being culturally shaped by Indians or, in other words, the anxiety over internalizing the critique offered by the Indians in the first part of the chapter.[9]

Section I: Indians as Modern Critics of the *ancien régime*

One of the more frequent and longstanding critical gestures in eighteenth-century studies is the attempt to locate the origins of what has been described as individual personal identity or the "modern self"; the foundational work of E.P. Thompson and Ian Watt, as well as more recent works by historians Linda Colley, Dror Wahrman, and many others, contribute to the narrative of subject formation in the eighteenth century by tracing the economic, aesthetic, historical, and cultural origins of British modernity.[10] Feminist and postcolonial scholars such as Laura Brown and Srinivas Aravamudan have looked more closely at the important and ambivalent role of alterity in these origins,[11] and this chapter similarly looks at the relation between the Indian and the British subject. Following Michel Foucault's description of the "invention of man" in *The Order of Things* (1966) and the narratives of identity formation put forth by philosopher Charles Taylor (1992) and cultural historian Wahrman (2004), I will examine the role that representations of Indians played in the trajectory of personal identity towards modern forms. Of particular use is Wahrman's description of what he calls the *ancien régime* of identity, which he traces as the dominant form of subjectivity in Britain up until the Revolutionary War. This earlier form of identity, he argues, was emphatically "*not* characterized by an axiomatic presupposition of a deep inner core of selfhood." Instead, the "specific categories of identity ... could prove to be mutable, malleable, unreliable, divisible, replaceable, transferable, manipulable, escapable, or otherwise fuzzy around the edges."[12] According to both Taylor and Wahrman, this form of identity would change towards the end of the eighteenth century, leading to what Taylor describes as a "sense of inwardness" and a "radical subjectivism and an internalization of moral sources."[13] For Wahrman, the change in subjectivity is tied to the broader transformation of other "categories of identity" such as class, gender, and race. These categories, he claims, would become hardened and more deeply connected to ideas of the self because the Revolutionary War brought with it a confusion over identity and distrust of disguise. While the specific causes of this shift in his account are often contested, this story of the "modern self" is not unique to Wahrman or Taylor, and can be seen in the formulations of others. In *The Complexion of Race*, for example, Roxann Wheeler describes the fluid nature of race through most of the eighteenth century, preceding the rise of strict categories of racial difference in the end of the period, while Deidre Lynch suggests in *The Economy of Character* that novels moved from an emphasis on generic character types for most of the century to greater individualization and interiority in the Romantic period. Michael Mascuch also claims that the "individualist self emerged in London ... in the final decade of the eighteenth century."[14] Taking the broader argument of these writers, this section will now examine literary encounters between Indigenous North Americans and Britons who exemplify the earlier, more fluid sense of identity. I will argue that Indians in these works, and as frequently represented in other places in British literature of the period, embody a subjectivity that bears a striking resemblance to elements of the "modern self." Rather than a sentimental or neo-classical trope, the Indian is more often a radical departure from and critique of the standing order.[15]

Bampfylde-Moore Carew: An Imposter Among the Indians

An inescapable feature of fiction from the first half of the eighteenth century is a preoccupation with the malleability of identity and the seeming ease with which disguise can switch and shape character. This is evident not only in theatre, which to a certain extent lends itself to such identity play by its very nature and can be seen in works such as John Gay's *Polly* (1729), but also in novels such as Defoe's *Roxanna* (1724) and Fielding's *Tom Jones* (1749). While those who were able to shift selves in these works often found themselves on paths to social ascendancy, they also manifested a cultural anxiety. The threat of the Stuart Pretenders to the throne and anti-Jacobite paranoia haunted the first half of the century, particularly in the wake of the Rebellion of 1745. Charles Stuart's apparent ability to mask himself was informed by and also fueled the slippery nature of identification. Various characters, both fictional and otherwise, were mistaken for him in novels and narratives, including Tom Jones, Smollett's Count Fathom, the Indian Cannassatego in John Shebbeare's *Lydia, or, Filial Piety* (based on the historical Onondaga chief Canassatego), and the character to whom I now turn, the notorious rogue Bampfylde-Moore Carew, a pretender in his own right to the title of the "King of the Beggars."[16]

While a lesser-known work in subsequent centuries, *An apology for the life of Bampfylde-Moore Carew* was one of the more popular texts from the 1740s and 1750s, and into the nineteenth century.[17] Carew was an actual historical figure, born in Devon in 1693. He was from a respectable family and was well educated, but he ran away from school and joined a band of "gypsies" as a teenager. The second edition of his narrative in 1750 was largely re-written and heavily embellished by a hack writer, most likely printer Robert Goadby, expanding its transatlantic incidents and overall critique of English society.[18] The interest in impostors and quacks throughout the century, most pronounced in the first half, is symptomatic of the era's more fluid understanding of identity and fascination with its seemingly unbounded possibilities.[19] At the same time, however, these impostors underscore the potential danger in an unstable and unknowable character; indeed, many narratives of impostors find them punished for their deceits, placed in prison or, as in the case of forger Japhet Crooke, also known as Sir Peter Stranger, who is put on the pillory while the hangman "cut off his ears, and with a pair of scissors slit both his nostrils," severely marked.[20] Imposters can indicate the threshold of identity, and while imposture was not in and of itself a crime,[21] the perpetrators are often captured and punished by the laws of the civil society they flaunt.

The *Apology* of Carew is, however, decidedly celebratory in tone,[22] and his freedom of movement across cultural and societal boundaries shows that the great are no different from the poorest soul, "for strip them of their gaudy Plumes, and we shall not be able to distinguish them from the lowest Order of Mumpers" (1749 ed., 88). His title as "King of the Beggars" itself transgresses the limitations of the social hierarchy, and he speaks to the desire for mobility among the "lower orders" that were restricted by punitive vagrancy and poor laws.[23] Carew's identity as a "gypsy" places him outside these repressive forms of authority and he joins a "marginal, outsider group that embodies a now lost British freedom."[24] Gypsy society offers an escape from the cruelties of enclosure and, as John Barrell notes, represents "a political utopia founded as much on a modern critique of modernity as on the vision of an imaginary and ideal past."[25] While the *Apology* pre-dates the Romantic and Victorian fascination with gypsies as nostalgic cultural icons in Britain, it does very clearly present them as honourable and free subjects.[26] Yet this utopian society is ultimately untenable in its current form, and is under constant threat by the laws of the land that seek to constrain their movement.

Carew is eventually caught by the British authorities and sentenced to transportation to Maryland for seven years for idle vagrancy.[27] Upon arrival he is sold into indentured servitude and, after attempting to flee, is given an iron collar or "pot hook" around his neck, which "is usually put about the Necks of the runaway [sic] Slaves" (91). The immediate commodification of his body, followed by its containment in an instrument of torture and shame, are indictments of the threat to liberty that the laws and regulations of England can pose, even across the Atlantic. And while there is not an obvious critique of slavery beyond an acknowledgment of its existence, Carew's experience suggests that it diminishes the freedom of all British subjects. If the gypsy represents both lost British liberty and a rational reform of civil society, a gypsy in a slave's shackles indicates that the current economic and legal structures diminish mobility and instrumentalize life.

After some of his friends come across him but are unwilling to risk a fine and imprisonment for removing the iron collar, they tell him to seek out "the friendly Indians," who will help him remove it. It is telling that it is only Indians who can liberate him; like the gypsies to whom he turns in England, the Indians allow for a freedom outside of unjust legal structures. They are a society on friendly trading terms with colonial North America, but who are more deeply invested in liberty than in unjust laws and will provide safety for the rogues and outcasts of commercial society.[28] And while he is warned of "two other Sorts of Indians" that need to be avoided because they are "very cruel to the Whites" and who "will certainly murder you" (33–4), Carew is willing to risk such dangers. Immediately following this rather stark warning, the author notes that "here the Reader will, we make no Doubt, be pleas'd to see some Account of the *Indians*, among whom our Hero was treated with so much Kindness and Civility, as we shall relate in its proper Place" (34). What follows is an extended, fifteen-page ethnographic account taken directly from the 1741 edition of John Oldmixon's sprawling history *The British Empire in America*, first printed in 1708.[29] Beginning in the early seventeenth century, the inserted text combines accounts of exploration and settlement with observations on the manners and customs of the Indians around Maryland. While the backwardness of their religion is emphasized, at the same time the account discusses their moral and aesthetic advantages. Just as the *Apology* provides ethnographic information on gypsies, however dubious it may be,[30] it also offers a broader contextual account of Indians to solidify their role as cultural critics. The text also contains the story of

Pocahontas (or "Pocahonta"), well before it became the American cultural touchstone of Indigenous benevolence and self-sacrifice for the early European settlers. While Goadby inserted Oldmixon's text verbatim, the material sets up Carew's encounter with the friendly Indians and historicizes their kindness and favour to the individual European men who go among them. Significantly, as I will discuss below, the ethnographic account ends with an observation on the language of the Indians, noting that it is "lofty, but narrow"; while the English language contains slippages and equivocation, the Indians speak in words that are certain and "as sonorous as any in Attica" (49).

Thus the imposter, criminal, and outcast Carew, with history nonetheless on his side, flees in search of the friendly Indians. He eventually spies five Indians in the distance, and "to his inexpressible Joy distinguish'd they had Guns in their Hands, which was a sure Sign to him they were the friendly *Indians*" (53). It is the recognizable European weapon that ensures these Indians are integrated into the networks of trade which define their relationship to the British. While Carew may be a rogue, he is nonetheless dependent upon the colonial activity of his nation to make the world a more cosmopolitan and hospitable place. The irony that this hospitality is represented by a weapon of violence is perhaps intentional, though Indian weaponry such as tomahawks and scalping knives were seen as much more brutal than the more efficient European firearm.[31] Europeans frequently distinguished their identities from Indians through weaponry, warfare, and violence, more than any other factors, as I will discuss in the final chapter.[32] An Indian with a gun is a more welcoming sight than one with a scalping knife.

The king of the Indians personally removes the pot hook with Carew's tools, indicating his own investment in individual freedom. He introduces himself with the unlikely name of George Lillycraft, and claims his father was one of the Indian kings who visited Queen Anne in 1710. He shows his European guest "some fine lac'd Cloaths, which, he said, were made a Present of to him by the last King *George* of *England*, (meaning his late Majesty King *George* the First)" (54).[33] The relation to the lineage of the Indian kings, as in the case of the *Universal Spectator* essay, ties King Lillycraft's voice and subjectivity to the already established trope of the original *Spectator* essay. But while the Four Indian Kings in Addison's work help shape a desirable model of Britishness based on already inherent qualities and global ambition, the next generation of Indians present themselves as models for the shapeless character with diminished freedoms.

With his decidedly Anglophone name and finery, King George Lillycraft is set in contrast with England's own King George. He is in a position of resemblance, not difference, and he questions Carew about "his Brother Kings of *England*." The Indian king applies his "natural sense" to British monarchy and is appalled by what he hears. When he learns, for example, that less than a thousandth of the populace of England have ever even seen the king in their lives, and that the king spends most of his time sequestered in his palace, Lillycraft flies into a passion, declaring "[h]e was certain he deceived him, and belied his good Brother of England, for how, adds he, can he be the King of a People, whom he hath no Knowledge of?" (56). He adds,

> *I know, and am known by all my Subjects, I appear daily among them, hear their Complaints, and redress their Grievances, and am acquainted with every Place in my Kingdom.* Being told, the People of *England* paid their King yearly, vast Sums out of the Profits of their Labour; he laughed, and cry'd, *O! Poor King!* Adding, *I have often given to my Subjects, but never received any Thing from them.* (56)

A footnote explains that "[t]he Indian *Kings are obliged to provide for the Subsistance* [sic] *of their People*." This model of kingship exemplifies the liberty embodied in many British writers' conception of themselves earlier in the century, and indeed later in the century by Jacobin writers in the 1790s, and offers a critique of the king who is not answerable to his people. King Lillycraft inserts modern values and rationality into the older institution, values which frequently found voice in literature on the peripheries of empire, and were troubled and also reinforced by indeterminate figures such as Bampfylde-Moore Carew. As Kathleen Wilson suggests, "the eighteenth-century Empire was … a crucible of eighteenth-century modernity."[34] Like Moll Flanders or Robinson Crusoe, Carew can explore or acquire new riches or new selves in the colonies.

Carew is an elusive man while among Europeans, and is able to switch identities simply by changing his clothes. Among the Indians, he is unwilling or unable to dissimulate, and he follows their laws and customs in ways that he would never do among his own countrymen. In Britain, the only way to be free is to transgress laws, yet Indians reveal a way to align liberty and legality. He hunts alongside the Indians every day, and King Lillycraft offers him a close relative as his wife. Carew, however, "notwithstanding these Honours, could not forget his native Country, the Love of which glow'd within his Breast" (57). While the European is able to switch identities, the narrative insists that he maintains a core identity loyal to his nation. The limitations of fluidity at this point lie at actual miscegenation, which poses a greater threat to the loss of identity than cultural exchange, and which becomes the site of satire in the case of William Johnson discussed below. Despite his freedom and esteem among the Indians, Carew seemingly cannot leave of his own free will, and so must plot his escape. He is not a captive, but a free citizen, and yet presumably the hold of Indian society is so great that one cannot simply walk away. One day while he is out hunting with his brethren, they come across another group of Indians. They "got some Rum amongst them" and begin to drink together, and eventually "fell to Singing and Dancing after their Country Fashion" (58). It is only through the introduction of a European trade good that the Indians' grip on Carew can be loosened, even though they still maintain their fundamental identities as manifested by their cultural practices. Carew slips off with one of their canoes and eventually makes his way to Newcastle, Pennsylvania. Here he "transform'd himself into a *Quaker*, pulling off the Button from his Hat, and flapping it on every Side, put on as demure and precise a Look, as if his whole Family had been *Quakers*, and he had never seen any other Sort of People" (57–8). As soon as he leaves the Indians, he again finds the fluidity of self with which he has thrived to this point in his life. The narrator notes,

> Here Reader, it will be necessary to remark, that as our Hero is no longer among the simple and honest *Indians*, who are not enough polish'd to forget the Dictates of Nature, but follow her in all their Ways, who have not Art enough to deceive, but speak what they think, and act what they say; as he is no longer amongst such, but amongst a polish'd People, whose Knowledge has taught them to forget the Ways of Nature, and to act every thing in Disguise; whose Hearts and Tongues are almost as far distant from one another, as the North from the Southern Pole, and who daily over reach one another in the Occurrences of Life: We hope it will be no Disgrace to our Hero, if among such he appears as polish'd as the best, and puts on a fresh Disguise as often as it suits his Conveniency. (58)

The Indians are the natural progression beyond social limitations, and present an alternative to the uneasy British self caught between social graces or transculturation. The "polish'd" Europeans have no stable core in terms of their social behaviour, and switch ideas at their "conveniency." Though it was printed several years later, Burke makes a similar observation in *A Philosophical Enquiry into the Origin of Our Ideas of the Sublime and Beautiful* (1757); he notes that the languages of "most unpolished people ... have a great force and energy of expression," since "[u]ncultivated people are but ordinary observers of things, and not critical in distinguishing them" (261). Burke does not go so far as to suggest that this is a superior condition, but argues that people from these cultures "express themselves in a warmer and more passionate manner" as compared to the "polished languages" which "are generally deficient in strength." Hugh Blair, in *A Critical Dissertation on the Poems of Ossian* (1763), notes the "serious" condition of those less cultivated, and that the "American tribes ... have been noted by all travellers for their gravity and taciturnity" (23). During the "infancy of societies" and in contemporary societies not in the "refined state," he writes, people "display themselves to one another without disguise," and, because they lack the linguistic refinement to control their passions, "[a]n American chief, at this day, harangues at the head of his tribe, in a more bold metaphorical style, than a modern European would adventure to use in an Epic poem" (2). While both Burke and Blair view Native North America as representing an earlier or less refined state of society, they both point to the potentially liberating and alternative ways of expression and identity embodied by their lack of "polish."[35] Gypsies, too, provided a glimpse of the unconstrained self, and Carew's *Apology* included a cant dictionary of their "very expressive" language to show, as Janet Sorenson suggests, "a community enjoying a liberty once shared by all Britons."[36] Curiously, gypsies would become appropriated into the British landscape in the 1790s and subsequently romanticized. No longer considered foreign, they would "become English" and be turned into a "symbol of nostalgia and longing" by Victorians.[37] While I will not develop this analogy further, there is a compelling similarity between this and representations of Indians, as subsequent chapters will show that they too would be appropriated and then mourned.

Indians at the Masquerade

If the case of Bampfylde-Moore Carew is an instance of a figure of the so-called *ancien régime* of identity encountering Indians in their homeland, the anonymous *Universal Spectator* and *London Magazine* essay explores the possibility of an Indian encountering British cultures in their place of nativity. While it poses as a continuation of Addison's *Spectator* letter from one of the Indian kings who visited London in 1710, the essay takes place in the time of its publication in 1742. The author reflects on the power of curiosity as both a powerful desire and a productive force in discovery, and admits to his own taste in reading about people who are "govern'd and directed by Nature," whose "blunt Simplicity shews them to be utter Strangers to that Politeness we value ourselves so much upon" (1). Politeness is, to the author of the article, a means of maintaining the artifice of the social order. He thus wonders "what would be their Opinion of us, were they to inspect our Manners and Customs," and claims to have obtained the continuation of a letter by "that Serene Monarch, *Sa Ga Yern Qua Rash Tow* [*sic*], one of the *Indian Kings*, who was here in the Reign of Queen *Anne*." The author hopes the Indian's observations can reveal the faults which self-love and "the Prevalence of Custom have long made [the reader] blind to," and that women in particular can look past the "*hideous, hideous* Indian" to "view herself in the Glass he presents, and discover her own Likeness in the Picture he draws of *Affectation*." Like Carew, who is critical of the "polish" of Europeans as compared to the Indians who he lives among, the author sees Indians as "regulated only by the Instructions that Nature gives them." The first place he sends them to is the masquerade, the ultimate celebration of affectation during the period.

Wahrman suggests that "[i]t is hard to overestimate – though easy to forget – the cultural significance of the masquerade in eighteenth-century England."[38] Terry Castle similarly claims that the masked assembly was "a social phenomenon of expansive proportions and a cultural sign of considerable potency."[39] Castle writes that these events were "in the deepest sense a kind of collective mediation on self and other, and an exploration of their mysterious dialectic," which resulted in a "material devaluation of unitary notions of the self."[40] It was at the masquerade that social distinctions collapsed, or at least had the potential to do so; the *Country Journal* for 30 July 1737 reports that the English masquerade is "*a Comedy of Mankind*," in which "a confused Jumble of all Ranks, Ages, Sexes and Conditions ... mix together." The numerous, competing advertisements for masquerade habits indicates the massive popularity of the events, and costumes could be let to those who could not afford to buy. An ad in the *London Daily Post* in 1740 for "Lee's Masquerade Habits," one of several ads in the same issue, boasts costumes such as "fine peasants," "running-footmen's habits," "a fine Morocco Dress," and "fine Indian habits, for Men and Women, with feather'd Lamberkeanes."

The Indian kings are taken by their landlord "about Midnight" to a large room lit by candles. The king writes that "we had no sooner enter'd it than we were seiz'd with a mortal Fright: We saw, on every side of us, the most monstrous, ghastly, horrible Figures that Imagination can form." When these figures begin to speak like humans, the kings are calmed, but "[w]hat gave us the more Courage was that we saw several of our own Countrymen (as we thought by their Dress) not in the least terrified at these deform'd figures, but walking amongst them with great Intrepidity." The kings are dismayed to find out, upon speaking to these Indians, that "they were not our Countrymen, but Cheats and Counterfeits, that had assum'd our Habit, and would have pass'd upon the Company for us." They are about to "lay Hands on them in order to punish them for their Villainy" when their landlord intercedes, explaining that they "only chose that Habit to disguise their real Persons, as it was always customary for those to do who frequented such Assemblies." The Indian does not initially understand why this custom is practised until he sees "one of the pretended *Indians* make a Sign to a Female, who follow'd him into a private Room." He concludes that these events are meant for lovers to "gratify their Inclinations … and to avoid the Notice of the Publick Magistrate." Dissimulation is here represented as an act meant to conceal more base desires, and identity play collapses under the scrutiny of the Indians. Wahrman and Castle cite the marked decline of masquerades near the end of the century as evidence of a shift to more essentialized notions of subjectivity and individual interiority, yet already here the Indian is performing the work of modernity.

The Indian king finds little to admire in Britain in the *Universal Spectator* essay, and throughout it his masculine superiority is asserted over the feminized English population. Following the masquerade he attends a play and observes in the audience the "beaus," who are "the most tawdry, conceited, ridiculous Animals I ever saw," but are nonetheless admired by "coquets," who "took abundance of Pains to spoil that remarkable Beauty which Nature had bestow'd upon them." The "beaus" speak in "an effeminate tone of voice," shave their beards too closely, and wear too much "borrow'd Hair upon their Heads," in contrast to the masculine king, who is the "[v]oice of Nature and Reason." The first part of the essay ends after his encounter with these people, and the next issue continues with the kings being escorted to a musical entertainment. The "[c]ommon People," the king writes, do not come to such events because it is too expensive and "above their Taste." He marvels at the changing scenery on the stage, which replicates the natural seasons, and watches as two men come onstage, "with high Plumes of Feathers on their Heads, higher and more grand than that wore by *Te How Bash Ban Ka Kochee*, King of the *Nine Nations*." The king is mesmerized by their "majesty" and longs to hear "their rough, manly Voice, worthy [of] their Mein and Figure," but is dismayed to hear their voices sound "like the Notes of our Birds," which would be pleasing "had it been more natural." After discussing the non-English origin of these castrati, who "had an outward human Form, but were not *Men*," and the rapturous response of the audience, the king concludes that the English "have a strange Love for *Novelty*, and will prefer whatever is *Foreign* to that which is the Produce of their own Nation, even though their own is much more valuable." Of course, the author's use of an Indian to articulate this critique is driven by this same love of the foreign, but the Indian's cultural tenacity and unambiguous masculinity is held against the shifting interests of the English elite. The reader is asked to occupy the gaze of the Indian as a means of revealing the disturbing emptiness underlying European dissimulation.

The Indian king concludes his critique with his observations on political discourse and systems of governance. He is disturbed by the politicians who seem more concerned with foreign affairs than their own, by the existence of a standing army even during times of peace, and the countless laws which most people do not understand. While he admires the vast amount of trade which the nation carries on, he notes upon observing the countless goods at the custom house, "*This, the People say, is the Effect of* Liberty; *how careful ought they then to be, to preserve so inestimable a Treasure!*" The reduction of liberty to the availability of goods will be discussed in chapter 4, but here the Indian is criticizing the conflation of consumer power with political freedom. His final stop is at the nearby stock exchange, where he is troubled by the merchants "with a kind of fierce Madness in their Eyes" and who "all made hideous Outcries to something or other, call'd *Stock: –* This, we were inform'd, was the *Idol* of the Place." He concludes that he "[does] *not care for staying in so odd a Place, where savage Brutes bore the Resemblance of a human Form.*" In the end, the Indian king takes on the arrogant voice of the colonial official or the authors of manners and custom texts, while the modern trappings of Britain in effect reduce the humanity of its citizens to a lower state.

Tombo-Chiqui, the Middle-Class Savage

Cleland's play, like the *Universal Spectator* piece, picks up the thread of an earlier precedent and, most likely, an actual Native North American visitor to Britain. The title, *Tombo-Chiqui*, is presumably taken from the Creek leader Tomochichi (or Tomo Chachi, as he was widely known in Britain at the time) who visited London in 1734,[41] while the content is mostly a translation and adaptation of the popular French play *Arlequin Sauvage*. Tomochichi was widely known at the time of his visit and in the years following, and he was the subject of various sympathetic articles and poems, including Samuel Wesley and Thomas Fitzgerald's "Tomo Chachi: An Ode" (1736) and Francis Hawling's extended poem on Indian virtue, "A Discourse from King Tomo Chichy, to his Nephew Prince Tonahohy" (printed 1751). However, Cleland's protagonist is a young gallant and not, as the historical Tomochichi was, an old man at the time of his visit, and little else besides the name resembles the visit by the Yamacraws to London.[42]

The play was never performed, but was reviewed favourably in the *Critical* by Smollett, who excerpted several scenes and concluded that it "is written with a spirit, which no where flags," and that "there is a strain of pleasantry [that] runs through the whole, which, in our opinion, would have ensured it success on the stage under the conduct of a Garrick."[43] While Smollett believed that scenes from the play tended to run too long at times for the stage and would need to be cut, he noted that the "American savage ... talks very rationally: his character seems to be that of uncorrupted integrity, such as Adam was before the fall. His ignorance and innocence are well pourtrayed" (199). Smollett's focus on the subjectivity of the Indian points to Cleland's central concerns in the play, which is not so much the plot as the cultural encounter between an Indian and the metropolis.

The play follows a young "American savage" who has been brought to London by Captain Clerimont. Clerimont was rescued by the Indian in a shipwreck, and, while his main purpose is to claim his fiancé Sylvia, he hopes to be entertained by the observations of Tombo-Chiqui, which are by now familiar in depictions of Indians: "[T]he quickness of his perception, and the native shreudness of his answers, gave me the first idea of bringing him to Europe in all his ignorance. I had a notion it would divert me to observe pure simple nature working in him, in comparison with the laws, arts, and sciences amongst us. The contrast will doubtless be singular" (6). The rest of the plot primarily follows

Figure 2.1 Tomo Chachi Mico, or King of Yamacraw, and Tooanahowi [*sic*], His Nephew. Artist: John Faber the Younger after William Verelst, c. 1734. Mezzotint on paper. Yale Center for British Art, Paul Mellon Fund. Used with permission.

Tombo-Chiqui as he is repeatedly mystified by the laws and cultural practices of Britain, and attempts to gain the affections of Sylvia's friend Violetta. At one point he runs into a "Jew Pedlar," who offers Tombo-Chiqui some of his wares.[44] The Indian takes all that the pedlar offers gratefully, but is confused and angered when the man demands payment, since he has no concept of money. They argue, and the pedlar tells Tombo-Chiqui that he will complain to a Justice of the Peace, who has the authority to have him hanged. Tombo-Chiqui notes that "the honesty of these people is not voluntary, it goes against the grain; they would not be honest but for fear of these same laws" (21). They proceed to argue and Tombo-Chiqui resolves to "scalp the dog," but is left with only the man's wig in his hand. In the next scene the young American reflects that "as far as I can see, the people here are nothing of what they appear to be, and every thing is artificial amongst them, goodness, wisdom, wit, and even to the hair of their head" (21–2). As in all the examples above, the Indian represents the authentic expression of identity, what we might consider the modern self projected onto the uncivilized, North American Indigenous subject. While Cleland tempers his critique of commercial society by making its representative a racialized other, he condemns the arbitrary nature of its enforcement in the following scene when the constables believe Tombo-Chiqui is the one who has been wronged because "he has cried rogue first" (23). However, when he admits he beat the man and took his wares, thinking he is in the right, they realize what has occurred and insist on taking him to a judge. Not understanding the authority of the law, he insists that he must first go to meet a "pretty girl." They seize him, and at that point Clerimont enters. Clerimont explains that it is his fault for not explaining the law and currency of the land to the "savage," pays his debt, and has him released.

Following this event, Tombo-Chiqui is profoundly disenchanted with both Clerimont and his countrymen, complaining that "every thing is false and hollow amongst you" (27). Clerimont explains the concepts of private property, credit, and money to the young man, who responds

[Y]ou are poor, because you confine your notion of riches to money, or to the trash that money can procure, instead of enjoying pure nature as we do, who desire nothing, that we may freely enjoy every thing. You are slaves to your possessions, which you prefer to your liberty, and to your fellow creatures, whom you would hang, were they to take any the least part from you, of that which is useless to you. In short you are ignorant,

because you make your wisdom consist in knowing the laws, at the same
time that you are strangers to reason, which would teach you to do without laws as we do. (31–2)

The collective law produces the shallow individualism of consumerism, as opposed to the individual reason of the Indians, which is seen to
erase the artificiality of social distinction and private property. Though
the historical Tomochichi could be understood as a king in British eyes,
Cleland's Tombo-Chiqui does not occupy a similar claim to royal lineage. As such, his dissection of British culture is not tempered by his
own lofty social position; he is not a "noble" savage in the literal sense,
but is instead an "American savage," offering an alternative vision of
social and political governance enjoyed by all the Indigenous people of
North America.

While the logic of the consumer market so adeptly exploited by Cleland in the case of *Memoirs of a Woman of Pleasure* (1748–9), popularly
known as *Fanny Hill*, somewhat effaces the ideological connections
between the pornographic and the (post?)colonial, and the novelistic
form of *Fanny Hill* and the dramatic presentation of *Tombo-Chiqui* carry
with them distinct implications, there is nonetheless a relation between
the sex worker and the "American savage." Felicity Nussbaum has
shown that *Fanny Hill* "relocates England's colonialist agenda to the
human geography of the female body which is characterized as a ship
that travels from man to man, country to country."[45] Cleland was himself invested in the colonial project, serving with the British East India
Company for twelve years, from 1728 to 1740. Nussbaum notes that
he likely wrote part of the *Memoirs* while in Bombay, engaged primarily in commercial activities; she speculates that Cleland's depiction of
the prostitute's body as both a means of exchange by comparing it to a
ship, and as territory to possess, can be connected to the large amount
of "[b]uying and selling, trading and shipping" which he conducted
while in India.[46] While *Tombo-Chiqui* was written significantly later,
and the author's days with the East India Company were long behind
him, he began planning the play at least four years earlier. In a letter
to David Garrick of 31 July 1754, Cleland discusses a play he has just
begun called *Clown Polished by Love*, in which "[t]he principal character is … a young, raw, untutored rustic, with good sense at bottom; a
diamond in the rough."[47] He does not expand on the plot beyond the
comparison between the "rustic" and his rival, "one of those detestably
gay, double-refined fops, one sees daily and pesterably swarm about

town and Court." This play, still a "barely yet embryo of a production," in all likelihood became *Tombo-Chiqui* over the next several years. Cleland's specific interest in North America and Indians was no doubt, like his interests in Bombay, primarily commercial, though Tombo-Chiqui does not become objectified or instrumentalized in the same way as his "woman of pleasure." And yet the Indian, like the prostitute, is an object of desire for both the reading and viewing audience, and also functions as a critic of moral and political hypocrisy. Furthermore, the Indian similarly provides a more fixed and defined gendered sexuality from which to offer critique.

What makes *Tombo-Chiqui* unique is that the eponymous Indian visitor is not, as I have already noted, meant to be a king or other form of savage royalty, despite the high status of his namesake. While Berkhofer claims that "[n]either the rational nor the sentimental Indian ever achieved the popularity in England that he did in France, perhaps because that country had already had its revolution in the previous century,"[48] Cleland's play presents one of the more influential noble savages from France in an English context. Indeed, Rousseau believed the original play was important for its depiction of the contrast between nature and culture, and admired the way it "encourages [the audience's] way of thinking, which is to search and love new and unusual ideas."[49] Laura Brown defines the "fable of the Indian prince," one of the key "fables of modernity," as a narrative in which "the non-European becomes an influential model for the European man of feeling."[50] In Brown's description, however, "[t]he native visitor to London is ... decisively a 'prince' in contemporary English parlance: the natives who attract the attention of the London population in the eighteenth century are consistently understood in terms of European categories of elite status."[51] While this is generally true in the case of actual visitors and the public spectacles surrounding their visits, it is also usually more broadly the case in fictional visits, which themselves are generally based on actual accounts. Cleland's departure from this trope hints at a potentially unstable moment of identification for the British reader and audience, a rupture in sentimental identification that challenges elite sentimentalism.

These texts were produced well before Wahrman's quite precise location of the emergence of the modern self following the American Revolution, but they already contain key elements of his description of modern subjectivity; their distrust or bewilderment over disguise and dissimulation, their confidence in national origins, and the assumption of essential (and gendered) identities. We can also see in these texts what Taylor describes as a "radical subjectivism and an internalization of moral sources." The idea of the noble savage has often been understood as a morally superior alternative to or critique of Western life; but if placed within the context of the history of personal identity, in a way similar to Said's description of Orientalism as an enabling discourse for Western nationalism and empire, the figure of the Native North American plays a much more significant role in eighteenth-century British literature and culture than has previously been acknowledged. Finally, while the well-documented effects of colonialism on Native subjectivity and culture were profound and continue to be negotiated, I am interested in the other side of colonial domination. As part of the postcolonial exploration of eighteenth-century British literature, I believe it is important to explore and assess how representations of Native people determined and undermined aspects of British identity.

Section II: Ambivalent British Subjects Becoming Ambivalent Indians

This section will discuss the representations of British subjects engaging with Indian ways of life, or, to use Mary Louise Pratt's popular terminology, representations of "transculturation." In *Imperial Eyes*, Pratt borrows the term from ethnography, where it is meant to describe "how subordinated or marginal groups select and invent from materials transmitted to them by a dominant or metropolitan culture."[52] Pratt asks, in addition to the dynamic of subjugated peoples integrating other cultural materials into their lives, "[H]ow does one speak of transculturation from the colonies to the metropolis?" How, in other words, can we describe metropolitan subjects being shaped by their engagements with the colonial cultures encountered on the frontiers of their empire? Furthermore, how can this discussion be productive when the colonial cultures are abstracted, commodified, or even invented by British authors and travellers? As this section and the fifth chapter will suggest, these sites of interaction changed greatly during the shift to modern forms of identity.

For most British authors in the mid-eighteenth century, the white person who "goes native," whether out of coercion as a captive or by choice, is not to be seen as proof of the superiority of life among Indians, away from the temptations and corruptions of civilization, but as a personal failing of that individual.[53] Boswell, for example, includes the following passage in his *The Life of Samuel Johnson* (1791):

> Johnson. "When we talk of pleasure, we mean sensual pleasure. When a man says, he had pleasure with a woman, he does not mean conversation, but something of a different nature. Philosophers tell you, that pleasure is *contrary* to happiness. Gross men prefer animal pleasure. So there are men who have preferred life among savages. Now what a wretch must he be, who is content with such conversation as can be had among savages! You may remember an officer at Fort Augustus, who had served in America, told us of a woman whom they obliged to *bind*, in order to get her back from savage life." Boswell. "She must have been an animal, a beast." Johnson. "Sir, she was a speaking cat." (II, 200)

Dr Johnson's antipathy towards "savage life" is a recurring topic in both his own work and in Boswell's accounts of their conversations, so it should come as little surprise to see him disapprove of the white people who choose to live "among savages." Notwithstanding Johnson's personal affection for his cats, we can assume he sees this woman as less than human, a "wretch" who prefers the "animal pleasure" of savage conversation. William Smith witnessed an event similar to that described by Johnson, or indeed perhaps the same event, in which white people living among Indians had to be bound in order to stay among the English during Colonel Henry Bouquet's expedition to repatriate captives in 1764.[54] In this well-known episode, which is described in the following chapter, Smith notes that "some women, who had been delivered up, afterwards found means to escape and run back to the Indian towns." He concludes that such people must be either from "the lowest rank" or have never known a good life. That Boswell, Johnson, and Smith should be so distressed by the seemingly willing transculturation of a white woman points to the uneasy relationship between racial mutability and sexuality, and the allure of savage life for these British men is tied to the moral degradation of some women. Unspoken by these men is the anxiety that life among savages offers a fulfilment for women which the refined and emasculated British male cannot offer, and the Indian's masculinity lures them away from civilization. However, these cases of white women living among Indians were, with the exception of some Puritan captivity narratives popular in New England, rarely mentioned in British texts until the nineteenth century.[55] More common was the representation of cohabitation and intermarriage by white men, as in the case of William Johnson and others, as well as depictions of male captives.

The Transculturation of Peter Williamson

One of the more prominent sites of Britons interacting very closely with Indigenous cultures in literature is in captivity narratives, texts which became increasingly popular in Britain in the 1750s and 1760s, as the conflict in North America between the English, French, and Indians allied with each side escalated. I will discuss these works in the following chapter, looking at the ways in which transculturation itself becomes part of the drama of survival, a necessary but nonetheless deeply ambivalent aspect of captive life. And though they are freed or escape in the end, the captives rarely emerge unchanged by their experiences, despite their claims to have been unaffected upon escape.[56] Indeed, in many respects the genre of captivity is a nationalist project to re-write the durability of British selves in the face of brutal cultures, but these attempts to reclaim the desired power relations in the colonies ultimately reveal the darker side of the colonial project.

The most well-known redeemed Indian captive in eighteenth-century Britain was Scotsman Peter Williamson, who would become a public figure known as "Indian Peter" in the decades following his time in North America, and he embodies the conflicts at the heart of transcultural relations in the period.[57] This section will look at the ways that Williamson's supposed transculturation unfolds by examining both the text of the many editions of his narrative, and the circulating image of the frontispiece. It will look to unpack the remarkable contradiction between his anti-Indian narrative and his public appropriation of an Indian identity. This dynamic is an important lesson overall in Indigenous representation and appropriation, and the unstable circulation of his portrait will demonstrate that the permeability of identity in this period could both unsettle and reinscribe cultural difference.

The first edition of Williamson's captivity narrative *French and Indian Cruelty* was printed in York in 1757, and by 1762 it had already reached its fifth edition and had received significant revisions from its author. The general narrative, however, remained primarily intact: Williamson is born to humble yet "reputable" parents outside of Aberdeen, and as a young child he is sent into that city to live with his aunt. When he is eight, he is spotted by two men "employed ... by some of the *worthy* Merchants of the Town, in that villainous and execrable Practice, call'd

Kidnapping; that is, stealing young Children from their Parents and selling them as Slaves in the Plantations abroad" (3). Williamson is sold to a
Scotsman, who was himself captured as a child, and brought to Philadelphia. His master allows him to attend school in the winters, and, upon
his death when Williamson is sixteen, leaves him a small inheritance.
Williamson, now a free man, marries the daughter of a successful planter
and settles with her on land his father-in-law gives them on the Pennsylvania frontier. They live there happily until 1754, when Indians "in the
French Interest" begin terrorizing the colonial settlements. This coincided
with the beginnings of the French and Indian War, which began in 1754
and led to the Seven Years' War in Europe. While Williamson primarily blames the French and the lack of loyalty of the Indians who at first
appear allied with the British, or "*French Chicanery* and Savage Cruelty"
(10), he admits that some Indians were easily won over to the French
side because they had been "cruelly treated by those who pretended to
be their Protectors and Friends" (10). These Indians eventually set upon
Williamson's homestead while his wife is away, burning his possessions and forcing him to accompany them. He spends a harrowing few
months with them, witnessing and documenting their cruel way of life
until he eventually escapes, running naked through the night. Much of
what follows involves him carrying out vengeance on the Indians as a
soldier, though in that role too he is captured, this time by the French.
They send him back to Britain in exchange for other prisoners, where he
arrives broken and penniless, having to publish his tale to make money.

As an abducted child and indentured servant, Peter Williamson is
caught in the transatlantic trade in bodies, already instrumentalized
by the colonial apparatus before his role as a settler on the disputed
frontier. He is, in his telling, just as victimized by European expansion
and ambition as the Indians whose land is increasingly encroached
on by North American colonists. His depiction of the exploitation of
poor British children by greedy merchants had a much greater impact
at home in Scotland than his vivid descriptions of Indian cruelty; he
was sued by Aberdeen merchants after the initial printing of his narrative, and all copies of the text were ordered burned. He successfully
appealed the decision and was given a settlement, and he included
the court proceedings against him and a "Discourse on Kidnapping"
in later editions. This material shifted the focus of the text away from
the "French and Indian cruelty" promised in the title, and he ends
the fifth edition with the promise to those "groaning under the yoke
of tyrany" that "Providence will throw friends in their way, their

oppressors shall hide their heads, and the cruelties they have committed be retaliated upon" (147). Merchant greed, not colonial violence,
is the broader issue in the end, and it is possible that Williamson's
subsequent transculturation can be seen as not simply a crass commercial move or colonial appropriation, which it no doubt was, but
also in part as a strategic occupation of a colonized subjectivity meant
to draw attention to the wages of empire.

What makes Williamson unique among British captives from the
period is that he would come to openly embrace an Indian identity
in Britain, though the foundations of this subjectivity were decidedly
shaky.[58] At no point in the text of his narrative, whose veracity itself is
strongly in doubt, does Williamson willingly act like an Indian; indeed,
after being forced to accompany them under threat of death following
their ransacking of his home and possessions, he is regularly tortured
and abused. During his first night among them Williamson is tied to a
tree and the Indians begin to dance around him, "whooping, bellowing,
and crying, in a frightful Manner, as is their Custom" (13). They then
proceed "in a more tragical Manner," burning him with coals and sticks
from the fire, "and at the same Time threatening to burn me intirely, if
I made the least Noise or cried out" (14). He can only shed silent tears,
which the Indians observe "with a shocking Pleasure and Alacrity"
and "take fresh Coals, and apply near my Eyes, telling me my Face
was wet, and that they would dry it for me, which indeed they cruelly
did" (12). This brutal rite of initiation constitutes a key event in representations of transculturation among North American Indians,
described by Charlotte Sussman as "running the gauntlet."[59] Sussman
notes that "[t]hese rituals, although violent, were seen by eighteenth-
century observers as the means by which Native American tribes
appropriated and transformed foreign cultures." She suggests that
"Europeans saw these rituals as evidence of a tribe's ability to retain
its social coherence in the face of a colonizing invasion – a quality
they found admirable as well as threatening."[60] This type of "corpo-
realizing cultural change" is seen also in Smollett's *Humphry Clinker*,
which in turn borrowed its scenes of colonial violence from earlier
sources such as Cadwallader Colden's *The History of the Five Indian
Nations* (1727). Sussman notes that in Smollett's novel the focus on
torture and dismemberment is meant to literalize, in an attempt to
neutralize, "the cultural anxiety surrounding transculturation."[61]
While Williamson does not explicitly acknowledge that this torture is
meant to bring him into the society of his captors, he writes that, following his cruel treatment, the Indians feasted and offered him food

which he "was ... forced to seem pleas'd with" (14). Thus the process of becoming other is accounted for as a performance necessary for survival, and as an inscription of corporeal cultural signifiers accomplished through torture.

The cruelty of Williamson's Indians knows no limits, and while he escapes the most brutal tortures, he describes other victims who are dismembered and otherwise taken apart by his captors. Whole families, including infants and children, are arbitrarily scalped, one family is cut to pieces and fed to pigs, and in one particularly gruesome scene,

> two of [the prisoners] were tied to a Tree, and a great Fire made round them, where they remained 'till they were terribly scorched and burnt; when one of the villains with his *scalping* Knife, ript open their Bellies, took out their Entrails, and burnt them before their Eyes, whilst the others were cutting, piercing, and tearing the Flesh from their Breasts, Hands, Arms, and Legs, with red-hot Irons, 'till they were dead. (19)

Williamson is tasked to dig the graves of his countrymen. Sussman describes scenes such as these as a "nightmarish version of social absorption" in which the European is either adopted or consumed (though Williamson does not focus on instances of cannibalism per se, but rather on annihilation).[62] In this context, it is difficult to locate Williamson's motivation to become an Indian. Yet amidst his diatribes against his captors, in which he vividly describes scenes of pornographic violence, he occasionally expresses an admiration for the Indians; he notes at one point that some nations "might be more happy, if, in some Instances, they copied them, and made *wise Conduct, Courage, and personal Strength*, the *chief* Recommendations for War-Captains, or *Werowances*, as they call them" (26). In the first edition of his narrative, Williamson's depiction of Indians is irreconcilably ambivalent; the inconceivable savagery of the "noxious creatures" who capture him and the gentle humanity of the elderly Iroquois chief Scarrooyda, alias Monokatcathy, who speaks in an "affecting manner" with tears in his eyes when pleading for military aid from the Quaker colonists in Philadelphia, present a radically different picture of Native people. Indeed, Williamson's earlier description of the "barbarous and extraordinary" way in which Indians execute old people whom they no longer deem useful, by having a small child slowly bludgeon them to death with a tomahawk while being lifted by an adult (27–8), adds to this ambivalence. If some savage acts can be understood as an aspect of resistance to invasion, rather than a determining characteristic of Indigenous cultures, others seem fundamental articulations of inhumane cultural values. How then can we understand Williamson's adoption of an Indian identity upon his return to Britain? What appeal could a culture of violent cruelty, even if largely invented, hold for a British subject?

Williamson's shift towards identification with his cruel captors begins with the fourth edition of the book (1759), the first printed in London, which was sold by *Monthly Review* editor Ralph Griffiths and dedicated to William Pitt, thus allying it closely with the Whig agenda of focusing on the war in North America.[63] This dedication also signalled Williamson's ultimately unrealised ambition to move from abject soldier and entrepreneur to legitimate statesman, seen also in his appendices on French activities in the colonies and other publications on military strategy.[64] In the dedication he writes that he hopes to rouse his fellow Britons "from sloth and dull delays" so that they can rescue the colonists in Pennsylvania, and explains that he evokes Pitt's name because his "support of our rights and privileges as men and Christians" have made him famous and Williamson is thus "desirous of appearing cloathed with your protection" (iii). But the most striking feature of this edition is that the new frontispiece depicts Williamson "in the Dress of a Delaware Indian with his Tomohawk, Scalping knife, &c." He is literally clothed like the "savage *Indians*" whom he is hoping to mobilize his readers against, seemingly undercutting any claim he may have had to the patronage of the protector of "the Protestant cause." Given the brutal nature of Williamson's depiction of "Indian cruelty," it is surprising to see his supposed transculturation foregrounded. Again, nowhere in the text does he hint at this transformation, or even mention donning Indian clothing; while he does concede that the white family to whom he flees upon his escape are alarmed because they "took me to be an Indian" (35), he is also notably without clothing at that moment. Like Crusoe in his motley dress in the first editions of *Robinson Crusoe*, Williamson begins the text with his own body depicting the drama of survival in a far away colonial setting. The surprising provenance of this frontispiece can itself illuminate the slippery contours of transculturation in the period.

The portrait of Williamson is, significantly, the first image in which a British subject is supposed to have "gone native" among North American Indigenous people.[65] Williamson stands in the foreground, his painted face bearing the blank expression of the ethnographic subject. His clothing is an accurate rendition of the "Indian fashion," including a mix of Native objects and European trade goods.[66] He is clutching a

Mr. Peter Williamson
in the Dress of a Delaware Indian

1. Tomohawk. 2 Scalping-knife. 3 Powder-horn. 4 Shot-
bag. 5 Belt. 6 Purse of Wampum. 7 Gun. 8 Bush-
Fighting. 9 War-dance. 10 Indian Canoe.

Figure 2.2 Mr. Peter Williamson in the Dress of a Delaware Indian, 1759.
Frontispiece engraving. John Carter Brown Library, Brown University. Used
with permission.

"scalping knife" in one hand and a pipe-tomahawk in the other, fraught transcultural icons, as we will see in a following chapter, of Indian difference, while his gun hangs on his back. The headdress and palm trees speak to earlier methods of exotic representations in British art,[67] but the costume that Williamson is wearing is contemporary. Indeed, the pipe-tomahawk is an especially current accoutrement, and this portrait contains one of the first pictorial representations of this weapon.[68] In the background we see a tropical setting decidedly unlike the backwoods of Pennsylvania where he was supposedly captured, and groups of Indians paddle in a canoe, perform a "war dance" around a palm tree, and engage in "bush fighting."

The broader history of the frontispiece in eighteenth-century texts can help unpack this incongruous illustration. Williamson borrowed heavily from the popular literature of the period, especially the "narratives of unfortunates," so it is not difficult to place him alongside other "factual fictions" and novels.[69] Janine Barchas suggests that, in the early novel, "extra-narrative" pages such as frontispieces were used "to negotiate the tension between textual authority and fictional identity," as in the portrait of Gulliver at the beginning of Swift's *Travels*. These "transparently counterfeit" portraits challenge the truth claims of the novel; as Barchas notes in the case of Gulliver, "[i]t is difficult to imagine that the man who now finds human contact so repulsive would sit for a portrait cloaked in the velvet trappings of the Yahoo culture he disdains."[70] Indeed, the portrait of Williamson presents the same challenge, contradicting the very premise of his narrative. And while Williamson claims to offer a true account, assuring Pitt his relation is "genuine," the portrait suggests otherwise.

In the frontispiece to the first edition of *Robinson Crusoe* (1719), Crusoe strikes a similar figure to Williamson; his eyes are cast down to the right of the viewer, his expression is difficult to read, his objects of survival evoke battle and violence, and the scene is not an especially faithful representation of the narrative. This portrait, which David Blewett rightly describes as "strangely evocative," depicts an uncertain moment in time for the castaway, and the intact ship in the background heading out to sea is a detail not mentioned in the narrative itself. Blewett suggests that this "haunting" engraving portrays the "'theatre' of Crusoe's mind," and we see Crusoe "not at an actual moment in time but as the timeless figure of the castaway, strangely dressed, thinking about his fate and his deliverance, symbolized by the background ship." This kind of "synoptic illustration," popular in earlier religious paintings

Figure 2.3 Robinson Crusoe, 1719. Frontispiece engraving, John Carter Brown Library, Brown University. Used with permission.

and illustration and still used in the eighteenth century, depicts several different moments in time simultaneously, causing "several problems of interpretation" but ultimately helping to sum up the experience of Crusoe.[71] Barchas notes that this summative illustration "renders Crusoe's wishes and memories as concrete objects open to the viewer's/ reader's gaze," aligning it with allegorical texts such as Bunyan's *The Pilgrim's Progress*.[72]

If the scene of Williamson stoically posed among the Indians is read the same way, it becomes the universalised experience of the white captive, performing a foreign subjectivity for their survival. Or perhaps it is a nightmare, registering the greatest fear of the suffering captive who to the end insists upon their cultural, if not bodily, integrity. Can it be a projection of Williamson's own desire to become an Indian, hidden somewhere deep in the narrative's foremost claims of Indian degeneracy? Unlike Crusoe's synoptic pose, the illustration of Williamson is disruptive rather than illuminative; the narrative trajectory of the text in terms of transcultural contact runs from fearful captive to vengeful soldier to abject colonial in Britain, and nowhere is there a moment in which Williamson lives as an Indian during his brief captivity. Barchas suggests that by the 1750s and 1760s, the frontispiece, like the novel itself, had begun to be less interested in "private identity" and turned towards "socially determined subjectivity."[73] There was an overall decline in their use, and those that do appear less often depicted the singular subject of the work but rather attempted to draw attention to broader social formations. Perhaps, then, we can in part see Williamson's portrait as existing somewhere between the earlier mapping of a private (fictional) subject and the more expansive concerns of later literature, an individual captive clothed in the forces of transatlantic circulation.

There is, however, further context for this image. Upon his return to Britain, Williamson had begun to perform publicly as "Indian Peter" shortly after the first edition of his narrative, and had gained a modest level of fame and fortune. He would dress in Indian regalia and perform his "war whoop" for crowds of people, travelling as far afield as Dublin, London, and elsewhere to entertain people in private homes and coffeehouses. He would later open his own Indian-themed coffeehouse in Edinburgh in the Scottish Parliament building in the early 1760s, with a sign declaring him to be "The Indian Captive From Another World."[74] There he continued entertaining patrons, including Robert Fergusson and Benjamin Franklin, with stories and performances, and would perform intermittently as an Indian for the rest of his life. The fourth edition of his narrative was the first printed in London, and coincided with Williamson appearing in the city. The Dublin periodical *Gentleman's and London Magazine* for June of 1759 also printed the image ahead of his appearance and reported that his performances involved "displaying and explaining their [the Indians'] method of fighting."[75] This frontispiece of him in Delaware dress acts as a promotion of his public performance, and more importantly as a dissemination of the character of "Indian Peter," the transculturated subject. It provides both a preview and a claim to authenticity. Yet while Shannon suggests we might gain historical insight into what Williamson's performances in racial drag consisted of by looking at this image,[76] it turns out that this portrait, perhaps either allegorizing or commodifying the experience of the captive, is itself an act of appropriation.

In inventor and showman Benjamin Martin's *Miscellaneous Correspondence*, an article from January of 1759 contains an image of a "Mohawk Indian Warrior, with his Tomax, Scalping-Knife &c."[77] The article explains that this unnamed warrior, about whom there seems to be no surviving historical evidence, "is lately arrived from *America*," where he was one of William Johnson's guards and was renowned for his "singular Valour in taking the *French* General, *Monsieur Desseau* [Dieskau], Prisoner" (1).[78] The capture of Dieskau in 1755 was a significant victory for the British, and resulted in Johnson being knighted, so the warrior's appearance in London was a direct connection to colonial triumph. Martin proclaims that this Mohawk man "(for the Gratification of the Curious) is expos'd to public View, dress'd in the same Manner with his native *Indians*, when they go to War, with his Face and Body painted, his Scalping-knife, and Tomax, or Battle-axe, and all the other Implements that are used by the *Indians* in Battle." The *Public Advertiser* carried an ad for his appearance at the "New York and Cape Breton Coffee-house" at a cost of one shilling per person, almost every other day for all of January, until he had to "embark for America" in early February. It notes that this warrior is "[a] sight worth the curiosity of every true Briton" and falsely claims he is "[t]he only Indian that has been in England since the Reign of Queen Anne." But even if the writer was aware of the Cherokee in 1730 and Tomochichi and the Yamacraw shortly afterwards, as Samuel Johnson notes in his *Idler* no. 41 for 20 January 1759, advertisers recognize that "[w]hatever is common is despised," and so they need to "gain attention by magnificence of promises" (121). Johnson read

The MOHAWK INDIAN Warrior,
with his Tomax, Scalping-Knife &c.

Figure 2.4 The Mohawk Indian Warrior, with his Tomax, Scalping-Knife &c.
Artist: Anthony Walker, 1759. Engraving. The William Ready Division of Archives
and Research Collections, McMaster University Library. Used with permission.

the advertisement for this Mohawk warrior in the *Public Advertiser* and noted that it

> is a very powerful description; but a critic of great refinement would say that it conveys rather horror than terror. An Indian, dressed as he goes to war, may bring company together; but if he carries the scalping knife and tomax, there are many true Britons that will never be persuaded to see him but through a grate. (122)

This is far from the sublime experience of managed terror, and he adds, "I could not but feel some indignation when I found this illustrious Indian warrior immediately succeeded by 'a fresh parcel of Dublin butter'" (122). The crass levelling effect of the classified advertisements page is no place for the fierce dignity of the Indian warrior, though Johnson sees this Mohawk man as equally constructed by the "masters of the publick ear" to appeal "too wantonly to our passions" (123).

The image of Williamson is clearly based on the print of the Mohawk man from the *Miscellaneous Correspondence*, done by well-known engraver Anthony Walker.[79] The man holds the same objects as Williamson, and the background evokes the same exotic setting. Both men are wearing linen shirts and are wrapped in trade blankets, typical of the hybrid fashion of dress among both Native people like Joseph Brant and colonial officials such as William Johnson. There are some distinctions between them, but the most noteworthy is that Williamson, and not the Mohawk man, is the one who more accurately reflects the "Indian fashion," from his gorget closely resembling others painted during the period, to his powder horn and headdress. Even Williamson's moccasins accurately imitate the beaded examples already in British collections at the time. The Mohawk, by contrast, wears laurels and a style of dress less current at the time, resembling a hybrid of North American and Classical European civilization. Even the man's weapon, a "tomax," is incorrectly identified. Williamson's portrait effectively displaces the Mohawk, a "real" Indian, as a representative of the transatlantic world, fulfilling the British expectations of Indian difference through a visual appropriation. This would become more apparent over time as it circulated during the latter half of the century.

The first depiction of Williamson in a London publication, with his "warlike and hunting implements," appears in the *Grand Magazine of Universal Intelligence* for 30 June 1759. This is months before the printing of Williamson's London edition, and the *Grand Magazine* was, like the London edition of *French and Indian Cruelty*, printed by Ralph Griffiths. Presumably Griffiths included this portrait to build publicity for the forthcoming narrative. Williamson's portrait in his own text, however, most likely reached the widest audience, and it appeared in subsequent editions of the narrative. Its quality degraded over time, but the main characteristics remained intact. What is more interesting, however, is the way that it circulated during the latter half of the century, becoming something quite different from either the Mohawk man or the costumed Scotsman.

In the 1766 Dublin edition of Charlevoix's *A Voyage to North America*, the frontispiece features a by-now familiar sight: "A Delaware Indian, with his Tomohawk, Scalping knife, &c." The same year, Williamson was in Dublin to promote the seventh edition of *French and Indian Cruelty*, the first printed in that city, and, ironically, to address the appearance of a counterfeit edition of his work.[80] It appears as though the printers of the Charlevoix text simply traced the Williamson engraving, since it is an exact mirror image of the "original."[81] And so, though he could never become one in life despite his desire to, Williamson circulated in print as a genuine Indian. And the Charlevoix text was not the only place; other British texts claiming to provide illustrations of Delaware Indian costumes also based their images around Williamson. In the fourth volume of *A Collection of the Dresses of Different Nations, Antient and Modern* (1772), the image of the Delaware is, once again, "with his Tomohawk, Scalping knife." Finally, in volume 5 of *A New Moral System of Geography*, first printed in Bath in 1790, there appears a small print of a Delaware Indian who, though unlabelled, is clearly holding the ubiquitous pipe-tomahawk and scalping knife.

The circulation and adaptation of this image, from Indian to European and back again, suggests, on the surface, that printers were not particularly concerned with the sources of their images, and it was easier to copy or adapt a picture than to find one's own. This is of course true, but it also points to the slippery means of signification in identity; the image, like Williamson himself, circulated through various texts, and would be redefined depending on each context. It was not until years after his captivity that Williamson fully appropriated his identity as "Indian Peter," raised from infancy among Indians. This is due in part, as the fourth chapter will argue, to the enabling shift to a modern way of identification during and following the 1770s. His ostensible portrait in Native garb accomplished this much sooner; while he meant

A Delaware Indian.
with his Tomohawk Scalping knife. &c.

Figure 2.5 A Delaware Indian. with his Tomohawk Scalping knife, &c., 1766.
Frontispiece engraving, John Carter Brown Library, Brown University. Used
with permission.

bit of a Delaware Indian with his Tomohawk Scalping Knife.

Indien de la Rivière Delaware armé de la Haché a du Couteau pour lever la chevelure.

202

Figure 2.6 Habit of a Delaware Indian with his Tomohawk Scalping Knife, 1790. Engraving (after Anthony Walker?). Wellcome Library. Used with permission.

Figure 2.7 A Delaware Indian,
1792 edition. Engraving. UCLA.
Used with permission.

it to enforce his own transcultural identity, the reliance of the *ancien régime* on performance and external dress for the assertion of identity (or non-identity) transformed his portrait back into an actual Indian, a stable subject.

Williamson is in some ways an idiosyncratic case for his time, but many people following him historically have similarly taken on Native identities; Linda Colley places him in the tradition of Englishman Archie Belaney, more widely known as Grey Owl, who became a popular environmentalist in the first part of the twentieth century after he took on a Native identity.[82] Shannon, for his part, suggests that Williamson falls within the discourse of British imperialism, demonstrating "the irresistible expansion of the British Empire and its inevitable incorporation of distant peoples and distant lands around the globe."[83] Given Williamson's own unstable social position, this seems to be an overstatement. His transformation into the spectacle of "Indian Peter" in his own life and into an actual Indian in the circulation of printed images reveals the complex and at times arbitrary distinctions between races and cultures in consumer and print culture of the eighteenth century. This transformation also suggests that even in its first graphic representation, the appropriation of Indigenous cultures, then and now, reinscribes the cultural difference it attempts to unsettle.

Sir William Johnson, Lismahago, and the Corrupt Transcultural Subject

In North America, figures on the periphery of national and cultural identities were not uncommon, and those on the frontier experienced transcultural exchanges frequently.[84] As Wahrman notes, the colonies "became the setting for conspicuous figures who in their very persons and lives embodied the limitations of familiar categories of identity on this permanent cross-cultural frontier."[85] People such as Mohawk leader Hendrick and Irish gentleman William Johnson blurred the lines between English and Indian; Hendrick was a Bear clan sachem who was an important English ally and who often dressed in the British fashion,[86] while Johnson regularly dressed in full Mohawk regalia and had a Mohawk family, but was also a baronet and important military official for the British empire.

Though portraits of Johnson tend to depict him dressed in clothing suitable for a British merchant and colonial official, Cadwallader Colden reports seeing him in 1746 at a Covenant Chain treaty conference "riding at the head of the *Mohawks*, dressed and painted after the manner of an *Indian* War Captain."[87] It was widely known in British print that he had been adopted by the Mohawks in the 1740s and given the name "Warraghiyagey" or "Doer of Great Things," and a large part of his success as the head of Indian Affairs was attributed to his ability to speak to Indigenous allies in their own language. The *Gentleman's and London Magazine* for September of 1755 emphasizes his transcultural abilities, noting "he is particularly happy in making himself beloved by all sorts of people and can conform to all companies and conversations," while the Mohawks among whom he lives "esteem him as their common father."[88] At the same time, his immersion in Mohawk life and his marriage to Molly Brant, Joseph Brant's older sister, was seen by some as a problematic, even morally questionable, choice of lifestyle.

In Charles Johnstone's *Chrysal; or, The Adventures of a Guinea* (1760), Johnson's transcultural brotherhood is satirized as a licentious and egotistical foray meant to satisfy his carnal desires. This popular novel, which quickly went through five editions and has received increased attention in recent years as part of the resurgence in studies on the "it-narratives" it inspired,[89] tracks the circulation of a gold coin as it changes hands across countries and oceans. The coin, an appropriate narrator to examine the effects of commerce on British people through- out the empire, reads the minds of the people who possess it, with Smollett noting that "we hope, for the sake of humanity, that the writer has beheld nature reflected by a false mirror."[90] With this bleak view of human nature, in the second book of the novel the coin enters the hands of a British commander in North America. This man (likely Braddock or Amherst) is governed solely by his "pride and avarice," and wants only to accumulate wealth without regard to public interest now that he has been given a position in the colonies. He meets a British gen- eral whose "whole deportment was in the unaffected ease of natural liberty, above the hypocritical formality of studied rules of behaviour devised only to deceive" (II, 139). This general tells the other British officer that he has adapted the "common sense" and "natural reason" of the "native *Americans*," and that they are "in general above our level, in the virtues which give real preheminence [*sic*], however despicably we think of, and injuriously we treat them" (II, 141–3). He has "become quite a stranger to that *dissimulation*, which is called *politeness*, among *civilized* nations; and must make use of words, in their original inten- tion of conveying my thoughts" (II, 145). It becomes clear by his loy- alty to and high opinion of the Indians that this is meant to be William Johnson, and the coin follows him to his home among the Indians, where he rules as a sovereign but at the same time is welcomed "with sincere joy and respect" (II, 147).

Johnson is a stark contrast to the other British officer, who believes, like Amherst, that "it would be an advantage to the world, if the whole race of them was exterminated" (II, 142). Johnson instead believes that the Indians who "converse much with *civilized Europeans* ... learn many things from them, which are a disgrace to their own *Savage* nature, as you call it" (II, 142). Yet if the other commander is the ultimate artic- ulation of the bigotry and greed of colonialism, Johnson represents a different kind of self-interest. The coin notes that while the general's authority over his American subjects comes in part from his treatment of them with respect and honesty, it also, "like that of the first rulers of the earth, was founded ... on the relations of nature, and supported by its strongest ties, he being literally the father of his subjects, the king of his own family" (II, 147–8). The narrator explains that, in order to gain esteem among these people he decided to set aside "all such rules of conduct as seemed to him to be contradictory to natural reason, and the publick good" (II, 148). Key among these rules of conduct which Johnson set aside was "the custom of restraining the commerce between the sexes, and confining individuals to each other, after the desire which first brought them together had ceased" (II, 148). The coin does not speculate on whether this decision came from reason or "(as is often the case) whether he sought for reasons to support the dictates of inclination," simply noting that in either case, "the effect was the same"; his subjects grew in numbers and "there was scarce an house in any of the tribes around him, from which he had not taken a temporary mate, and added a child of his to their number" (II, 149–50).

By the 1750s Johnson had become the most widely known British colonial officer serving in America, and his interest in Native women became equally established among colonists. One friend noted that "Sir William like Solomon has been eminent in his Pleasures with the brown Ladies," while a colonist observed that Johnson "knew that Women govern the Politics of savages as well [as] the refined part of the World and therefore always kept up a good understanding with the brown Ladies."[91] In Britain, however, his reputation remained strong in contrast to the failed campaigns of officers such as Braddock, and his success was attributed by some to his ability to accommodate himself to the customs of the Six Nations. Thus Colden remarks in the 1755 edition of *The History of the Five Indian Nations* that he "was indefatigable among the *Mohawks*; he dressed himself after the *Indian Manner*, made frequent Dances, according to their Custom when they excite to War, and used all the Means he could think of, at a considerable Expence, (which his Excellency had promised to repay him) in order to engage them heartily in the War against *Canada*" (II, 126). While his transcultural inroads were clearly done in the service of the British and colonial governments, Johnstone's satire points out the slippery nature of Johnson's colonial enactments, and the suspicion that, while Indians were widely seen as virtuous, the Europeans who chose to live among them were decidedly not. For his part, Johnson enjoyed the tales of his sexual prowess, and owned a copy of *Chrysal* himself.[92]

Following his return to the village in which he is connected to most families through his productive relations with the women of the community, Johnson asks his subjects to join the British army in a campaign, which they "readily and sincerely assented to" (II, 150). He then returns to his "domestick concerns," and the coin describes his new master's family life. Johnson has a small compound with a number of cottages, where "the females of his present family" live. He does not in any way prevent them from leaving him for other men, and in fact keeps in contact with them, even giving them presents when they leave. His wives raise their children with him in these cottages, and while the women lack the "delicate sensibility" of European women, "custom, that reconciles all things, had made them agreeable to him, especially as no comparison could there be made to their disadvantage" (II, 152).

It turns out, however, that even when there is a European woman available, Johnson opts for his adoptive people. When some of his community discover a "*European* lady, whom they found wandering in those unfrequented wilds" (II, 159), Johnson, feeling a strong sense of patriotic attachment and duty to the woman, makes her comfortable and makes sure that all of her possessions are accounted for. Once she is settled, Johnson asks her how she came to be in "the midst of those desarts so far away from every *European* settlement" (II, 160). She explains that her husband was a high-ranking English officer who was killed near the beginning of the war, "before *England* had exerted herself in such a manner, as to intitle her to success" (II, 160). The widow was so distraught by the news of her husband's death that she travelled to North America "for the melancholy pleasure of one last view of his dear remains" (II, 160). She manages to accomplish her goal, but "not so much to her satisfaction as she could have wished," since

> the body being in a state of putrefaction, [it was] not possible to be approached without disgust and abhorrence; nor to be distinguished from any other mass of corruption, when she had caused it to be dug out of the grave, in which it had been buried on the spot where he had been killed, among the other victims of the day[.] (II, 161)

While Johnson has managed to accommodate himself and even thrive in the colonies by appropriating ostensibly Indigenous practices, the British officer is consumed by the earth, losing any sign of individual signification.[93] The mouldering body of the English soldier, unable to be looked on "without disgust and abhorrence," is a reminder of the hidden and ignoble aspects of colonial conflict, and the ways in which colonialism corrupts the British subject is literally represented by the soldier's rotting corpse. His widow's attempt to memorialize him with "melancholy pleasure" uncovers the failure of sentiment in the face of colonial reality. At the same time, as a fellow high-ranking

British officer, Johnson himself is mirrored in this "mass of corruption" for also having lost the markers of British subjectivity.

Johnson sees the woman's actions as indulgent, demonstrating "immoderate grief," but offers nonetheless to help her, telling her she can stay in his home "and have the conversation and attendance of his women" (II, 161). She is grateful, but after a series of delicate questions about "his women," he offends the sensitive widow by declaring "they are all native *Americans*, by whom I have had children; and in whose unfeigned affection, and easy complying tempers I find such satisfaction, that I never shall quit them to attach myself solely to any one woman, however superior to them in the advantages of beauty and education" (II, 163–4). She declares to Johnson, "I have not the least desire for the conversation of *Squaws*, and am in haste to leave this savage place" (II, 164), and the coin changes hands in this moment of conflict between the self-righteous metropolis and the degenerate colonies. Johnson gives the widow some gold "to defray any accidental expence" on her journey home (II, 165), and following her reflections in the next chapter on her simultaneous repulsion and attraction to Johnson, the guinea moves on to England.

The widow's desire for one last site of her beloved husband is met with a putrid mass of human remains, and her encounter with Johnson's frontier family is an unsettling reminder that the British self is unable to remain uncompromised in the "desarts" of America. Consumed by the violence of war or the temptations of life among the Indians, British bodies occupying colonial space in *Chrysal* cannot resist the forces operating in the contact zone. Only the coin, the object-narrator of the novel, is able to circulate unmarked by the various sites and cultures it encounters while unifying geographic space and human relations through commodification.[94]

Perhaps the most well-known transculturated British subject in the eighteenth-century novel is Lieutenant Obadiah Lismahago in Smollett's *Humphry Clinker* (1771), who I will briefly turn to for the sake of comparison to the men above.[95] Like Williamson, Lismahago is a Scotsman who is violently captured by Indians. In his captivity, however, he is formally adopted by the Miami Indians who take him. Initially both he and Murphy, another soldier, are captured, and the tribe intends to adopt Murphy, who is "the younger and handsomer of the two," and to "sacrifice the other to the custom of the country." However, following their torture, which is a rite of initiation, Murphy is "rendered unfit for the purposes of marriage" while Lismahago's torture "had not produced emasculation." He is, however, brutally tortured in a scene reminiscent of many contemporary captivity narratives:

> A joint of one finger had been cut, or rather sawed off with a rusty knife; one of his great toes was crushed into a mash between two stones; some of his teeth were drawn, or cut out with a crooked nail; splintered reeds had been thrust up his nostrils and other tender parts; and the calves of his legs had been blown up with mines of gunpowder dug into the flesh with the sharp point of a tomahawk. (193)

Sussman suggests that this emphasis on the physical mutilation of Lismahago's body is meant to emphasize the corporeal nature of transculturation in North America, and thus "the diffuse operations of cultural change are reduced to discrete, physical losses."[96] Tara Ghoshal Wallace argues that Smollett's inclusion of the gunpowder and the "crooked nail" are meant to evoke "artifacts of the industrial world brought to America by Europeans," and the scene is therefore "a monstrous reenactment of European incursions into American territories [in which] Indians use the invader's weapons to penetrate and destroy them."[97] At the same time, this violation of Lismahago's body is a literal act of transcultural exchange; the European goods are not used on their own, but alongside Indian objects. Thus the gunpowder is dug into his legs "with the sharp point of a tomahawk," combining the two iconic weapons of European and Indian warfare. While his mangled body forever displays his cultural adoption, the tools that bring about this transformation suggest that European efforts to transform Indigenous cultures only create a menacing hybridity.

Following their running of the gauntlet, Murphy is devoured by the tribe, while Lismahago is married to Squinkinacoosta. Both these fates, as Sussman has shown, present positive and negative visions of the same act of incorporation. Tim Fulford argues that Smollett emphasizes Lismahago's survival as being a product not of his heroic fortitude, but his adaptability. As such, "colonial encounters empower the man of few principles rather than the chivalric hero."[98] The same can be said for the depiction of William Johnson in *Chrysal*, who thrives only because he has shed conventional European standards of morality. For Lismahago, the cultural transformation that allows him to thrive among the Miamis, where he becomes a sachem, also allows him social mobility in Britain when he is able to broker his experience into a marriage to Tabitha Bramble.[99]

Subsequent visions of heroic transcultural subjects began to appear in Britain in the late eighteenth century, as in Robert Bage's *Hermsprong* (1796), but this significantly comes after the Revolutionary War, when Britain was less invested in the North American colonies. Prior to this time, Britons among Indians challenged assumptions of cultural superiority and the inevitable expansion of British culture and territory. Their forays into Indian lives are always already compromised, and fail to produce the heroic subjectivity they perhaps desired. Only after the American Revolution, when Indians became much more abstract than real to most Britons, did the modern British subject emerge. Thus, in another act of transcultural incorporation, the image of cultural strength and resistance embodied by Indians in eighteenth-century British culture became a foundation for the hegemonic vision of empire and expansionism.

Conclusion

The Indians in this chapter appear in key cultural moments, in each instance rejecting the slippages in identity categories seemingly tied to a superficial and commercial culture. Yet their virtue and certainty remains out of reach to the imaginative realm of the British author, and the appropriation of an Indian identity is impossible or suspect at this stage. The closest to becoming a full and accepted hybrid Indian is the rogue Carew, who is warmly embraced and lives according to their customs and laws; yet, tellingly, it is his love of country that propels him back into a life of social circulation. Being British, for Carew at least, is to embrace the corrupt uncertainties of a performative identity rather than shed the "polish." For Peter Williamson, his attempt to claim an identity is undermined by the same forces he sought to exploit, and the print market unfixed his image as a Lenape through its circulation. There was not yet space in the British cultural imagination to allow for a positive depiction of transculturation among Indians, but the groundwork was being put in place. Indians in these texts provide fundamental and specific challenges to British subjectivity, rather than a reinforcement of imperial fantasy as in earlier representations. This became more evident during the Seven Years' War, when critical Indians turned into destructive ones who threatened to annihilate the subject. The next chapter will look more closely at captivity narratives, where the fears and desires of Indian culture are put to the fore.

3 Captivity Narratives and Colonialism

[C]olonization, I repeat, dehumanizes even the most civilized man; ... colonial activity, colonial enterprise, colonial conquest, which is based on contempt for the native and justified by that contempt, inevitably tends to change him who undertakes it; ... the colonizer, ... in order to ease his conscience gets into the habit of seeing the other man as *an animal*, accustoms himself to treating him like an animal, and tends objectively to transform *himself* into an animal. It is this result, this boomerang effect of colonization, that I wanted to point out.

– Aimé Césaire[1]

While on a mapping expedition for the British army to "sound the lakes" around Detroit in 1763, during what would turn out to be the onset of Pontiac's Rebellion, seventeen year-old Yorkshire-born Scotsman John Rutherfurd was captured by Ojibwa people (or, as Rutherfurd knew them, and as they are still called in much of the United States, the Chippewa). Several members of his party were killed, including the English baronet Sir Robert Davers, and Rutherfurd, escaping the gruesome fate of some of his countrymen, was made the property of his Ojibwa master, Peewash. After being taken into the man's family and ceremonially adopted into the place of one of his new father's deceased sons, Rutherfurd, renamed Addick, would eventually escape and join the fight against the Indians while his experience would belatedly join the larger body of work collectively known as captivity narratives.[2] The tropes of his story, of capture, ritualistic torture and/or cannibalism, of substitution for lost family members, and ultimately of escape and return to European society were familiar to British readers beginning in the 1750s. Rutherfurd was but one of many British captives who wrote tales of suffering at the hands of non-European peoples throughout the seventeenth and eighteenth centuries, but the singular shape or mode of Indian captivity most formed perceptions of British transcultural encounters and Indian culture in the decades leading up to 1776. With notable exceptions, many of these texts remain remarkably under-studied, despite the vast amount of scholarly interest in the relationships between European colonialism and literature. Captivity narratives document moments, real and imagined, where European subjects lose control of the boundaries separating themselves from "primitive" and "savage" populations and become entangled in colonial violence. While the previous chapter's subjects fail in their transculturation for a variety of reasons, the captives in this chapter fail to disavow its effects, attempting to produce a profound otherness out of "Indian cruelty" and British superiority, but producing instead abject subjects. Their failure to assert Indian difference in these earlier narratives in some ways foreshadows the lure of cultural hybridity in later texts, which will be discussed in the fifth chapter.

British Captivity Narratives and Male Bodies

In American scholarship, a captivity narrative is most often assumed to be a text written by a Puritan woman from the late-seventeenth or early-eighteenth century who is captured by Indians and must hold onto her faith in the face of savagery. Richard Slotkin's well-known description of the captivity genre claims that

> a single individual, usually a woman, stands passively under the strokes of evil, awaiting rescue by the grace of God. The sufferer represents the whole, chastened body of Puritan society; and the temporary bondage of the captive to the Indian is dual paradigm – of the bondage of the soul to the flesh and the temptations arising from original sin, and of the self-exile of the English Israel from England. In the Indian's devilish clutches, the captive had to meet and reject the temptation of Indian marriage and/or the Indian's 'cannibal' Eucharist. To partake of the Indian's love or of his equivalent of bread and wine was to debase, to un-English the very soul. The captive's ultimate redemption by the grace of Christ and the efforts of the Puritan magistrates is likened to the regeneration of the soul in conversion. The ordeal is at once threatful of pain and evil and promising of ultimate salvation. Through the captive's proxy, the promise of a similar salvation could be offered to the faithful among the reading public,

while the captive's torments remained to harrow the hearts of those not yet awakened to their fallen nature.[3]

While this influential mythology of captivity has been challenged by recent scholarship that looks to highlight cultural exchange in these texts,[4] it is important to note this framework since Puritan captivity narratives are often thought to have formed the first "uniquely American" genre of writing,[5] and captives still inform nationalist cultural narratives. Across New England, there are numerous commemorative sites and monuments dedicated to Puritan captives who escaped from Indians in the late seventeenth century; Redemption Rock in Princeton, Massachusetts, marks the site where Mary Rowlandson's release from captivity among the Wampanoag was negotiated in 1676, while Hannah Duston (also spelled Dustin or Dustan), who during her escape in 1697 killed and scalped a family of ten Abenakis in their sleep, including six children, has no less than six memorials scattered throughout the eastern seaboard. One of these monuments, which depicts Duston triumphantly standing with a hatchet in one hand and numerous scalps in the other, was built in New Hampshire in 1874 and is widely thought to be the first public American monument dedicated to a woman (another statue was erected in Massachusetts five years later). Mount Dustan, also in New Hampshire, was named after the former captive sometime before 1870 and has inscribed the very landscape with this act of violence.[6] Clearly the mythology of early Puritan narratives has played a role in American national self-definition, largely during the westward expansion of the nineteenth century and the widespread, often violent, displacement of Native people. This is mirrored in the single-minded quest for American origins in colonial texts that in many cases were read on both sides of the Atlantic, which is both anachronistic and ideologically suspect; as Michelle Burnham argues, this approach to the reading of captivity narratives, which we can attribute to a nationalistic philosophy of American exceptionalism, has "historically obscured [the texts'] colonialist origins."[7] This effacement of history is particularly problematic for Native people, as it renders violent colonization into originary myth and the "devilish" Indian becomes reinscribed by the interpretive act. Moreover, captivity scholarship lacks an understanding and appreciation of the temporal and geographic variety within the broader captivity tradition, and more specifically within North American narratives. The singular focus on Puritan texts has downplayed or ignored later writings, particularly those produced in the 1750s and 1760s,[8] works that have long been described as degraded and/or commodified versions of the Puritan originals, or simply as anti-Indian propaganda meant to encourage colonial domination.[9] Yet I believe and will argue that these later, predominantly male narratives unmask the violence of colonization and question the stability and durability of the British self and body, which in these texts is written upon by resisting Indians battling against colonial hegemony.

Unlike Slotkin's description of Puritan narratives and their depiction of spiritual salvation, the British taste for Indian captivity was decidedly secular. Indeed, Mary Rowlandson's *The Soveraignty & Goodness of God, together, [sic] with the Faithfulness of his Promises Displayed* (1682) was printed the same year in London as *A True History of the Captivity & Restoration of Mrs. Mary Rowlandson*, while Quaker Elizabeth Hanson's Philadelphia edition of *God's Mercy Surmounting Man's Cruelty* (1728) would appear in London as *An Account of the Captivity of Elizabeth Hanson* (1760). Captivity itself, not God's grace, was what interested British readers, and the threat and thrill of cultural emersion provided the fundamental fascination of the texts. The re-titling marks a generic shift from a Christian Providence tale to a captivity narrative, already an established genre in Britain.[10] God's will becomes less important than the truth of the account in order to appeal to a broader audience, though the reading public of the narrative in Rowlandson's case likely remained the Nonconformists who enabled the text to cross the Atlantic.[11] Verisimilitude, not piety, was emphasized in the packaging, which would become an emphasis on bodily, not spiritual, suffering in the later narratives. These later texts emerged out of a period in which struggles for land in North America reached a level of intensity higher than at any other previous point in the eighteenth century. The French and Indian War, which was in part the North American theatre for the Seven Years' War in Europe, lasted from 1754 to 1763, while Pontiac's Rebellion, a resistance launched by various Native peoples dissatisfied with British colonial policy, continued from 1763 until 1766. The "middle ground" previously negotiated between various Native peoples and the French and English had by this time collapsed into a "battleground," and old alliances between the competing European empires and Indigenous nations dissolved into often brutal warfare.[12] These conflicts created a seemingly endless war for the British, in which for the first time large numbers of Britons, and not just colonists, were killed or captured by Native people,[13] leading to a greater domestic interest in, and corresponding proliferation of, texts about Indians. This context of the rise in textual representation and actual, often violent, contact is important to bear in mind when considering the propagandist value of captivity narratives during this time; these texts are filled with hyperbolic spectacles of violence, including lengthy and elaborate scenes of torture and suffering at the hands of cruel Indian masters who are generally commanded by or closely tied to French Catholic forces. Peter Williamson, whose widely read (though perhaps largely fictional)[14] *French and Indian Cruelty* we have encountered already, describes a scene where a prisoner is buried neck-deep in the ground, scalped, and left for several hours "in the greatest Agonies." The Indians then light a fire near his head and he pleads for them to kill him, "for his Brains were boiling in his Head." However, "[i]nexorable to all his Plaints, they continued the Fire, whilst, shocking to behold! his Eyes gush'd out of their Sockets."[15] To be sure, the villainous Indian is a construction informed by wartime ideological needs, but texts like Williamson's nevertheless remain troubling to both colonial discourse and British identity itself. The sight later on in the narrative of a newly redeemed Williamson and his fellow soldiers "cutting, hacking and scalping … dead *Indians*" with such a relish that they are forced to "cast lots for this bloody, though agreeable piece of work"[16] destabilizes the moral superiority of the suffering captive and the widely embraced domestic image of British soldiers as humane and reasonable practitioners of war.[17] The title page's promise that the narrative will provide an account of the "scalping … committed on the English" by the "Savages" is tempered by the actions of the British soldiers, and when Williamson boasts that they were "rewarded handsomely for the scalps of those savages" upon arrival to Boston, he exposes the entanglement of violence and profiteering at the heart of the business of empire.[18]

Perhaps the most troubling case of captive violence is Robert Kirk's *The Memoirs and Adventures of Robert Kirk* (1770), in which the eponymous narrator is captured and adopted by a tribe in place of a dead man and given an "adopted wife and a fine boy who my brother told me was my son" (12). The captivity portion of his narrative is mostly unremarkable and was possibly written from borrowed material, as Kirk witnesses the cruel torture and death of companions, adapts to his situation while insisting on his internal resistance, provides some manners and customs descriptions of the Shawnee, his captive hosts, and eventually escapes along with another adopted European. He acknowledges that, once adopted, the Shawnee "used me with so much affection, that at first I could not help regarding them very much," but goes on to assert that "there is something in the manners and inclinations of Europeans so different from them, that it is not possible they should long agree together" (11). He disavows the possibility of a transcultural community. Like other captives he joins in the battle against the Indians, but in Kirk's case he participates in a massacre, admitting to joining in a plot to "kill every one without mercy" in an Indian town, afterwards reflecting, "[T]hus the inhumanity of these savages was rewarded with a calamity, dreadful indeed, but justly deserved. This was I believe the bloodiest scene in all America, our revenge being compleated" (45). Shortly after this event, Kirk claims that his commanding officer, the well-known Major Robert Rogers – author of the play *Ponteach: or the Savages of America, A Tragedy* (1766) – butchers an innocent Indian woman whom they captured from the town and "divided and cast lots for the shares which were distributed to each an equal part; we then broiled and eat the most of her; and received great strength thereby" (47–8). While Kirk's tale may be dubious,[19] it nonetheless participates in the failure of the captivity genre to assert Indian difference through cruel acts by magnifying British violence.

With the exception of Elizabeth Hanson, the most popular narratives on both sides of the Atlantic during this period were written by men, most of them young and strong soldiers or labourers in the colonial project.[20] The captives' own involvement in imperial enterprise or enforcement often complicates their accounts of Indian cruelty. Henry Grace is a soldier captured while guarding wheat fields planted on land recently taken by force from local Indians; Robert Eastburn is a tradesman working on English forts who takes up arms and fires upon Indians in a skirmish, killing one and wounding another, before he is made captive; and John Rutherfurd, an employee of a trading company seeking to exploit Indian trade following the defeat of the French around Detroit, is seized while on a military mapping expedition. However unwittingly, captives are often actively engaged in colonial struggle at the time of capture. This context sharply contradicts the generic demands of captivity narratives based on Puritan texts, which calls for a passive female subject,[21] and these male bodies, so important to the British Empire in producing labour and military force, are taken and used by Indians as servants and warriors, or, worse, taken apart and annihilated. One officer in Rutherfurd's narrative, a Captain Robertson, has the skin of his arm turned into a tobacco pouch after he is killed, "leaving the first joints of the fingers by way of tassels," and his remains are devoured in a night of feasting and dancing by his Indian captors.[22] At least one white captive also takes part in the feast. The captive British body therefore becomes an important site, as it is inscribed with the violence of the contact zone. Captive bodies are tortured, mutilated, dismembered, or marked in other ways by the Native people whose land is meant to be surrendered and whose presence is an obstacle to that possession. This struggle for land is carried out on the body of the captive. Michel Foucault writes that in eighteenth-century European societies "the condemned man published his crime and the justice that had been meted out to him by bearing them physically on his body."[23] The criminal's body becomes a site upon which is written both the truth of his or her crime and a demonstration of the sovereign's power; truth and the exercise of power are thus united on the body of the condemned. Adam Smith observes in *The Theory of Moral Sentiments* (1759) that sympathetic identification with this violence to the body is central to the machinations of justice, writing that "[i]n order to enforce the observation of justice, therefore, Nature has implanted in the human breast that consciousness of ill-desert, those terrors of merited punishment which attend upon its violation."[24] The captive is thrust into a similar role, in which his body too becomes a site of truth and power, and an object of sympathetic identification. But whereas the criminal's body demonstrates a judicial truth, the captive body bears the anxieties of empire and the truth of colonial violence. For British readers, to observe the suffering and tortured captive was both to identify sympathetically with him and to reflect on the cause of that violent punishment. Williamson gestures towards this understanding when, in the midst of his military party's butchering of Indian bodies with the "utmost Chearfulness" using the ostensibly Indian practice of scalping, he observes that he and his fellow soldiers are so eager to do this "work" because they wish to articulate their vengeance towards the Indians by "shewing it on their lifeless trunks."[25] The language of justice and the menace of the contact zone in captivity narratives, and possibly all contact literature, are written on the body.

Resisting Transculturation and Feigning Indian

A central element of the transgressive potential and the appeal of most captivity narratives is the possibility of a captive "going native."[26] Yet compared to other British captivity narratives, such as those written by captives held in Islamic societies from the seventeenth and

early-eighteenth centuries, pre-Revolutionary North American narratives offer few instances of obvious transculturation. There are no captive authors during this time who write about intermarrying or having
children with the Native societies they are captured by, and the time
periods chronicled in these narratives are seldom more than a few
months. Despite these relatively short durations, resisting the incomprehensible brutality of Indian life is a primary concern for both the
more widely studied captivity narratives from around the time of King
Philip's War in 1675 and the later texts from the 1750s up to the American Revolution, which points to the forbidden appeal of fully crossing
the cultural divide. Other texts, such as journals by English traders and
Indian agents, do attest to the permeability between British and Indian
cultures prior to 1776, suggesting that the anxiety over transcultural
subjects in captivity narratives is not necessarily a dominant cultural
force. Nevertheless, captivity narratives prior to the Revolutionary War
are consistent in their portrayals of Britons resisting the influence of
Indian cultures, similar to the literary encounters from the period. In
Puritan narratives, preserving one's self in the face of savagery and
Papist trickery becomes a drama of religious perseverance and redemption, and the eventual escape or release of the generally female captive
is, as in Rowlandson's well-known text, a visible sign of Providence
and the "goodness of God."[27] I have already noted the secular interests
in Britain, and mid-century narratives focus instead on preserving the
captive's sense of British identity. This transition in the genre comes in
part from the broader cultural shift towards a more cohesive and coherent sense of Britishness in the face of an ever-expanding empire,[28] and
an awareness of the stakes in losing colonists or soldiers in peripheral
spaces, where British bodies were needed to occupy land and displace
previous claims to ownership. Perhaps even more significant to this
nationalistic shift in writing narratives, however, was the widespread
desertion of British soldiers, traders, and settlers into different Native
societies. The troubling and sentimental scene of white captives having to be forcibly returned to the English in William Smith's account of
Colonel Henry Bouquet's 1764 expedition to Ohio definitively showed,
if there was any previous doubt, that the stability and appeal of life as
a British subject had severe limitations. While younger captive children
had known only an existence among the Indians, and thus could be
excused for "part[ing] from the savages with tears," the sight of white
adults separated from their Native spouses and families continuing
on for "many days in bitter lamentations," in some cases having to be

bound so that they might stay with the English, leads Smith to anxiously speculate that

[f]or the honour of humanity, we would suppose those persons to have
been of the lowest rank, either bred up in ignorance and distressing pen-
ury, or who had lived so long with the Indians as to forget all their former
connections. For, easy and unconstrained as the savage life is, certainly it
could never be put in competition with the blessings of improved life and
the light of religion, by any persons who have had the happiness of enjoying, and the capacity of discerning, them.[29]

Many Britons stubbornly maintained this belief in the poverty of
"savage life," as seen in part by the massive fundraising efforts to
save the "poor Indians,"[30] despite the mounting evidence that up to
this point "very few if any Indians had been transformed into civilized
Englishmen," yet "large numbers of Englishmen had chosen to become
Indians."[31]

It is with this particular anxiety in mind that the threat of transculturation must be read into mid-century captivity narratives. In order
to assure their readers, and indeed themselves, that they have avoided
the dangerous allure of "unconstrained" Indian life, any participation
in the captor's culture is externalized by the captives and depicted as
a performance that is essential to bodily survival. Thus Rutherfurd
writes in his narrative,

I found it was absolutely necessary for my safety to affect a relish for their
savage manners, and to put on an air of perfect contentment, which I had
often heard was the way to gain the affections of the Indians; whereas a
gloomy, discontented air irritates them, and always excites worse treatment, and sometimes occasions the death of the captive who is so unfortu-
nate as not to be able to accommodate himself to his situation.[32]

Williamson, whose account of his experience among his Delaware
captors changed greatly in subsequent editions and writings, also
claims that the Indians who captured him resorted to "threatening me
with the worst of deaths, if I would not willingly go with them, and
be contented with their way of living," which he "seemingly agreed
to."[33] Thomas Brown writes that "[l]ove of Life obliged me to comply" with Indian demands, and he admits, "I feigned myself merry."[34]
Gary Ebersole calls this kind of justification a "rational ruse" which,

in addition to ostensibly guaranteeing survival, also "confirmed the cultural prejudice of readers that life with the Indians could have no attraction for civilized persons."[35] But even if the necessity of collaborating with the captor's culture was wholly accepted as legitimate by the readership, there is clearly an understanding of the performativity of identity implicit in the moments of feigned transculturation, in the very moments where the captors are trying to assert the underlying strength of British identity.

The captive must mimic the Indians in order to survive, yet this mimicry fails to assert a mastery over the Other.[36] Mi'kmaq captive Henry Grace describes how "they made me stand up and practise dancing along with them till Morning, and I took a great deal of Pains to do as they did, though I performed very awkwardly, for which they beat me."[37] Rutherfurd writes that his master would occasionally "dress me out in the richest manner, putting all the ornaments belonging to the family upon me, taking me out to the plain and making me strut about to show myself, when the whole village were assembled, calling out to the people to look at the little white man." He understands his role as spectacle, noting that "[a]t this time I was only made a show of, and not suffered to join in the game."[38] Mimicry is, as Homi Bhabha suggests, always "profound and disturbing" to the authority of colonial discourse. Though Bhabha is speaking of the response of colonized peoples in reaction to the "civilizing mission," mimicry produces a similarly ambivalent note in captivity narratives. On the one hand, the more convincingly the captive mimics the captor, the better his chance of survival and even reward among the Indians. On the other hand, the more the captive resembles an Indian, the less uniquely British he is, and the more he becomes what Bhabha calls a "partial presence."[39]

The heroism of the singular male captive is therefore decidedly ambiguous, since his liberation is bought at the cost of compromising his own cultural identity. This self-conscious performance of Indianness intended to ensure the survival of the British body at the expense of British identity can be described as "feigning Indian," a trope which reveals the understanding that the body and the self are not mutually exclusive, and that the captive body can perform an alien subjectivity in the name of preserving its own. The action of feigning Indian destabilizes the authority of British identity and momentarily collapses the distinction between self and Other. At times it threatens to become a simulation; Jean Baudrillard distinguishes between "feigning" and "simulation," suggesting that "[s]omeone who feigns an illness can simply go to bed and make believe he is ill. Someone who simulates an illness produces in himself some of the symptoms." It is therefore the case that "feigning or dissimulating leaves the reality principle intact: the difference is always clear, it is only masked; whereas simulation threatens the difference between 'true' and 'false,' between 'real' and 'imaginary.' Since the simulator produces 'true' symptoms, is he ill or not?"[40] There are moments that suggest the captive's feigning becomes a simulation: Gamaliel Smethurst writes in his narrative of time spent among the Mi'kmaq in 1761, "[a]fter we had walked a league further, we pitched our tent for all night – Lay upon our mother's lap (the earth) – I was under some apprehensions at first, as I had never travelled with Indians before; however, I behaved as if I was not the least afraid."[41] His use of "we" and "our," as well as the casual appropriation of what appears to be an Indigenous view of the maternal earth, threatens Smethurst's claim that he is merely behaving "as if" he were content. The captive author often cannot separate 'we' from 'I,' which implicates him in the actions of his captors. Likewise, William Fleming admits to raiding the house of a fellow settler with an Indian; at first, he writes of the Indian that "he rumaged up such Things as pleased him best, … then he set Fire to the House" while Fleming "seem'd heartily to comply with [the Indian]," but he later slips in that "[w]e then made the best of our Way with the Plunder of the Place."[42] To paraphrase Baudrillard, since Fleming is in fact participating in an Indian raid, is he feigning or not? Iroquois captive Robert Eastburn, who piously refuses to participate in Indian cultural and religious practices, writes that when the French bring provisions, there is "great Joy [among the tribe], for we were in great Want."[43] And John Rutherfurd recalls that while among his captors, "[s]ometimes our Mother roasted a large piece [of meat] for the whole family," and he admits, "I soon came to eat as heartily as [my master] himself."[44] Though he insists he "feigned a satisfaction with their way of living and a particular fondness for my new dress," Rutherfurd is nonetheless adopted into his captor's family, as is Eastburn. Their performances are evidently so convincing that these two captives are eventually taken into Indian families, simulating the place of lost loved ones while insisting upon their internal resistance.

The trope of 'feigning Indian' differs significantly from what Philip J. Deloria has called "playing Indian"; while the former is meant to reiterate British subjectivity in the face of a perceived threat to its integrity, the latter is a form of conscious and often violent appropriation that depends on disparate power relations between Native peoples and an emergent American state seeking colonial domination. For Deloria, "playing Indian" is a fundamental aspect of American identity, beginning with the Boston Tea Party when a group of erstwhile British colonists dressed as Mohawks in order to make "a unique and privileged claim to liberty and nationhood."[45] In this case, the figure of the Indian is used as a means of differentiation from Britain, and the appropriation of Native culture by white colonists during the American Revolution and following independence is driven by the simultaneous and perhaps inseparable motivations of national self-definition and the large-scale expropriation of Native lands. Indeed, starting as early as the late 1770s there appears a body of captivity narratives which proudly displays, even celebrates, full transculturation into various Native societies while at the same time demonizing Redcoats. Though these documents purport to chronicle events that occurred in some cases decades before the Revolution, their belated production speaks to a new set of ideological imperatives from the colonists.[46] Terry Goldie has described this process in British settler-states such as Canada and Australia as "indigenization," noting that "it is only by going native that the European arrivant can become native."[47] Thus Colonel James Smith, officer from the Revolutionary War, could boast forty years after his captivity among the Delawares in the mid-1750s that one of the tribe proclaimed him "flesh of our flesh, and bone of our bone," and assured him that "every drop of white blood was washed out of [his] veins."[48] This new kind of American subject, a product of myth and regenerative violence, is very different from the abject British captive written about as recently as ten years earlier.

Abject Captives

Mary Louise Pratt insists that captivity is a traditionally "safe" form, since "the story is told by a survivor who has returned, reaffirming European and colonial social orders."[49] Yet this return in captivity narratives from the 1750s and 1760s is rarely celebratory, demonstrating instead that the performance of Indianness can have enduring effects, and that the colonial social order is deeply unsettled by the truth of colonial violence just as the European social order cannot accept the fragility of its own artifice, both of which are inscribed on and embodied by the British captive. In Peter Williamson's narrative, he escapes to a neighbouring farm, only to have the farmer and his family react to his appearance with utter horror and threaten him with a gun, for they "took me to be an *Indian*."[50] Rutherfurd ends his narrative with a reflection on its poor composition, noting that "having so long been confounded with hearing and speaking different languages, French, Dutch, Chippewa, Ottawa, &c &c that it is no wonder I should be at a loss to write or speak that of my native country."[51] These external cultural forms confuse the captive's identity shortly after his escape, which as Joe Snader writes, "transform[s] a long-hoped-for moment of cultural reunion into a moment of isolation, dislocation, and cultural confusion."[52] Captives often realize that they are not as comfortable in their old lives or bodies as they once were, and find it difficult to become stable European subjects.

Captives become outcasts from their own homes and families; the experience of captivity does not simply end after their escape, and they are marked by the trauma of the contact zone. Charles Saunders writes that after his captivity, his "[c]onstitution being quite broke, and being wounded in the Arm, I was advised to come to *England* my native place, in hopes of recovery." Though his body recovers eventually, he writes that "'tis humbly hoped the indulgent Publick will commiserate the unhappy fate of the Author, and contribute their endeavours to enable him to go to Sea again: He having lost upwards of Three hundred Pounds sterling by his captivity, is now reduced to the lowest degree of indigence."[53] Henry Grace also laments his post-captivity state; he writes that after leaving the army

> I procured my Discharge the 10th of *February*, 1763, and the Loss of the Year's Pay and Cloathing, and could obtain no Pension, though it has been granted to many who had not gone through any thing like the Miseries I suffered. When I came home, I was in Hopes to get some comfortable Settlement, but found it quite contrary, those who ought to have been my best Friends proved my worst Enemies, and my own Relations used their utmost Endeavours to ruin me.[54]

Robert Eastburn complains that "as soon as the *News* were sent Home, that I was *killed*, or *taken*, [my wife] was not allowed any more *Support* from my *Wages*, which grieved me much, and added to my other *Afflictions*." He returns home "*sick* and *weak* in *Body*, and *empty handed*, not having any Thing for my Family's and my own Support."[55] The redeemed captives are left to fend for themselves or depend on their sometimes treacherous friends and relatives. Grace, like Saunders, pleads for the charity of his readers: "I submit my Case, with the many Distresses I have gone through, and my present melancholy Situation, to the Consideration of the Humane and Benevolent, hoping for some Relief; and any Favours received, will be acknowledged with the utmost Gratitude."[56] Since he was not brought up with a trade, he must perform day labour for his sustenance. However, an injury sustained in captivity prevents him from working; his arm was forcibly tattooed when he was among the Chickasaws with his captors, and he "can feel the ill Effects of it to this Hour." Grace's tattoo, made when "Indian paint" was smeared over his skin after it was pricked with thorns,[57] is a permanent inscription of colonial violence on his body, and prevents him from participating in British society. There is little redemption after all, as the captive finds himself isolated and persecuted in his home. Captives are alienated from their own countrymen, and the physical transformation brought about by their captors' society, it seems, is more than simply external. If the body can no longer be relied upon as a marker for Otherness, the stability of the Self is compromised, and the enduring wounds and scars brought about by captivity are reminders of this circumstance.

We have already seen in the previous chapter how Williamson is a unique case among these captives because of the success of multiple, widely differing versions of his narrative and the greater historical record of his post-captivity life, but he too tells a tale of abjection. Williamson claims he is sent home from his military service due to a wound to his hand inflicted by a gunshot during a battle with French and Indian forces, which rendered him *"incapable* of *further* service" and left his hand partially paralysed. Like Grace, he complains in the first edition of his narrative, "I could not get any Provision made for me, by Pension, or otherwise," adding bitterly that he is given only six shillings "as a *Reward* for my Sufferings and Services."[58] Following the subsequent libel litigation by the Aberdeen merchants, Williamson reflects in the fifth edition of 1762, "I could not help considering myself in a more wretched state, to be reduced to such barbarities in a civilized country, and the place of my nativity, than when a captive among the savage Indians, who boast not of humanity."[59] Even though he won his case on appeal, was eventually awarded a settlement, and even achieved a modest celebrity for his Indian-themed tavern and his public performances in Indian dress, the editions of his narrative continue to depict his failed return to British life. By 1789, when Williamson was an established printer, he would claim in another piece of autobiographical writing:

I shall only leave it to the public to judge, if they can expect a learned discourse from a person, who, from his infancy, was brought up with those
Savages, and taught nothing else but the use of the tomahawk and scalping knife; for a printed book was alike to me with that of clean paper; and
the only opportunity I had to learn any kind of figures, was in the time of
snow, to imitate the Indians by the mark they made on trees, which much
resembles the Greek characters.[60]

Thus even the act of writing, the Eurocentric process meant to reclaim
appropriate power relations in travel writing and ethnography and to
mark the European subject, is in Williamson's account of his life subverted by a savage predecessor. His alienation from British life, or at
least his desire for a new kind of subjectivity, would be shown through
his body on one final occasion when, at his funeral, "by his own wish
he was interred in the full panoply of a Delaware Indian Chief similar
to those he had observed in Pennsylvania."[61]

It was a common practice in the mid-eighteenth century to sail British captives to England following their release, regardless of where
they were born, and those from the colonies would eventually board
ships for a return to the colonies.[62] For some, this was a profound and
moving experience, a reaffirmation of their essential Englishness following a threat to its integrity. These voyages also served as a means to
transport information on captivities and Native peoples back to England, and show the metropolitan population the stakes involved in the
colonial struggle. Jean Lowry was one captive who found hospitality in
"old England," and was brought into many homes as a welcome guest.
She notes that the English "discovered surprising regard unto a poor
disconsolate Stranger."[63] This same trip in Robert Eastburn's narrative
of 1758 fails to produce a comfortable merging of colonial and metropolitan British cultures. After Eastburn procures freedom for himself
and his son, they sail from Montreal to England before being returned
to Philadelphia. Though Eastburn had moved to the colonies at the
age of four,[64] and his son had likely never set foot in England, it was
nonetheless the country that defined them culturally and spiritually.
There are 300 other former captives on the ship, and they arrive with
"great *Joy*"; however, there is an outbreak of smallpox, which, laments
Eastburn, means "we were not allowed to go on *Shore*, but removed to
a *King's Ship* ... where we [were] confined on *board*, near two Weeks."
He and his son are left to suffer from their "near View of our *Mother
Country*, the Soil and Comforts of which, we were not suffered to touch

or taste." Having surrendered their coats to some of the sick since they were "expecting Relief" for themselves, Eastburn and his son return to winter in New England "almost naked," since "all Application to the Captain for any Kind of Covering [had been made] in vain."[65] Their nakedness is noteworthy because the unclothed body is a recurring signification for Indian difference, and the moment a captive is stripped of his clothes marks his entry into Indian culture. Henry Grace writes that "[a]s soon as we came to the Chief Man's Wiggwam they took away my Hat, and began stripping me of every thing I had in the World, and then put me on my Knees close to a great Fire." John Rutherfurd describes how his master's father took his clothes and told him that he "should wear them no more, but dress like an Indian." Finally, Eastburn himself notes that immediately after his capture, he "was surrounded by a great Number, who stripped me of my Cloathing, Hat, and Neckcloth (so that I had nothing left but a Flannel Vest, without Sleeves)."[66] Later, an Indian and a Frenchman strip him of his flannel vest too. Thus his nakedness following the failed reunion with England is another moment of fractured subjectivity and alienation. So while it is true that the subjects of captivity narratives are always released in the end, this release often turns out to be as empty or terrifying as life among their captors. Though the authors have located the enduring effects of Indian life on their bodies as a means of discounting these changes, clearly this external presence is lasting and in fact depicts the permanent inscription of colonial violence on the European body and the inability of the English character to accept it or erase it.

Conclusion

Captivity narratives produced in the mid-eighteenth century, as I have suggested, are often understood to be forms of anti-Indian propaganda meant to justify the continued conquest of Native lands and nations. Though I have in part demonstrated the ways in which British subjects entangle themselves in these constructions, I cannot wholly discount this assessment given the historical and current reality of colonialism and its effects on Native people. It is admittedly difficult to claim within this context that these narratives are subversive texts that undermine the colonial project. Linda Colley notes that captivity narratives are "ambivalent documents" because there is an "essential linkage between captivity on the one hand and the business of empire on the other."[67] This connection draws the captives into what Césaire calls the "antagonistic economies" of imperialism, yet at the same time these men frequently find themselves in states of abjection at the end of their captivities, recalling Anne McClintock's notion that "[a]bject peoples are those whom industrial imperialism rejects but cannot do without."[68] They are integral to and yet alienated from the riches of empire, making their narratives contradictory accounts of both terror and desire. The different investments of empire within the captivity genre make it a battleground, centred around the European body whose suffering threatens to mask the more widespread and genocidal violence directed towards Aboriginal populations. The captive's body ultimately cannot conceal the process of colonization, however, because it is implicated in it.

Though I believe these narratives must be situated within a broader Anglophone captivity genre, it is also important to emphasize their relation to the conquest and settlement of North America. Maori critic Linda Tuhiwai Smith argues that for Indigenous people, "[c]oming to know the past has been part of the critical pedagogy of decolonization," and we need to "revisit, site by site, our history under Western eyes" if we are to "transform history into justice."[69] These narratives call attention to the intense conflict and brutality surrounding them that has been largely absent from North American national histories, which in turn form an integral part of the subsequent and ongoing oppression of Native people. The contemporary disconnection from the violent claims of ownership asserted by various European and Euroamerican powers in North America over the last five hundred years, as well as the pervasive racism towards Indigenous people in Canada and the United States which is chilling in both its ferocity and casual acceptance, means that these spectres of colonial slaughter will continue to haunt the peripheries of North American cultural memory alongside the figure of the captive, whose damaged body cannot forget the colonial trauma inscribed upon it.

4 Novel Indians: *Tsonnonthouan* and the Commodification of Culture

I hope our happy constitution is too well founded to be in the smallest degree shaken by any wind of Indian doctrine.
      – Anonymous, *Memoirs of the life and adventures of Tsonnonthouan*

In Benjamin Bissell's study on American Indians in British literature of the eighteenth century, still often cited as the definitive work on the topic, Bissell claims that John Shebbeare's *Lydia, or Filial Piety* (1755) is significant because "[i]n no other novel of the century does the Indian figure so conspicuously."[1] However, in 1763, the anonymously written satire *Memoirs of the life and adventures of Tsonnonthouan, a king of the Indian nation called Roundheads* was published in London, and, though all but forgotten by contemporary scholarship and not even mentioned by Bissell, this novel displaces *Lydia* and all others for its singular devotion to Native North American people.[2] In this chapter I will look at the important intervention which *Tsonnonthouan* makes into the culture of its time; using ethnographic texts, "it-narratives," and *The Life and Opinions of Tristram Shandy* as source material, I will show how the novel constructs its eponymous Native North American character not as a stoic Indian chief or cruel savage, but rather as an enthusiastic consumer of foreign commodities, namely brandy, and a ready convert to various religions and sects. This book therefore both mocks British colonial endeavours and projects some of the fears and fantasies associated with the newly emergent cultural force of early capitalism onto the Indigenous people of British North America.

Tsonnonthouan in part reveals the ways in which the trope of the North American Indian functioned as a construction of imagined, "modern" subjectivity, which is explored in the second chapter in a different context; Peter Weston suggests that "[w]e might ... see the story of the noble primitive as intimately connected with that critical point of bourgeois ascendancy in the late seventeenth century," since "[t]he concept of a free, unitary bourgeois subject, source and origin of meaning and morals, legitimator by free choice of 'society', was a radical concept which powerfully subverted social values based on inheritance and tradition."[3] Various European writers and philosophers explored the limits of their cultures using what has been traditionally labelled primitivism, beginning at least with Montaigne's "Of Cannibals" in 1580. Moreover, the myth of the "Golden Age" was often re-deployed in eighteenth-century Britain through the figure of America, and "directed both against the restrictions resulting from inherited rank and against the destructive effects of the so-called free market." And yet, paradoxically, while the spread and influence of gentry capitalism and luxury in Britain produced an ideal cultural milieu for a corresponding primitivist response, the conventions of the eighteenth-century British novel, Weston notes, are not conducive to an articulation of a primitivist critique of social values. As a result, texts such as Shebbeare's *Lydia* relegate the potentially radical critique of landed property and inherited privilege to the margins of the text; the romanticized Indian chief Cannassatago, whose observations while in Britain condemn the poverty and toil which the labouring classes are forced to endure, is effaced from the novel in favour of the British heroine Lydia's marriage to a benevolent nobleman.[4] He also represents a drastically different kind of Indian than Tsonnonthouan because of his uncomplicated sentimentality and moral superiority, much more in keeping with the Indians who offer visions of modern subjectivity uncorrupted by affectation and consumerism. Furthermore, the noble primitives who do appear in literature are often meant to be kings, queens, princes, and so forth, which limits their critique and domesticates the image of uncivilized egalitarianism.[5] The more radical noble savage evoked by French thinkers such as Lahontan, Rousseau, and Voltaire, whose Indians embody their critiques of inherited title, does not find a popular voice in English literature until near the end of the century.[6] While there are novels that represent the potentially leveling effects of commerce, such as Defoe's *Robinson Crusoe* and *Moll Flanders*, the eighteenth-century British novel prior to the 1790s generally affirms the pre-existing, socially stratified society out of which it emerged.

Tsonnonthouan is an exception to this rule because, as in Bakhtin's well-known description of Menippean satire, it blends, or "devours," genres and contains "an extraordinary freedom from plot"; through satire, the text is able to critique not only the subject matter of the novel, but also the genres from which it borrows.[7] While eighteenth-century texts such as Addison's letter from one of the Indian kings in *Spectator* no. 50 and the *Universal Spectator* article discussed in the second chapter use Indians and other non-Europeans as vehicles for satire, they do not offer the multilayered satire which *Tsonnonthouan* accomplishes by appropriating other genres in order to pillory the methods of narrative and ethnographic representation central to the construction of both Indians and Britons. Moreover, like the earlier texts, the novel satirizes British culture by using the perspective of a naive "natural man" to point out the "unnatural" and pretentious ways that Britons imagine themselves. At the same time, the book projects British culture outwards, onto the natural man, to examine the ways in which colonialism participates in and reproduces Britain's own cultural degradation. As such, *Tsonnonthouan* uses satire to mock the sentimental impulse which created the "romantic Indian," and to deploy the radical potential of the noble savage in narrative form. This is largely accomplished thanks to the eschewing of typical methods of novelistic representation. As Weston notes, "[t]he radicalism of this novel is more effective as a result of its formal rupturing of the conventions of expressive realism," while Bakhtin similarly observes that Menippean satire deploys a "bold and unrestrained use of the fantastic."[8]

Tsonnonthouan tells the story of a clever though capricious member of the Roundheads, a fictionalized version of the Atikamekw people, known by the French as the Têtes-de-Boules because, according to Charlevoix, they "think a round Head to be a great Beauty; and it is very probable that the Mothers give this Shape to the Heads of their Children in their Infancy."[9] It is due to this round head that the title character can better grasp systems and ideas, since a sphere allows for a larger mass within it; yet it is also the reason why he cannot commit to one ideology: "In whatever figure [ideas] strike the pericranium, it is certain that they will affect a lesser space of the scull of a round head, ... and consequently make a less forcible and lasting impression" (I, 32). Thus the narrator notes that "his mind seemed to be a mere *tabula rasa*, a sheet of white paper" (I, 9), which sounds indeed like what Weston calls a "paradigm of [the] bourgeois subject."[10] Tsonnonthouan is not quite, however, an ideal Lockean empiricist due to his "extreme mutability and inconstancy" in regard to his religious principles and his attraction to systems that are the most "improbable or incredible" (I, 10). While this trait is no doubt a jab at the ever-changing systems of philosophy and theology being produced and adhered to in the period, it also speaks to the increasing role of fashion and novelty in popular culture and consumer practices. The Round-head name also surely evokes the Parliamentarians of the Civil War, and their connection to Whiggish principles further serves the Tory writer's satire of the "inconstancy" of the protagonist.

The disjointed narrative of the novel tracks Tsonnonthouan's journey as he worships different manitous, converts to various faiths and sects, and encounters unsavoury people and situations. The way in which Tsonnonthouan circulates throughout the colonies, becoming, as Weston suggests, less a character than a "site," and the absence of a central plot, is similar to the popular "it-narratives" of the period, which were fictional texts that created narratives for objects and commodities such as coins, pincushions, and coaches as they changed hands and masters.[11] While the targets of the book's satire are varied, the novel is interested in the effects of colonialism and consumerism on culture and subjectivity; like it-narratives, to borrow Aileen Douglas's phrase, *Tsonnonthouan* "mediate[s] the consumerism [it] exploit[s]."[12] I will argue that it subverts many of the most significant representational practices and Protestant missionary fantasies of British writers depicting Native people during the period, and is important because of its unique distillation of various developments in the commodification of culture itself during the mid-eighteenth century.

Indians and Consumers

Eighteenth-century Britain witnessed what Neil McKendrick describes as a "consumer revolution," and the "birth of a consumer society" has become a well-mined field of inquiry. The "eruption of new prosperity," McKendrick writes, in addition to "an explosion of new production and marketing techniques," meant that more people than in any previous society were able to "enjoy the pleasures of buying consumer goods."[13] This "revolution" had, of course, its apologists and detractors, and others who both celebrated the expansion of trade and mourned the loss of rural simplicity. The figure of the North American Indian emerged during this time as a contradictory figure that mediated between the promise of colonial hegemony and the disappearance of the state of nature. Stephanie Pratt notes that the iconographic representation of Indians in European culture is "overwhelmingly concerned with [Indians'] existence outside any commercial or mercantile frame," despite the "long-established inter-tribal trading networks and the successful colonial exploitation of this extensive North American economy."[14] Indeed, for Samuel Johnson, the "rude Indian" is the other to the city-dwelling consumer, whose natural instincts have been dulled by the "labour of a thousand artists."[15] He notes that those who dwell in London "have scarce an idea of a place where desire cannot be gratified by money," and it is only by spending time "in a distant colony" that one can get a sense of the "artificial plenty" that city life allows (400). While Johnson believes that the labour of others allows one to find "leisure for intellectual pleasures, and enjoy the happiness of reason and reflection" (402), he also notes that there are negative consequences to the "variety of merchandise and manufactures which the shopkeepers expose on every hand" (398). Despite the availability of all wants in the metropolis, happiness is still unattainable because "new wants likewise are easily created" as one integrates more "instruments and conveniences" into his or her life. Thus, Johnson remarks, "our desires always increase with our possessions; the knowledge that something remains yet unenjoyed, impairs our enjoyment of the good before us" (401). Yet this compromised happiness is still better than "a savage life," in which the Indian must "provide by his own labour for his own support," doomed to "preserve his existence in solitude" (401). Johnson rejects the radical critique offered by the "noble savage," whom he sees as an isolated individual without the benefits of society. The fact that many of the "popular and modish trifles" overflowing the shops of London and propelling British consumer society originated in North America seems lost on Johnson here, and for him it is exchange value and consumer desire which transforms the elements of bare survival for the Indian into the "artificial plenty" of the metropolis. Thus the figure of the noble savage can, on the one hand, provide a critique of inherited title and luxury, but on the other hand can mask the source of colonial wealth.

The middle part of the eighteenth century witnessed a massive proliferation of texts about North American Indians, owing in part to the expansion of the print industry, but also to the increased involvement of Britain in affairs in the colonies.[16] Horace Walpole wrote to Richard Bentley in 1754 that the war "has thrown me into a new study: I read nothing but American voyages, and histories of plantations and

settlements." He notes that, "Among all the Indian nations, I have con-
tracted a particular intimacy with the Ontaouanoucs, a people with
whom I beg you will be acquainted," adding that he "was as barbarous
as any polite nation in the world, in supposing that there was nothing worth knowing among these charming savages."[17] There was an
increase in not only the quantity of information, but also, as Walpole's
specific interest in one tribe suggests, in its content; Britons lived and
died among Indians, had children with them, and engaged in other
types of material and cultural exchange (notwithstanding the denial of
this fact in literary texts, as previous chapters suggest). Alexander Farquharson, for example, was a Scottish soldier who served in the Seven
Years' War as a Lieutenant from 1758 until he died in Havana of fever
in 1762; during his time in the colonies, he regularly wrote letters to his
family back in Scotland, telling them of his experiences among various
Native nations. Farquharson wrote to his kinsman in 1760 that he and
his fellow soldiers were "often amused in our passage by viewing the
manner of life and oeconomy of several Indian Nations viz Mohawks,
Oneidas, Onondages, Senekas etc."[18] That he would mention the specific names of some of these nations, all members of the Iroquois confederacy, to a relative in Britain suggests a more sophisticated level of
contact than existed even a few years earlier. In Smollett's *The Expedition of Humphry Clinker*, published in 1771, Jerry Melford writes of the
Duke of Newcastle mistaking him for Sir Francis and asking him to
be sure to look after "[o]ur good friends of the Five Nations," whom
he lists as "[t]he Toryrories, the Maccolmacks, the Out-o'-the-ways, the
Crickets, and the Kickshaws" (112). Anyone versed in foreign affairs by
that time could have no doubt listed the members of the Five Nations,
who were by that time Six Nations, and the Duke's comical failure to
name them implies the actual knowledge most of Smollett's readers
had of Native affairs.

Cadwallader Colden's *The History of the Five Indian Nations*, a relatively sympathetic and sophisticated account of the Haudenosaunee
confederacy, was first printed in New York in 1727, but was revised and
reprinted in London in 1747, 1750, and 1755. It became the standard
reference work on Native people and, as such, provides a key insight
into British representations. Colden writes that

> [t]he *Five Nations* are a poor, and generally called, barbarous People, bred
> under the darkest Ignorance; and yet a bright and noble Genius shines
> through these black Clouds. None of the greatest *Roman* Heroes have

discovered a greater Love to their Country, or a greater Contempt of Death, than these People called Barbarians have done, when Liberty came in Competition. (v)

Unfortunately, Colden notes, members of the Five Nations "greatly sully … those noble Virtues, by that cruel Passion, Revenge" (vi). This contradiction is key to representations of Native North American people, and, indeed, the term "noble savage" itself embodies this contrast, marking a tension between a virtuous life that is equally uncivilized and unconstrained.[19] Colden, however, makes this murkier, suggesting that the Indians have "become worse than they were before they knew us":

> Instead of Virtues we have only taught them Vices, that they were intirely free from before that Time. The narrow Views of private Interest have occasioned this, and will occasion greater … Mischiefs, if the Governors of the People do not, like true Patriots, exert themselves, and put a Stop to these growing Evils. (vi)

In other words, it is the effects of commodity exchange that have corrupted and debauched the Native people. Their taste for European goods, specifically alcohol, threatens not only their way of life, but also the stability of the colonies. The "narrow Views of private Interest" cannot be the basis for a successful colony, but instead the Indians, according to Colden, need to be civilized through sober Christian virtue. It is to this contradiction, between the corruption and redemption of European influence, that I will now turn, for it is the effects of religion and commerce that most interest the author of *Tsonnonthouan*.

Tsonnonthouan

The publication of *Tsonnonthouan* was noted in most of the major periodicals in London, while the Whig *Monthly Review* and the Tory *Critical Review* published widely differing assessments of the novel.[20] The critic for the *Monthly* writes, notwithstanding its own extended review of Charlevoix three years earlier, that "we imagine the generality of Readers know too little of the Indian manners and customs, to enter into the spirit and design of our Author." More comically, the reviewer took issue with the lack of realism, noting that the depiction of bears as carnivorous animals was false since "we are told, that, tho' when attacked, or insulted, these creatures will give rather a closer hug than is agreeable to delicate constitutions, they never set their teeth into human flesh living or dead." The *Critical* had heavily praised the novel two months earlier, though some aspects, in particular its critique of religion and monarchy, extended too far.

Smollett and Goldsmith's *British Magazine* excerpted one of the earlier chapters of the novel and praised the book as "witty and ingenious" and "a truly original performance" in the style of Cervantes and Swift.[21] It also appears in the catalogues of several booksellers, clergy, and gentlemen, as well as in the collection of circulating libraries such as that of bookseller William Earle in Soho. Among these men who owned the novel was Malachy Postlethwayt, economist, enthusiastic celebrant of British empire and commerce, and author of *The Universal Dictionary of Trade and Commerce* (1757). However, *Tsonnonthouan* seemingly did not reach a wide enough audience to warrant the continuation that the author promises throughout the book, though a re-issue, with the printer's name removed, appeared around 1781, and two French editions were printed in 1778 and 1787.[22] The translator viewed the novel as "a demonstration of the wanton straying of the human mind and as evidence of what the freedom of the press made English authors dare to write."[23]

The author of *Tsonnonthouan* uses the preface to draw attention to the ways in which his text has become commodified; he explains the various interventions of his bookseller, who "has not as yet read a sentence of the following work, and in all probability never will" (v), but nonetheless composed the title page. The bookseller insisted that "memoirs" be added to the title to make it seem more fashionable, and that Tsonnonthouan be dubbed a king because "notwithstanding some late incidents," it is a title which "has still some regard paid to it, amongst us" (vii). While the author insists that "such an office was entirely unknown among the Indians," the bookseller believes that "an English reader would have a much greater curiosity about the adventures of a crowned head, than a private person" (vii). This detail shows an awareness of the radical potential of the noble savage, suggesting that the reading public prefer instead the more palatable and domesticated plot that affirms the class order. The author notes later in the novel that the Cherokees who visited London the previous year were also mistakenly described as "kings," as was Tsonnonthouan when he visited England, but he could not fathom the concept of such a "preposterous" notion as hereditary rule (II, 76). Implicating both the bookseller and the English reader, the preface begins a sustained exploration of the effects of consumerism by questioning the integrity of the text itself, ensnared as it is in a web of consumer desire, commodification, and compromising editorial concessions. The author is unmistakably complicit in this process, despite his protestations, which illuminates the otherwise uncontested authorial voice so important to both the narrative power of formal realism and the objective authority of manners and customs writing.

The printing industry was a key site in the development of capitalism and culture in eighteenth-century Britain; as Laura Brown notes, the economic changes wrought by the capitalist development of the bookselling industry "intersect with cultural production in a way that brings the power of capital into an unusually close proximity with the imaginative constructions of literary culture."[24] Bookselling, which was an industry that developed under the scrutiny of the public eye, demonstrated in a visible way the power of capitalist development through the cultivation of a marketplace, the importance of consumer demand, advertising, and profit, the commodification of writing, and the increased professionalization of authors. Many authors responded anxiously to their positions as cogs in the machine of the print industry beginning early in the eighteenth century, as in Pope's *Dunciad*, which, as Brown suggests, "uses Grub Street as a rhetorical springboard to assimilate a variety of contemporary responses to its analysis of the modernizing powers of capitalism."[25] *Tsonnonthouan* foregrounds this response in its preface, despite the fact that in the body of the text itself there is little explicit mention of it. The author instead mimics and satirizes other popular forms on the literary market to explore the relationship between consumption and culture, and the mutual implication of author and reader/consumer in the commodification of the book.

One of the visible signs of the commodification of writing in the 1760s was the diffusion of Sternean stylistic elements throughout the fiction of the period, with an unprecedented number of *Tristram Shandy* imitations, commentaries, and forged continuations entering the literary marketplace shortly after the publication of the first volume in 1759. Furthermore, the typographical play of Sterne was easily mimicked and appropriated by lesser talents. As René Bosch suggests, it was already evident by the end of 1760 that "there was a tendency to incorporate [*Tristram Shandy*] in a more superficial culture of cynicism and commerce."[26] Hence the author of *Tsonnonthouan* claims in his preface that the reason his book does not have a running title throughout all of its pages is that his bookseller tells him that, should the book not find success, he can simply insert a new title page into the already printed copies that reads, "*A Continuation of the Life and Opinions of Tristram Shandy*" (viii). His bookseller also complains that there is too much "solid matter" in the novel, which, "if it had been properly managed, would have made four of Tristram Shandy's volumes" (x). Thomas Keymer notes that Sterne's small volumes "soon became a byword for the deceptive packaging of slender matter,"[27] a point not lost on the bookseller, who explains that, despite not having read the book, he has been told "a great deal of Tristram Shandy's wit consists in the distance between his lines, in the shortness of his chapters and paragraphs, in the great number of his breaks and dashes, in his blank leaves, and even in misreckoning his pages" (x–xi). Many authors contributed to the scramble to cash in on Sterne's rapid rise in fame and fortune, with books and pamphlets such as *Explanatory Remarks Upon the Life and Opinions of Tristram Shandy* (1760), *Tristram Shandy's Bon Mots* (1760), and *Yorick's compleat Jests* (1761), not to mention numerous productions claiming to be the next volume of *Tristram Shandy*, all vying to satisfy the public's desire for Shandean texts. The typographic effects used by Sterne are, for the author of *Tsonnonthouan*, a superficial and "irksome ostentation," and while Sterne may have sought to differentiate himself through form, this is precisely what made his work so appealing to the market and so easy to imitate. The number of Sterne imitations entering the literary marketplace was unprecedented even by the standards of the rapidly expanding print culture of the 1760s, and these texts, some of which claimed to be by Sterne himself, were by and large written by anonymous Grub Street "hacks" whose aims were mostly commercial.[28] This large body of imitations has been mostly forgotten by scholarship, and, ironically perhaps, *Tsonnonthouan* has been counted among them; bibliographic entries tend to list it, as in the *English Short Title Catalogue*, as "an imitation of Sterne's *Tristram Shandy*," while Joseph Sabin's sprawling nineteenth-century catalogue of "Americana" describes it as "[a]n imitation of Sterne's *Tristram Shandy*, then of course in publication. The scene of the story is laid among the Têtes de Boule of Canada, and its object was to parody Sterne, especially in his indecency."[29]

While he insists the plot was conceived long before the appearance of *Tristram Shandy*, the author accepts that his text will circulate within the world of the literary marketplace, and offers that if "any Grubstreet continuator should undertake it, he will find hints in the first chapter, to which he is heartily welcome, and if he does, I sincerely wish him all the success he may deserve" (xv). Indeed, the text contains a surplus of narrative detail, and it is filled with plot developments that are mentioned but which do not occur directly in the book itself. Most of Tsonnonthouan's religious conversions, for example, do not happen until after the period of the novel, as is the case with his many travels. His trip to Britain is only tantalizingly alluded to, as well as the experience of his son, who eventually goes to London for education and lives with the narrator. The constant movement to background contextual material in Sterne becomes in *Tsonnonthouan* an anxiety to get the entire story out as soon as possible, even as the pages dwindle and the plot only narrowly moves forward. While this satirizes the shallow literary culture among hack writers and booksellers, it also mirrors their practices by giving the reader an excess of narrative product.

The author of *Tsonnonthouan* closely read French ethnographic texts, widely available in English translations, to provide the source material which was then burlesqued. The name of the novel and protagonist comes from the French name for the Seneca Nation, members of the Iroquois confederacy, who are mentioned by Charlevoix; the Jesuit notes that among some Native nations it is common for a man to marry multiple women, but "there prevails in the Iroquois canton of Tsonnontouan a much greater disorder still, namely a plurality of husbands."[30] This detail lends itself to the purposes of the author and shapes the interest of the text, again following Sterne, in emasculation. At times the book borrows so heavily from the ethnographic sources that there is little distinction between them, which implies that the author perceives ethnography itself as a contingent narrative construction.[31] The *Monthly Review* dismisses *Tsonnonthouan*'s ethnographic passages, complaining that, if this is what passes for a romance, then "Charlevoix himself may pass very well as a Romance writer for years to come."[32] However, such generic distinctions were often blurred, even in the pages of the *Monthly*. Three years earlier, in a review of Charlevoix's text, the *Monthly* noted that the Jesuit's Indians shared similar opinions to "the learned and profound Mr. Tristram Shandy's father."[33] The writer adds

> Now, tho' Mr. Shandy may pretend, for the honour of his family, that this opinion was the native production of his father's genius and reflection, we cannot but think there is some reason to suspect he might have adopted it from the systems of some of the Iroquois, Algonquin, or Michillimakinac Philosophers. (425)

Both Walter Shandy and the philosophical "savages" of French ethnography are textual constructions mediating and criticizing the fruits of enlightened modernity. This is exactly what *Tsonnonthouan* suggests, with the added inference that, like fiction, ethnographic texts are constrained by the marketplace and other external forces, and hold no more claim to truth than a "humorous romance." English writers frequently criticized French ethnography for its pro-Catholic bias, even as they depended heavily upon it as source material. Colden complains that "[h]istories wrote with all the Delicacy of a fine Romance, are like French Dishes, more agreeable to the Palate than the Stomach, and less wholesome than more common and coarser Diet" (xiv), and it is his intention to begin a British response by writing about "our Indians" for English consumption. Yet this effort is equally questionable for the author of *Tsonnonthouan*, whose narrator, an unnamed English physician, frequently compromises his own reliability as an objective voice. When he first meets Tsonnonthouan, for example, he is among the Miami Indians on an unspecified "commercial adventure" (II, 5) and, after treating the Roundhead for an injury by giving him copious amounts of brandy, attempts to charge him "ten times the market-price, which I think is a very moderate surgeon or apothecary's profit" (II, 17). The authoritative yet effaced narrator of ethnography is revealed to be constrained and compelled by the same forces and desires as the Indians who consume their goods and the reading public who consume the Indians. *Tsonnonthouan* uses ethnography and, more specifically, North America, as a vehicle and site for imagining the effects of British culture on the (transnational) self.

Worshiping Objects

It is frequently argued, as I have discussed above, that the "modern subject" evident by century's end is a rupture from earlier modes of self-imagining; the self became individually rather than collectively defined, and this modern self, as numerous critics have stated, was shaped and imagined by the consumption of commodities.[34] For the British, this was a problematic development since, as an island nation, part of its mythology was as a land of exception, free from the religious and political tyrannies of continental Europe. At the same time, there was a vulnerability and anxiety in this smallness that contributed to the rapid expansion of a vast empire, the fruits of which became essential products of British identity itself. Charlotte Sussman notes that the

British fantasy of self-sufficiency was undermined by colonial commodities, whose consumption posed a transcultural threat to Britain.[35]
Moreover, in McKendrick, Brewer, and Plumb's analysis, consumerism
was seen as a threat to the stratified society in which it thrived, and
goods once only possessed by the rich descended down the social scale
through the practice of social emulation.[36] Thus the "artificial plenty" of
Johnson's London, while providing greater leisure to those able to take
it in, also threatened the society it propelled.

The love of objects takes a literal turn in *Tsonnonthouan*, and, in a
distortion of actual Indigenous practice, the Indians each possess
individual manitous or gods which they begin to worship when they
are between eight and ten years old. Borrowing from Charlevoix,[37] as
well as the large body of sources forming what Thomas Preston calls
"the general storehouse of 'Indian matter'" available in Britain at the
time,[38] the narrator describes the process through which a young person chooses his or her manitou: after a period of fasting for five days
or more, the child worships the first object which they dream about,
and, if they do not dream, they continue the fast until a manitou is
chosen. Following the selection of a manitou, the child is given her or
his name. When he was ten, Tsonnonthouan was asked to begin fasting so his manitou and name could be selected. Shortly before his fast
began, his father accidentally killed a bear out of season and set this
"great delicacy" aside for the feast following Tsonnonthouan's fast.
After only two days of fasting, the young Tsonnonthouan claimed he
dreamed of sucking a bear's paw, and the right paw of the bear was
cut off and hung around his neck. Years later, when the narrator questions Tsonnonthouan as to whether he had invented this dream to "put
an end to this disagreeable ceremony," the Roundhead claims that
he can no longer remember (I, 41). Thus his "virgin divinity," which
Tsonnonthouan nonetheless worshiped for ten years, was chosen to
fill an immediate want. His name was chosen following this, and he
was given his Iroquois maternal grandfather's name; the author notes
that "it is remarkable that Tsonnonthouan, though he often changed his
manitous, never once altered his name" (I, 40). Despite his fluidity and
constantly shifting religious alliances, his own character remains stable;
similarly, though Tsonnonthouan switches belief systems constantly, he
adopts each one zealously. Thus, as Bosch suggests, "Tsonnonthouan's
instability ... does not temper his need of certainties."[39] While other
Indians frequently change their names, Tsonnonthouan remains the
same, confident in his own character even as he switches the systems

that give it meaning. If, as in Wahrman's analysis, the "modern self" as described by the political and philosophical discourse of the late eighteenth century can be seen as less fluid and more certain of its essential origins, the figure of the Indian during the mid-eighteenth century, as the second chapter argues, can be seen as a mediator between the less certain *ancien régime* of identity and the more unified personal identity of the Enlightenment.

Tsonnonthouan's next manitou enters his life following the introduction of an Indian trader, the transported Briton Diggory Bunce.[40] Bunce is of humble origins, but was taken in by a dowager countess in London as her steward. This creates a scandal among the "honourable tea-tables in this metropolis," and the dowager's numerous suitors encourage this gossip. These suitors take him into their "select society," where he proves no match for the skill and experience of his "noble adversaries in the mysteries of whist and piquette" (I, 55). Bunce gambles away his lady's fortune, and he is forced to become a highwayman after she fires him. He is caught and sentenced to death but, after his lady's intervention on behalf of her own good name, his death sentence is commuted to transportation for life in North America and he becomes an Indian trader. Prior to his acquaintance with Bunce, whose name is appropriately slang for money or extra profit (though "Diggory" is derived from the French *égaré* or "lost"), Tsonnonthouan is faithful to his bear's paw for many years. However, while out walking one day, the two men encounter a bear "in pursuit of a beautiful Indian young lady" (I, 57). Tsonnonthouan shoves a brandy bottle into the animal's mouth and proceeds to fight it. Bunce, who as a gambling man is an expert on boxing, enthusiastically circles the combatants as though at a boxing match in a "certain house in St. James street." Tsonnonthouan beseeches the man for assistance, but Bunce declares, "The bear shall have fair play, damn me if he shan't" (I, 59). He accordingly cheers both fighters on, while taking bets from an imaginary crowd of "noble and honourable members of the worthy club" (I, 60). Fortunately for Tsonnonthouan, Bunce is unaware of the brandy bottle shoved in the bear's mouth, and does not take action to remove it. Eventually the bear suffocates when the cork of the bottle comes out and the brandy begins "gushing … into his lungs" (I, 61). Seeing that he owes his victory to this lucky bottle, which still contains ample brandy, Tsonnonthouan discards his bear paw, since he suspects it aided its kin in the battle, and adopts the bottle as his new manitou. Thus Tsonnonthouan's impious journey through the worship of different objects into the "metaphysical or systematical sort of theology" (I, 63) begins with the providential assistance of a harmful European trade good.

Alcohol is an important commodity in *Tsonnonthouan* because it is representative of the destructive effects of colonialism and trade. There are countless eighteenth-century texts that depict Indians being debauched by alcohol acquired from English traders; in captivity narratives, British captives frequently hide in terror while their Indian captors get drunk and fly into uncontrolled murderous rages, ethnographic accounts from mid-century rarely neglect to mention the deleterious effects of rum or brandy among the nations that the Europeans visit, and missionary texts lament the physical and spiritual degeneration that professed Christians are introducing among the Indians. Robert Beverley noted in 1705 that "[f]or their Strong drink, they are altogether beholding [*sic*] to us, and are so greedy of it, that most of them will be drunk as often as they find an opportunity," adding that "they go as solemnly about it, as if it were part of their religion."[41] Colden remarks in the second edition of his 1750 *History* that the only vice among all Indian nations, which was unknown prior to their "[a]cquaintance with the *Christians*," is drunkenness. He writes, "[i]t is strange, how all the *Indian* Nations, and almost every Person among them, Male and Female, are infatuated with the Love of strong Drink; they know no Bounds to their Desire, while they can swallow it down, and then indeed the greatest Man among them scarcely deserves the Name of a Brute" (13). This was not new knowledge, since British traders and colonists had long observed the effects of alcohol in Native communities; a newspaper report from London's *Post Man and the Historical Account* on 11 October 1701 similarly notes that the Native people who are "[n]eighbours to the Christians" are dwindling in numbers because the Christians "sell them a sort of liquor call'd Rum, which they love exceedingly, and so kill themselves by too much drinking." While countless texts depict Indians being debauched, alcohol was in many ways superior to material goods such as cloth and guns because, unlike those objects, it was in constant demand thanks to a regularly shrinking supply.[42] Many Native people demanded that colonial officials intervene on their behalf to put a stop to the alcohol trade; Charles Thomson wrote in 1759 that one chief complained during negotiations,

> Your Traders ... bring scarce any Thing but Rum and Flour: They bring little Powder and Lead, or other valuable Goods. The Rum ruins us. We beg you would prevent its coming in such Quantities by regulating the

Traders ... These wicked Whisky-Sellers, when they have got the *Indians* in Liquor, make them sell the very Cloaths from their backs.[43]

The reality was, as the colonial officials in Pennsylvania admit in Thomson's text, that traders had come to use rum and other liquors as "the principal Article of their Trade." Other Native voices, some real and some the ventriloquized thoughts of British writers, arose in objection to the spread of alcohol in their communities. One such example is the pamphlet *The Speech of a Creek-Indian, Against the Immoderate Use of Spirituous Liquors*, printed in at least two editions in London in 1754. The text of the speech, as well as the other compositions meant to be written by Indians in the same edition, is supposedly taken from a book printed in New York,[44] and, "being a Place of the greatest Commerce with the *Indian* Nations, we cannot doubt of their Authenticity" (iv). The words of the Creek man, whose name is given as Onughkally-dawwy Garangula Copac, are meant to illuminate the vice of "immoderate *Drinking*," which "rears its shameless Front, and reels from Street to Street in broad Day" (v–vi). He tells his brethren that there is a "*lurking Miscreant*" among them, which is "that pernicious Liquor, which our pretended *white Friends* artfully introduced, and so plentifully pour in among us" (12). He emphasizes the damage alcohol brings to not only the Creek nation as a whole, but to the "domestic bliss" of each individual's home. While the authenticity of this document is very much in doubt, there was undeniably a movement among various Indigenous nations to rid their communities of alcohol and, even more dangerous for British colonizing efforts, all European goods. The Delaware (Lenape) prophet Neolin told his people in the mid-1760s to shed all European influence from their lives, but "above all, you must abstain from drinking their deadly *beson* [medicine], which they have forced upon us, for the sake of increasing their gains and diminishing our numbers."[45] It is striking that Neolin's anti-colonial strategy is very similar to consumer boycotts of imported goods in Britain, with the shared goal of cultural preservation, purification, and drastic political change.[46] Samson Occom offered a more apologetic voice, but nonetheless encouraged his fellow Christian Native people to break free of the "destructive sin" of drinking, which was encouraged only by "develish men."[47]

British colonial officials wanted to integrate North American Indigenous people into the systems of commerce and religion. By ensuring Native people were producing and consuming goods, and practicing a rational Protestantism, the colonies could function more profitably and peacefully. These two overarching systems were fundamental aspects of British identity by mid-century, as Linda Colley and others have shown,[48] and nowhere were they more inter-implicated than in the colonies. This can be seen most obviously in missionary texts, which urged Britons to invest financially in schemes to convert and "civilize" the Indians, making them into better trading partners. The pamphlet *A Brief Narrative of the Indian Charity-School* (1766), meant to raise money in Britain for Eleazar Wheelock's school in Connecticut, argues that "[i]f they can be civilized" there will be "an Increase of the Demand for British Manufactures," making the project vital to "the Commerce of Great Britain and the Colonies" and a "Source of Opulence to the whole Empire!"[49] As both a trade good and a cultural force, alcohol threatened this vision of a productive future. It provided the counter-narrative to one of progression towards enlightened civilization, suggesting that with commerce and increased contact with the English came moral vacuity and degeneration. Historian and Virginia planter Robert Beverley writes in his 1705 text that the "harmless" Indians live "in their Simple State of Nature," but have growing reason to "lament the arrival of the *Europeans*," who have "introduc'd Drunkenness and Luxury amongst them, which have multiply'd their Wants, and put them upon desiring a thousand things, they never dreamt of before."[50] This carries a stirring resonance with Johnson's description of mid-century London, though Johnson celebrates rather than laments the possibilities of consumer desire.

Trade was in some ways more important for a functional colony than proselytization; unlike other European countries colonizing North America, namely France and Spain, the British placed a unique emphasis on trade over religion.[51] In their self-imagining, they colonized not by willfully destroying Indigenous culture, but by integrating other cultures into networks of mutual exchange. Or, as Horace Walpole writes in a letter of 1755, upon reflecting that the cost of the purchase of Maryland from its "savage proprietors ... was a quantity of vermilion and a parcel of Jews-harps," "*we* do not massacre, *we* are such good Christians as only to cheat."[52] Thus the only named Briton in *Tsonnonthouan* is Indian trader Bunce, while the only Frenchman is Father Pego, whose name represents in Spanish both trickery and violence. The liquor trade was therefore seen with decided ambivalence, since it integrated Native people into the economy of trade, generating a huge market for European goods, but it caused a great deal of harm to Indigenous communities and, more significantly, it built resentment among them and, on a discursive level, spread fear throughout white colonial settlements of drunken, destructive Indians.

The Indians in *Tsonnonthouan* do not angrily resist the influence of alcohol in their lives and communities, but rather celebrate it through drunken orgies and the glorification of traders who distribute it among them. The sole kind of alcohol they consume is brandy, which was in reality an increasingly important commodity for British trade in northern locations. The Hudson's Bay Company, for example, sold a mere 70 gallons of brandy in 1700 at their post in Fort Albany-Eastmain; by 1753, the combined amount sold at their three major northern posts had grown to 2,300 gallons, and remained around 2,000 gallons per year until 1763, the year of the publication of *Tsonnonthouan*.[53] Charlevoix notes that "an Indian will give all he is worth for one glass of brandy," and this has been exploited by the "avarice of our dealers" and hindered the success of missionaries.[54] In *Tsonnonthouan*, the author claims that "an Indian is so sensible of the power of brandy over himself, that he very readily allows for, and excuses all its effects in others" (I, 71). As a result, if one is drunk on brandy, they can physically assault others with impunity; the unscrupulous Bunce does just this, feigning drunkenness so he can attack Tsonnonthouan, giving him a furious beating after the Indian insults the trader's hero, David Garrick, and is subsequently forgiven.

The reality of the destructive effects of alcohol was apparent not only to Native people and British settlers and colonial officials, but also to any Briton who was well-versed in accounts of North America. And yet nowhere does there appear in the novel a clear sense of this reality; at one point Tsonnonthouan and his fellow Roundheads raid the entire supply of tobacco and liquor from English trader Bunce, and do not stop until they "had arrived at the most perfect state of happiness, which Indians are capable of, namely, that of complete intoxication" (I, 72). The tone is ironic in its celebration of consumption, but is unique in its lack of explicit concern over the deleterious effects of alcohol among Native peoples. Instead the narrator notes that in describing the scene following the drunkenness, "those who have seen what has passed at our gin-shops … will form a better conception of it than I can supply them by words" (I, 74). The text here enacts a denial of difference, providing instead a reflection on the exporting of British debauchery abroad. Despite the initial cost of furnishing the Indians his supply for their "elegant entertainment," Bunce is compensated when they buy his remaining stock, at the urging of Tsonnonthouan, at a very high price, thus rewarding him "in a mercantile way" (I, 79). In addition, his name becomes proverbial: a man who is "excessively intoxicated" is said to be "drinking with Diggory Bunce, or he has been at Bunce's brandy-warehouse," and all forms of strong liquor that are consumed at no cost become known as "Bunce's brandy" (80).

Transported criminals were frequently blamed for the debauching of the morals of Native people; Thomson, writing in 1759, cites one colonial administrator who regrets "the miserable Situation of our *Indian* Trade carried on … by the vilest of our own Inhabitants and Convicts imported from *Great-Britain* and *Ireland*, by which Means the *English* Nation is unhappily represented among our *Indian* Allies in the most disagreeable Manner."[55] Yet this explanation itself implicates the imperial project and capitalism, since Britain is, in effect, exporting its own moral degeneracy to North America. But while transported criminals reflect the flaws in both the poorer classes and the justice system that circulates their "vileness," the backstory of Bunce suggests that the kind of debauchery he peddles was in fact learned among the wealthiest class of people in London. His life is akin to Tom Rakewell in Hogarth's *A Rake's Progress*, though Bunce has humbler origins. Like Rakewell, he earns the favour of a wealthy older woman, and squanders her fortune in a gaming house. But while Rakewell goes to prison, where he loses his mind, Bunce's career is salvaged by transportation to the colonies. He buys his redemption by debauching the Indians in North America, a place which, as Sussman rightly points out, functions as "a convenient offstage site for capital accumulation, or as a respectable outlet for entrepreneurial energy" in eighteenth-century novels.[56] *Tsonnonthouan* makes this economy visible and central.

Despite his flaws, then, when compared to the Europeans in the novel, Tsonnonthouan is an exemplar of virtue. Bunce is the lone Englishman in the novel besides the narrator, and he debauches and cheats Tsonnonthouan before he, at a later date, becomes a Quaker and converts the Roundhead. The other significant European is Father Pego, a French priest who lusts after the wives of the medicine men in the tribe he is attempting to convert; he succeeds in converting Tsonnonthouan to Roman Catholicism, and he then helps the missionary to bed the women he desires. The Jesuit later convinces Tsonnonthouan that it was the English who crucified Jesus Christ, and he sets out on a crusade against them. He is eventually captured and, as the novel ends, converted to Presbyterianism by Tribulation T'otherworld, "parson

of Tottipottimoy and professor of divinity in the university of Catara-
coui." But it is Bunce and Pego, an Englishman and a Frenchman, who
represent the corruption of North America by the colonial powers who
turned it into a warzone over the previous decade and sought to establish their own moral superiority among Indigenous people.

In this way, *Tsonnonthouan* adopts an anticolonial position similar to
that adopted by Samuel Johnson in *The Idler* no. 81, in which he imagines
the words of "one of the petty Chiefs of the inland regions."[57] Johnson
writes that the Indians hope to see "the cruelties of invasion ... revenged,"
with his unnamed fictional chief declaring, "The sons of rapacity have
now drawn their swords upon each other, and referred their claims to
the decision of war; let us look unconcerned upon the slaughter, and
remember that the death of every European delivers the country from
a tyrant and a robber." The one military campaign in the book, besides
Tsonnonthouan's singular conquest against the English, comes to similar
conclusions as Johnson's essay, but in a decidedly different manner, as
we will see below.

If the brandy bottle represents the avarice of British traders and the
dangers of commodity fetishism, Tsonnonthouan's third manitou highlights the book's depiction of North America as not so much a warzone
(which in reality it still was) but as a space of debauchery and degeneration between cultures at sites of contact. Following his marriage to
Sasteratsi, the Indian maiden he rescues from the bear, Tsonnonthouan
is unable to consummate their union because of "how devoutly he had
addressed his manitou, not only the bottle itself, but also its contents
the brandy" (I, 114–15). Since Indians in the novel, like Moses in the
old Testament, demand physical proof of a bride's virginity, and the
"tokens of virginity" are not in Tsonnonthouan and Sasteratsi's marriage bed, the zealous shaman or, as Indians call all priests and minis-
ters, juggler, Doctor Chickamichabou demands the bride be "scalped
and tomahawked" unless she submits to an examination. The narrator
notes that if the English were to adopt such a custom, only one bride
in a thousand would be proven a virgin and spared her life, owing,
he believes, to the "extreme humidity of our atmosphere, and a conse-
quent relaxation of fibre" (I, 111). The modest Sasteratsi refuses to allow
the doctors to examine her, and Tsonnonthouan asks that her delicacy
be spared until he is able to acquire a new manitou, which will restore
his vigour. He tells the village divines that, after he drunkenly smashed
his brandy bottle manitou, he dreamed that Sasteratsi "was whipping
him with a bull's pizzle over the back and hips till the blood ran down

to his heels" (I, 115). Though Doctor Chickamichabou remains uncon-
vinced, the rest of the canton applauds Tsonnonthouan and allow him
to go on a quest to find his new manitou.

Tsonnonthouan sets off with some Catawba warriors who were
moved by his speech in defence of Sasteratsi, and they eventually
arrive in the Quaker back settlements of Pennsylvania. Here they proceed to kill a great many oxen, who are of course lacking the "necessary appendage" (I, 119), until they eventually find and kill a virile bull.
This provides Tsonnonthouan with his new manitou, with which he
happily returns home. However, this bull, and most of the slain oxen,
belonged to a powerful Quaker named Ezekiel Soady, who "forgot
one of the original tenets of his sect, namely, when his cloak was taken
away, to give his coat also" (I, 120). He honours his religion's insistence "never to fight himself," the narrator notes, and uses his influence
to "incite the Pensylvanians [sic] to commence hostilities against the
Indians." He succeeds, and the colonists declare war on the innocent
Indians who happen to be nearest to them, the "Chickesaws" (I, 120). In
the resulting warfare, many English women and children are "scalped
and tomahawked," including the Quaker's wife, and the nation of the
"Chickesaws" is almost wiped out; Soady himself is able to "secure his
own person" (I, 121). The narrator vows not to go into greater detail
of this "bloody war" because Tsonnonthouan, though the cause, was
not directly involved in it, but he reflects on "what minute and uncon-
nected circumstances roll the most important events of this world"; if
Tsonnonthouan had been able to consummate his marriage, or had he
dreamed of a different object, the Quakers would still have their wives
and children, and the Chickasaws would still be a "flourishing nation."
Similarly, the narrator continues, if a "certain great man" in Germany
had been able to consummate his marriage, "or to take those divertise-
ments with the fair sex, so innocent in a person of his station," he would
not take such pleasure in "the toils of ambition, and the horrors of war
and bloodshed" (I, 121–2). War, then, is the sublimation of erotic desire,
and Frederick II's reputed celibacy or homosexuality is contrasted with
Tsonnonthouan's brandy-fueled impotency as a catalyst for armed
conflict. But while Frederick II's sublimated sexuality is more directly
transformed into violent ambition, Tsonnonthouan's thwarted desire
becomes a quest for another materialization of divinity, manifested in
the form of a phallic tool of corporal punishment. This is what marks
the colonial war: the materialization of phallic drives and ideological
motives, in the form of land, trade goods, resources, and other forms

of wealth. It is, in other words, a commodified version of the wars of Europe, in which the Native people are necessarily drawn in by the European economies of consumer goods and religion.

Consuming Religion

If colonialism must be about more than "private Interest," as Colden insists, then it must be driven by a central principle. To that end, missionaries and colonial officials such as Sir William Johnson maintained that conversion efforts would lead to more equitable relations between Indians and Europeans. One of the major targets of the author of *Tsonnonthouan* is therefore organized religion. The *Critical Review*, while celebrating the novel as "one of the best executed modern romances," boosted by the same "keen satirical strictures which distinguish the works of Swift," worried that this "dangerous tendency of the work" could be a "poison which may have a bad effect upon weak minds," while the *Monthly Review* complained that the author was "frequently as gross and indelicate in his satire, as he is mistaken in the objects of it," to the point that he is "bordering sometimes … on blasphemy."[58] The novel questions the very foundation of revealed religion, mocks the miraculous feats described in the New Testament, and implies that religion in general is an "infection" that spreads through all peoples. The inconstant Tsonnonthouan leaps from faith to faith, adopting each religion or belief system "[w]ith all the fury, heat and enthusiasm of a bigot"; we are told "[h]e was first a papist, then a presbyterian, next a cacatorian, then a merrydancer, next a jew, then a mutilator, after that a methodist, and lastly, a quaker" (I, 12). Towards the end of his life, after many other conversions, he "would do as every wise man ought to do, conform to the religion of his country, and worship paws, horns or rags, as his friends and relations did" (I, 13). However, before that time, because of religion, he is castrated and, later, while in England, pilloried and sent to beat hemp in Bridewell (I, 14).

Indian manitou worship is repeatedly compared to Christianity in the novel, with the suggestion that both require blind faith and a dependency on a false attribution of positive qualities to arbitrary objects or ideologies. The narrator observes that, in fact, manitou worship is better than Christianity because "this species of madness is not so near so contagious amongst them as it is in other nations," since each worships his or her own deity and "they do not worship one common universal manitou, as is the custom in most other countries" (I, 170).

In one episode, Tsonnonthouan believes he has been saved from a herd of rampaging buffalo by his devout prayers to the hide of one of the animals. He was actually rescued by his fellow Indians, but they do not try to convince him otherwise by "using reason and argument" because, "knowing that in any thing where religion, or a manitou, are concerned, they would only render matters worse, rivetting the person … more firmly in his madness, and making him more obstinate in pursuing its suggestions" (I, 182). To argue against his faith runs the risk "of having the madness communicated to others, and, perhaps, the infection spread amongst nations." There is throughout the novel similar comparisons between the comical, arbitrary faith of Tsonnonthouan and the foundational tenets of all forms of Christianity.

The use of a North American Indian to critique religion is an apt choice, since some of the most prevalent writing about Native people was, since the mid-seventeenth century, written by missionaries and their supporters.[59] The missionary fantasy that Indians should, and in fact could easily, be converted to the Christian religion was found in many texts published by groups such as the Society for the Propagation of the Gospel in Foreign Parts (SPG), as well as in literary texts; Friday in *Robinson Crusoe* is perhaps the most well-known example. As the narrator of Behn's *Oroonoko* declares in describing her time among the Indians of Surinam, "it were not difficult to establish any unknown or extravagant religion among them" (122). The British interest in converting Native people to Protestantism was particularly high during the period in which *Tsonnonthouan* was published, with both the SPG and the Society for Propagating Christian Knowledge (SPCK) publishing accounts of their missionary efforts and continuing need for more funds. Three years after the novel's appearance in 1763, Mohegan preacher Samson Occom toured all of Britain in a highly successful fundraising effort for Moor's Indian Charity School, raising over £10,000 and showing that British people were prepared to invest in the education and conversion of the "poor Indians" of North America. The self-image of compassionate and righteous colonialism was an integral part of the ideological structure of the British empire, and it was widely believed that while the Spanish practiced violent slaughter and subjugation in their earlier conquest of the Americas, and the French exploited Native fears and superstition through a perverted religion, the British sought to introduce a rational faith through education and a genuine concern and pity for what Laura Stevens calls the "the figure of the virtuous but uninformed Indian."[60] Of course, as in the case of Eleazar Wheelock's

Indian Charity School, British sentiment was exploited to further the colonial apparatus: the funds raised through immense personal sacrifice by former student Occom during his two lonely years in Britain, away from his Mohegan family, did not go towards the expansion of the Charity School, as Occom and his donors believed it would, but rather mostly went to the establishment of Dartmouth College, an institution that primarily educated white colonists and graduated only nineteen Native people in its first two-hundred years.[61]

Nonetheless, the ideological foundation of Protestant colonialism, or the "reforming empire," as Christopher Hodgkins has called it,[62] was in part based on a genuine, though self-serving and condescending, pity for Indians. The extent to which *Tsonnonthouan* challenges this sentiment is made clear by the negative evaluation in the *Monthly Review*; the Whiggish critic writes

> [i]t would, doubtless, be extremely absurd and ridiculous in an European, to adopt the Indian manitou, and make a deity of a bear's paw, a bull's pizzle, a buffaloe's hide, a brandy bottle, or a red rag; but this circumstance in an untutored Indian, ought rather to excite sensations of pity and compassion, than those of ridicule and laughter.[63]

Thus, the writer believes that like Pope's "poor Indian" in *Essay on Man*, "whose untutor'd mind / Sees God in clouds, or hears him in the wind," Tsonnonthouan should be seen as a miserable figure, desperate for Protestant intervention. Of course, he does become a Protestant, numerous times in fact, and ultimately rejects the faith for his own. Furthermore, the *Monthly* reviewer fails to see the extent to which Tsonnonthouan's worship of objects implicates and imitates patterns of British consumption at home. Instead he sees the reality that, emptied of religion, the only successful British practice that colonialism effectively introduces is debauchery and commodity fetishism, in this case in the most literal sense. And while the satire of colonialism in *Tsonnonthouan* is not necessarily connected to broader emancipatory goals or movements and has more in keeping with the Tory critiques of Swift and Smollett, it can be approached through Laura Brown's dialectical approach, which aims for an understanding of "the necessary intimacy of structures of oppression and liberation."[64] While Brown is interested in the ways in which *Gulliver's Travels* critiques imperialism through frequently misogynist representations of corporeality, *Tsonnonthouan* similarly uses racist stereotypes about Native people to criticize not only colonialism proper, but the cultural and governmental institutions that give it meaning.

Conclusion

In addition to its obvious importance as a text which provides a unique access to eighteenth-century modes of interactions between Native people and British self-imaginings, there is a significant chance that *Tsonnonthouan* influenced others who in turn produced more canonical and influential texts. It is very likely that Tobias Smollett read it and is the author of the favourable review in the *Critical*. Foster notes that the review makes sense chronologically in Smollett's career, and the style is similar to other reviews known to be by him. Moreover, the political and artistic opinions of the reviewer are in keeping with what one might expect from him. As already mentioned, Smollett's *British Magazine* extracted a chapter of *Tsonnonthouan*, and both *The History and Adventures of an Atom* and, more significantly, *Humphry Clinker*, bear its influence. Just as Tsonnonthouan falls sick from eating too much bear, so too does Lismahago's Miami bride Squinkinacoosta, though she dies of the affliction; Lismahago claims the Miamis avoid the "articles of luxury" popular in Britain because "they were too virtuous and sensible to encourage the introduction of any fashion which might help to render them corrupt and effeminate" (195), while the narrator of Tsonnonthouan maintains that "Luxury and effeminacy have not, as yet, come to such a height amongst the Indians" (135). Smollett also saw the hopelessness in converting the Indians to British ways, complaining that the British "have a strange itch to colonize America, when the uncultivated parts of our own island might be settled to greater advantage" (256). Furthermore, "the Indians were too tenacious of their own customs to adopt the modes of any nation whatsoever" (195). Both authors are interested in the fruits of colonialism; while Smollett is disgusted by the tide of corruption and dependency brought into Britain from the colonies by "every upstart of fortune ... enriched they know not how," the author of *Tsonnonthouan* concerns himself with the ideological and representational practices of colonialism and the exports of greed, hypocrisy, and cynicism.

Tsonnonthouan is a peculiar book for its singularity and obscurity, but is important as a transatlantic text, giving unique insight into the ways in which North American Indians functioned in the British imaginary in a pivotal year in the colonies. Indians loomed large in policy and strategic importance, but few other texts satirize the very means through which information on them was disseminated. Smollett would take up some of the text's concerns over consumption in *Humphry Clinker*, but his Indians are too "tenacious" and virtuous to be dazzled by the wares of Europe, and demonstrate instead, as Sussman has shown, that the "colonial encounter violates Europe."[65] In *Tsonnonthouan*, the logic of colonial discourse and consumerism is extended to its extreme, and the novel mocks the pretensions of missionaries and traders who, in the end, are equally guilty of making "[Tsonnonthouan's] original notions ... warped, his knowledge improved, and ... his principles debauched" (II, 28). The novel does not, however, offer a way out of these cycles, since it highlights its own participation in crass consumerism as a commodity.

Tsonnonthouan's final manitou before converting to Christianity for the first time is a red rag, which is from the uniform of a British soldier who was captured by "French Indians" and "put to death by those Barbarians" after his wounds would not allow him to travel further (II, 1–2). The captive body, as the previous chapter argues, becomes an important site in captivity narratives of the time as a reminder of the costs in the colonial project and the thrills and perils of cross-cultural contact, but in this the case the captive is absent. His body was "long ago consumed by the birds and beasts," and the red cloth that remains appears "by its cut and shape, as well as other marks, to have been the seat of his breeches." The ideological apparatus of colonialism is the primary target of the novel, but here the underlying violence is evoked metonymically; all that remains of the British military, despite the recent historical victory of the French and Indian War, is the bawdy without the body. Even the damaged, abject soldier disappears in this case. The end product of colonialism is the vulgar and profane object, which replaces all value systems and people, or turns them into objects themselves.

5 Becoming Indians: Sentiment and the Hybrid British Subject

Be guiltless – Be an Indian.

– William Richardson, "The Indians, A Tale" (1774)

After the first reports of North American settler unrest reached London in the late 1760s, when the loss of the colonies became a distinct possibility, British writers began to romanticize North American Indians and cultural interactions with them in a way that split from earlier strategies of representation. While this is the same period in which various scholars locate a move away from more fluid ideas of race and personal identity, texts that represented Britons who had been fully and wilfully transculturated among the Indians appeared for the first time. As categories of identity were becoming hardened and less ambiguous, particularly as they related to race,[1] traits of Indians were paradoxically appropriated as an aspect of British identity in texts of this period, and the hybrid Indian-British subject became distinct and desirable during the apparent ascendancy of the confident and stable self. Forged in part through conflict and fear, this hybrid identity was articulated in the years after the most violent confrontations between Britons and Indians. The Indian in these later texts is, as I will argue below, often similar to the "impartial spectator" of Adam Smith's *The Theory of Moral Sentiments* (1759), though in Smith the savage is not subsumed into British and Anglo-American identity and remains an appealing but ambivalent subject. Indeed, for Smith, Indians are overly impartial, unable to sympathetically identify with others because of the harshness of savage life. This lack of sympathy among all savage nations prevents them from being ideal selves to occupy according to his moral treatise, despite their resemblance to the "man within the breast" who provides appropriate ethical and emotional responses.

This chapter will look at texts that present Indian-British identities as solutions to the critiques of British culture and subjectivity that Indians exposed in earlier literary manifestations. The Indian in these works becomes foundational to a corrective kind of subjectivity, a modern self that can navigate the terrains of imperial governance, effeminacy brought on by consumerism and immoderate sentiment, and individualism in the face of a fractured identity. It will first consider the anonymously written novel *The Female American* (1767), which uses the affective work of earlier missionary writing to create a hybrid identity for the purposes of converting the Indians and asserting governmental control. The chapter will then turn to Henry Mackenzie's *The Man of the World* (1773), a sentimental novel and sequel to *The Man of Feeling* that depicts a corrupted British man who is redeemed by his time among the Cherokee and internalization of their emotional fortitude. It will then look at fellow Scottish writer William Richardson's "The Indians, A Tale" (1774, adapted for the stage in 1791), a work that, while lesser known, circulated in various adaptations and presents Indians as equally tenacious and cosmopolitan in their beliefs. The next hybrid subject will be William Augustus Bowles, an Englishman born in the colonies who took on an Indian identity. Bowles is presented in a little known pamphlet, *Authentic memoirs of William Augustus Bowles, Esquire* (1791), as an ideal masculine subject whose aristocratic and savage tastes form a striking and heroic individualism. The Irish playwright John O'Keeffe claimed to base his play *The Basket-Maker* (1789–90) on Bowles, and while I challenge this assertion, the play centres on the similarly heroic King Simon and his ascendancy in power and wealth by taking an Indian identity. Finally, I will turn to Robert Bage's Jacobin novel *Hermsprong; or, Man as He is Not* (1796), a popular work that focuses on a European man who is raised among Indians and introduces reforms to the effeminate aristocracy of England. In these works, Indians became more aestheticized and, as in the American context, were appropriated into a nationalist narrative of identity formation.[2] While this transformation offers an image of Indians that is often more qualitatively positive and less ambivalent, it also obscures or erases actual colonial struggle. Moreover, it is always Britons, not Indians, who emerge from encounters with an improved sense of self. This shift in representation is, of course, not uniform, and there continued to appear texts that villainized Indians as cruel and bloodthirsty, in some cases with even less ambivalence than in captivity narratives. The polarized visions of noble and ignoble savages do not necessarily contradict one another, but offer competing interpretations of the same cultural fantasies. Both the inhuman savage and the sentimental chief consume British bodies, and fail to see either social or cultural distinctions among themselves or their enemies; each threatens to dissolve the individual signification of the Briton as autonomous subject or corporeal being. [3]

The British context is distinct from the American history of what has been described by Renée L. Bergland as "the national uncanny," in which the vanishing or even spectral Indian becomes a literary symbol of both a triumphant American state and a reminder of national guilt over this conquest.[4] Bergland argues that, beginning with texts by Puritan colonists in the sixteenth century, North American "land is haunted because it is stolen." She notes that "Native Americans, as a race, are absorbed into the white American mind as an aspect of American consciousness," which separates them from both the future and the past of the state.[5] Philip Deloria's "playing Indian" is an act of national self-definition in American history and cultural activities, while, in the context of Canada and Australia, Terry Goldie classifies white appropriations of Indigenous subjects in literature as "indigenization."[6] In Britain, this spectralization is not tied to the triumphant yet guilt-ridden occupation of a haunted landscape or a straight-forward act of appropriation and displacement, but rather, at least in part, supplements a melancholic sense of loss of North American colonial space. This phenomenon is also a development of discourses from the preceding decades, which saw a large strategic dependency on and fascination with the Indigenous people loyal to Britain. The experiments in subjectivity by peripheral figures such as Peter Williamson point to a latent desire to be Native in even the most pernicious texts about Indians, while subsequent appropriations often linked the Indian to radical politics emerging in Britain between the American Revolutionary War and the French Revolution. Indian subjectivities could also provide relatively safe sites from which to launch critiques or celebrations of other sites of empire.

The fetishization of Indians at the end of the eighteenth century highlights their unique position in the British imaginary. No other non-European group was so consistently seen as providing correctives and alternatives to British culture, while also being so demonized and despised in other contexts. This position certainly already existed prior to the Revolutionary War, but the growing disenchantment with empire that occurred following the loss of the American colonies and the Hastings trial in the 1780s[7] solidified Native people as ideal anti-colonial subjects in literary texts.[8] The depiction of Indians as melancholic and/or desirable subjects is challenged by a vision of inhuman savagery and fundamental cultural difference, but even the propagandist images often carry critiques of the moral failings of Britain at home and in the colonies.[9] North American Indigenous people provided a model of culture and selfhood which was both alluring and dangerous to the expanding British Empire; the perception of tribal identities as simultaneously fluid and stable, in the sense that non-Native people could be fully adopted into strong Native societies, provided the fantasy of an Indianised Briton who could enter a foreign culture, gain from it, and still retain the best qualities of British identity.[10] The savage could be internalised and sublimated, becoming less a real being than a discursive function.[11]

Hybridity in this chapter is not meant to evoke Homi Bhabha's well-known discussion of colonial mimicry, which describes the destabilizing ways in which colonized peoples appropriate aspects of dominant colonialist culture in reaction to the "civilizing mission."[12] This process, which is often "profound and disturbing" to the authority of colonial discourse,[13] can be seen in some captivity narratives as discussed above, but becomes neutralized in the texts I will be discussing. This is not to suggest that this hybridity is necessarily meant to produce an ideal model of imperial governance, though this can occur, as in *The Female American*. Rather, the hybrid provides a uniquely "modern" way of imagining subjectivity by appropriating the figure often used to critique earlier forms of self and culture, and who generally stands for unconscious or libidinal desires. The Indian as critic earlier in the century, and as tyrannical captor in captivity narratives, becomes subsumed into British identity as a means of correcting or transforming the shortcomings of European culture.

This chapter will explore the hybrid subjects produced beginning in the 1770s, but will start with a discussion of the changing representations of Indians as they began to fundamentally inform the development of late-eighteenth-century political and aesthetic movements, particularly Romanticism.[14] Robert Rogers's play *Ponteach: or the Savages of America, A Tragedy* (1766) is a striking example of this shift, given that it romanticizes the Odawa leader who led a massive anti-colonial uprising against the British only three years earlier. Anthropologist

Renato Rosaldo describes the phenomenon of "imperialist nostalgia," in which anthropologists, colonial agents, and missionaries participate in this "mourning for what one has destroyed" in the cultures they have encountered.[15] This is not dissimilar from the American "national uncanny," but, in Rogers's case, the ideological agenda is less clear; Ponteach as represented in the play is a powerful and developed character, not necessarily the abstracted and tragic representative of a doomed race.[16] Furthermore, the English colonists and soldiers in the play are almost uniformly despicable, forming a chain of corruption and greed that clearly implicates the British themselves in the colonial resistance, more so than the pride, ambition, and righteous anger of Ponteach. The four scenes in the first act focus, respectively, on corrupt traders who cheat Indians, hunters who plan to indiscriminately slaughter them, military officers who are complacent and dismissive towards Indian complaints of poor treatment, and the colonial governors who, like the traders, wish to cheat the Indians and horde the treaty gifts from the king for themselves. In three short years, the leader of a costly war against British interests had become a tragic hero in a play written by one of the colonial officials who fought against him.

Savage Contradictions

There is a stark contradiction between the sentimental Indians who appeared in British imaginative literature beginning in the 1750s and the depictions of cruel Indians in the British press between the 1750s and 1770s.[17] Indians generally appalled the press, and newspapers focused on Indian warfare and torture practices to such an extent that some readers began to doubt the accounts of Indian cruelty due to their hyperbolic excess.[18] Even more balanced travel and ethnographic texts, such as James Adair's *The History of the American Indians* (1775), were excerpted only for their accounts of torture and the harsh treatment of captives, while romanticized representations by the likes of Rousseau were rejected outright.[19] During the Revolutionary War, public opinion was almost universally opposed to the use of Indians as allies against British colonists, though this was not the case when the French were the enemy during the Seven Years' War. Edmund Burke's "Speech on the Use of Indians" from 6 February 1778, which lasted for more than three hours and "was universally thought the very best Mr. Burke had ever delivered," reflects this sentiment.[20] Burke argues that "the fault of employing [Indians] did not consist in their being of one colour or another, in their using one kind of weapon or another; but in their way of making war; which was so horrible, that it shocked not only the manners of all civilized people, but far-exceeded the ferocity of all barbarians mentioned in history" (521). The Indians, Burke claims, have no titles or distinctions for distinguishing themselves in battle, but instead "their rewards were generally received in human scalps, in human flesh, and the gratifications arising from torturing, mangling, scalping, and sometimes eating their captives in war" (521). The parliamentary record notes that Burke "repeated several instances of this diabolical mode of war, scarcely credible, and, if true, improper to be repeated." No doubt drawing on accounts he read in the press, Burke steadfastly believes that "to employ them was merely to be cruel ourselves in their persons." He excuses the British use of Indian allies in the colonial struggle with France as a necessary consequence of the close ties held by both European powers with various tribes, who were, at the beginning of European settlement, "comparatively, great and powerful states." Now, however, because they are so reduced in number, their only strength is their cruelty. In Burke's argument and in broader press coverage, Indians threaten Britons not only corporeally, through their savage warfare, but also in a more fundamental way; by associating with them, Burke argues, Britons lose their "reputation as a civilized people" (521).

During this same period, despite the prevalence of anti-Indian discourse, some authors were presenting radically different visions of Indians. Troy Bickham notes that only in the period following the war could there be this shift in imagination towards Indians as "lamentable victims and heroic resistors of imperialism."[21] However, we should also recall Johnson's "Indian's Speech to his Countrymen" in *Idler* no. 81 from November 1759, which presents an Indian articulately wishing that "the cruelties of invasion shall be revenged" against the French and British. More significantly, in literature and in periodicals around the time of the Revolutionary War itself, there was also a sympathetic representation of the Indian that ran parallel to the more prevalent cruel Indian. Positive representations certainly dwindled at the height of the tensions in 1776, but there nonetheless continued to appear less overtly negative depictions in the surrounding years. Adair's *History*, mentioned above, was printed in 1775 and offers a nuanced, often favourable description of Indians. He writes that the Indians could be valuable allies because "there is no such thing among [them] as desertion in war," and the English need not pay mercenaries like the Swiss or Germans for protection if they act nobly towards their Native allies. Indians are "[g]overned by the plain and honest law of nature, [and] their whole constitution breathes nothing but liberty."[22] He observes that "[w]e have frequent instances in America, that merely by the power of affability, and good-natured language, the savage Indian, drunk and foaming with rage and madness, can be overcome and brought to weep."[23] The brutal savage and the sentimental Indian are, according to Adair, never far apart, and he attempts to reconcile the polarized representations.

Mohawk leader and British ally Joseph Brant, or Thayendanegea, went to London in 1776, and was warmly received.[24] His interview with James Boswell, as discussed in the first chapter, appeared in the July 1776 issue of *The London Magazine*, not long after Burke would draft his impassioned plea before Parliament. Boswell notes that "[t]he present unhappy civil war in America occasioned his coming over to England," and Brant supposedly wished to meet "THE GREAT KING" in order to make up his mind on which side he should take in the conflict. While Boswell is unsure "[b]y what mode of reasoning this chief was convinced of the justice of the demands of Great Britain upon her colonies, and the propriety of enforcing them," he happily writes that Brant has promised his assistance by bringing 3000 men into the field. Even newspapers occasionally printed more positive stories, such as in the *Morning Chronicle and London Advertiser* for 10 June of that year, which tells the story of a Mohawk chief, a "child of nature" likely based on Brant, complaining about the favourable attention South Sea Islander and Captain Cook passenger Omai received during his visit. He wonders why "this she looking black, this Molly dressed thing of a man, should be brought to England, and more money spent upon him here than is given to all the Indian nations in America," despite the fact that, unlike the Mohawks, neither he nor his people ever assisted the British. The Indian voices the masculine, xenophobic voice of modern British chauvinism and remains safely out of its critique.

Elsewhere, depictions of cruel Indians were understood as ideological constructions. In the anonymous *Modern Midnight Conversation, or Matrimonial Dialogues* (1775), meant to be a humorous revelation of the secret thoughts of both the most influential and prevalent types of people in British society, including "Nabob Hunters," "Unemployed Artists," and "Speculative Stock-Jobbers," the terrifying savage is discussed in the dialogue, *"Between a POOR Manufacturer on the Point of emigrating to America and his Wife."* The husband, frustrated by his exploitation at the hands of the wealthy and powerful, suggests, "Let's

JOSEPH TAYADANEEGA called the BRANT,
the Great Captain of the Six Nations.
Engraved from an Original Painting of G. Romney in the Collection of the Right Hon.ble the Earl of Warwick by J. R. Smith.

Figure 5.1 Joseph Tayadaneega called the Brant, the Great Captain of the Six Nations. Artist: John Raphael Smith, after George Romney, 1779. Mezzotint on paper. National Portrait Gallery, Smithsonian Institution; gift of the Abraham and Virginia Weiss Charitable Trust, Amy and Marc Meadows, in honour of Wendy Wick Reaves. Used with permission.

to America repair, / To breathe a less infected air" (190). While he is able to convince his wife of the injustice and difficulty in commerce which he faces in Britain, she tells him, "Wild beasts, and Indians too, I dread, / The notion almost strikes me dead, / Such shocking things I've often read; / Their cruelties my fancy chase, / And make me shudder while I'm safe" (196). The manufacturer urges her to "[b]elieve not all you read, or hear," and suggests that "[t]he greatest brutes you'll always find, / Are polish'd brutes of human kind" (196). He assures her,

> Be not depriv'd of ease, my life,
> By tomohawk, or scalping knife;
> From such ideas, pray, refrain,
> Indeed they're groundless, weak and vain.
> Altho' it ne'er disturbs your head,
> We've savages at home to dread;
> Reason can at St. James's see,
> Many a drest up Cherokee,
> With gold lac'd coat and high toupee;
> And many a furr'd gown Catabaw,
> Here scalp us by the forms of law;
> Let's quit such savages this week,
> Less dreadful canibals [sic] to seek;
> And to America repair,
> Indeed you'll find less danger there.   (197)

The savages at the heart of British commerce and culture, the author wryly suggests, present inequalities far worse than the pathological depictions of Indian violence. Anti-Indian discourse, while prevalent, was clearly not unchallenged, and was at times seen as a projection of Britain's own political and moral failings both at home and in the colonies. Alexander Kellet's *A Pocket of Prose and Verse* (1778) contains two satirical captivity narratives, which, while far from romanticizing Indians, mock the tropes used to represent them. Kellet worked as a colonial official in Georgia for a time, which no doubt gave him a keen awareness of the gap between representation and reality. His fictional narrative "A true Relation of the unheard-of-Sufferings of David Menzies, Surgeon, among the Cherokees, and of his surprizing Deliverance,"[25] still often read as factual, tells the story of a Briton taken captive and given to an old woman. She rejects him, "instead of courteously inviting her captive to replace by adoption her slain child," and decides that they shall lard him instead (or boil his fat while he is alive). They perform it on one half of his body and lard some bacon with the results, but become too drunk on rum to complete the process (201). He seizes this opportunity and flees, setting fire to the Cherokee town on his way out. Since he is without any means of gaining food, he "sustained famished nature by the bacon that was saturated with the juices of [his] own body," and was thus "preserved by the very cruelty of the Indians" (203). He literally consumes the transcultural act on his body, and he remarks that he has received a "momentous benefit" from his treatment among the Indians: "I have got rid entirely of a paralytic complaint, with which I had been for years afflicted, in that left side of mine which was roasted" (204). The effects of hybridity ultimately prove corrective, unlike abject captives of the period like Henry Grace and his tattooed arm. The other fictional narrative in the collection, "The Innocent Suicide," is a short text in which a Highlander is given by the Spanish to a group of Indians in Florida. Before they torture him, he flatters them in a speech, insisting that he has "no personal enmity to the natives of America, whom in truth I venerate, on account of the incorrupt simplicity of their manners, and the similarity of their customs to many of my own country" (218).[26] The man goes on to convince the Indians that he is invincible to any weapon of war, and, as proof, he insists that one of them take his broadsword and deliver a blow to his neck. The Indians oblige, and decapitate the man in the process, after which they realize "that the subtle suicide had deceived them, in order to evade the impending tortures" (223). Both narratives provide a central role to Indian torture, which signals its ubiquity in captivity accounts, but also demystify it by making it a site of satire. By re-writing torture, Kellet challenges the fundamental categories of difference asserted by Burke in his speech to Parliament as well as the basis for the prevalent terror and loathing in the press.

There are more substantial representations during this period that provide sentimental scenes of Indians and Britons interacting; in his *Fugitive Poetical Pieces* (1778), Edward Jerningham describes a captivity episode in his poem "The Indian Chief." It tells they story of an English officer taken prisoner by the French Indians during the Seven Years' War, who "became the slave of an old Indian chief, who treated him with humanity" (25). After a year of teaching the Briton the skills of Indian life, such as skinning beavers, building canoes, and "scalp[ing] the shrieking foe," the chief reflects melancholically on the death of his own son and the grief that the soldier's father must feel over his loss. He decides that the world must still look bright for the Englishman, and proclaims to him, "Go virtuous stranger, to thy father go, / Wipe from his furrow'd cheek Misfortune's tear: / Go, bid the sun to him his splendor shew, / And bid the flow'r in all her bloom appear" (27). The allusion to scalping in this case does not diminish the overwrought sensibility of the chief and his ability to sympathize with the soldier. Indeed, the captivity narratives produced in the preceding decades always combined bodily violence and the pleasure of sympathetic identification.[27]

The sentimental masculinity of wizened Indian elders appears in other texts of the period as well, as in the anonymously written epistolary novel *The trial: or, the history of Charles Horton, Esq.* (1772). The character of Edward Simpson, writing to Charles Horton, is once again a soldier deployed to North America, leaving his family behind. After all his companions are killed in a battle with hostile Indians, Horton is wounded and taken captive. He is held for a number of days, uncertain of his fate, until he is taken by a mob of Indians and tied to a stake with a pile of wood at his feet.[28] Though he mourns the loss of his life on behalf of his wife and son, Horton resolves to bear whatever happens "with as much magnanimity as possible; and shew the savages, that even their tortures could not daunt a British spirit" (II, 51). Adam Smith's *The Theory of Moral Sentiments*, as I will discuss below, claims magnanimity is the defining characteristic of "savages," but here the British soldier asserts this fortitude as his own. He suffers in this position for some time, until the people divide and an old Indian enters and approaches him "with much dignity" (II, 51). After inspecting him closely and conferring with twenty other old men, he has Simpson released because "he found so great a resemblance in my face and person of his lamented child, that he was quite astonished" (53). After appropriating the courage and endurance of the Indians, the Briton begins to resemble one. This departed son, Tuskarora, was beloved by the people, and they rejoice when the chief tells them that they must spare they soldier's life because of the strong resemblance. The son's name is borrowed from the Tuscarora people, members of the Six Nations who were accepted as one of the Haudenosaunee in 1722. They had fled their southeastern lands for protection under the Iroquois following land displacement, conflict, and enslavement after European arrival to their territory. Part of the reason they were accepted into the Confederacy was a recognition of a distant shared history, and when petitioning the governor of New York in 1714 on the plight of the Tuscarora, members of the then Five Nations proclaimed that "[t]hey were of us and went from us long ago, and are now returned and promise to live peaceably among us."[29] Simpson's acceptance as a member of Indian society because of his resemblance to "Tuskarora" mirrors the Tuscaroa's own entry among the Iroquois, and the uncanny similarity between the young men combines the best of British and Native subjectivities. Simpson agrees to stay with the old man for a time to provide him some comfort, and after a month the chief agrees to let him return to his garrison. He sends two Indians with him as guides, and after they are treated well by the soldiers, they become allies of the British. The recognition of something Indian in the Briton's face validates English moral authority in the colonies.

Both this novel and Jerningham's poem contradict the more dominant representations of the time, and show Indians displaying humanity and compassion. They also revolve around familial drama and absent sons, with Britons able to fill the place of the departed men. The family unit is in these texts rendered flexible while at the same time universal, and Indians are desperate to maintain them even in new forms.[30] As Kellet writes in his partly satirical "Letter concerning the American Savages" (1778), "their love for offspring is so excessive as to replace their lost children by the adoption of captive enemies, the Whites not excepted" (20). This is effectively an invitation to appropriate Indian cultural forms as a literary device, and would prove appealing to the cult of sensibility.

Thus, while the romanticized Indian dwindled for a time during the Revolutionary War, he (and, less often, she) did not disappear completely. The contradictory impulses of fear and pity were themselves, at least in part, manifestations of the anxiety many Britons felt towards the civil conflict occurring in the colonies. The mourning of the absent son performed by the Indian chiefs is a displaced grief over the familial battle of the war itself, much as the heartless savages represent the brutality of conflict between fellow Britons. As Wahrman notes, both pro- and anti-American Britons began to "deflect the anxieties attendant upon an unnatural civil war, by associating and even conflating the enemy with the unnatural savagery of the Indians."[31] At the same time, the desire for unification with the sentimental Indian completes the need for healing the fragmented subject, split across the Atlantic and at war with itself.

Righteous Hybridity in *The Female American*

Within this context of incomprehensible otherness and the want of sameness emerges the hybrid British subject. While hybrids existed before in British literature, as seen in the previous chapter, they were forced to excuse and renounce their Indianness as an expedient for survival or a coerced performance, or they were treated with contempt and derision by the writers who created or represented them. Authors began to experiment with internalizing the critiques that Indians had offered in literature from earlier in the century, even at the height of anti-Indian propaganda during the 1770s. The precise cause for this change in the understanding of transculturation is difficult to pinpoint, but some likely factors include the increased awareness in Britain of actual examples of men and women who willingly chose to live among Indians, anxiety surrounding the loss of the colonies, and a growing group of political radicals who were dissatisfied with the corruption of the gentry and the lack of social mobility and liberty in British society. As the texts below will show, there is no singular political or philosophical agenda in the fantasy of the dual subject, but they all contribute in some way to subsequent cultural myths about Native people. For Britons, more fundamentally, this cultural fantasy contributed to the growing notion of the modern subject that could negotiate the difficulties of the transient world.

The Female American, by "Unca Eliza Winkfield,"[32] has become a popular text in contemporary criticism due in part to its unique depiction of a mixed-race woman as the primary narrator. Half-Native and half-English, Unca Eliza's identity is constructed out of actual historical figures from earlier English colonial history: Uncas, the prominent Mohegan sachem of the seventeenth century, and Jamestown settler Edward Maria Wingfield, whom Unca Eliza claims as her paternal grandfather. Kristianne Kalata Vaccaro notes that this merging of historical and fictional narrative fashions a lineage for the protagonist that becomes a performance and manipulation of both forms.[33] Unca Eliza's identity, as the child of an Indian princess and a fictional plantation owner descended from an actual person, is also a precursor to subsequent North American fantasies connecting the lineage of settlers to Indigenous North American "royalty."[34] There is also an echo here of the Pocahontas story, which would become more known later in North America, but was in circulation throughout the eighteenth century.[35] The Indians in this novel, however, are anachronistic, a melding of Egyptian and various cultural groups from both North and South America, and not in keeping with the huge amount of information available on Native people by the end of the decade, which witnessed most of the French and Indian War and Pontiac's Rebellion. This is in some ways typical of sentimental representations of Indians; they tend to exist outside of time and lack cultural specificity. In this text, the Indians have much more in common with Dryden's Indians one hundred years earlier than the vast majority of representations around its own time. At the same time, the protagonist's identity represents the contemporary reality of the mixed identity possessed by many people living in the colonies. These intercultural subjects were generally excluded from British texts, and therefore this novel is an important document in understanding the racial discourse of the period and the prospect of miscegenation between Britons and Indians.[36]

The Indians in *The Female American*, both in Unca Eliza's family and those she later encounters, lack the fortitude in their own beliefs which shaped other depictions of romanticized Indians, and as such are not as strongly contrasted with Britons. They are instead similar to the sympathetic figure of the "poor Indian" propagated by missionary texts, and the conversion efforts of the protagonist suggest this construction of malleable and sympathetic colonial subjects is necessary for these practices. The Indians do, however, articulate anti-colonial critiques at times; early in the novel, Unca Eliza describes how her father came among the Indians. Following the massacre of Jamestown settlers by Indians in 1618, in which her grandfather is killed, her father, William, is taken captive along with five others. William recalls the words of his brother in England, who told him that the English "have no right to invade the country of another, and I fear invaders will always meet a curse" (8). The six captive settlers discover, to their surprise, that they are mistaken in the belief that Indians are "men-eaters," which unsettles any claims to moral superiority in colonial struggle. The prisoners are then stripped and surrounded by a large circle of Indians, and a "venerable old man seemed to address them in a pathetic manner, for tears accompanied his words" (10). He is their king, and he asks his captives if they were sent by their god, the sun, to punish them. He continues, "[W]e know you not, and have never offended you; why then have you taken possession of our lands, ate our fruits, and made our countrymen prisoners? Had you no lands of your own? Why did you not ask? [W]e would have given you some" (12). When the Britons do not respond because they cannot understand the language, the king takes it as an admission of guilt, and proclaims that they must be killed for the sake of justice. Each is beheaded in turn, but one of the king's daughters intervenes to save Unca Eliza's father just as the executioner is about to deliver the same fate to him. Thus the violence in "early

American" texts from the Puritan period, which demonized Indians in captivity narratives and religious works, is re-written as a justifiable resistance to invasion. The settlers themselves, and not just the traders and others who profited from the colonial project, are implicated in the crime of displacement and land theft.

The author transforms the righteous anger and hatred expressed by New England Puritans and early colonists into sympathetic identification in its contemporary British context. And yet, though there is a critique of colonial settlement, this sympathetic identification is based upon a Christian ideology whose ultimate goal is religious conversion. The desire to convert rather than kill – to, as Stevens suggests, transform fear and disgust into pity[37] – is an important aspect of British colonialism. Despite the widespread failure of British missionary attempts, the rhetoric and fund-raising efforts by groups such as the SPG taught many Britons that their benevolence could bring good to the people who had been colonized by other Europeans. Unca Eliza's father, who is implicated as an invader by his own brother, falls in love with the king's daughter and converts her, which the novel depicts as an organic and inevitable process once he is taken into the Indigenous society. The princess asks him to marry her, but he tells her, "[M]y God will be angry if I marry you, unless you will worship him as I do" (20). In this endeavour, "he was more successful than he expected, and in a little time the princess became convinced of her errors, and her good understanding helped to forward her conversion." While he comes to "look upon the country he was in as his own ... and was ... willing to make [Unca] and her country his forever" (42), her easy conversion nonetheless points to the desirability and superiority of European culture. All the initial fear felt by Winkfield becomes transformed into a successful conversion. Unca's adoption of the Christian faith at the same time brings her into European culture, and when she is subsequently killed in a revenge plot orchestrated by her sister, who loves William and wants him for herself, the novel evokes the tragic fate of Indian women in earlier stories such as Pocahontas and Inkle and Yarico. However, unlike the Inkle and Yarico tale, it is the Indians themselves who cause the death of the Indian princess, and the desirable Englishman is not implicated in the crime. The stain of colonial betrayal which marked the earlier story of merchant greed is washed out by the missionary impulse.

It is important to note that what makes this text unique is that the hybrid subject is in fact a product of miscegenation, and not a white person who appropriates aspects of a Native identity following time in

North America. Roxann Wheeler suggests that during the period in which it was printed there was an increasing interest in British fiction directed towards intermarriage between Britons and non-Europeans because of the shifting policies of empire from a period of land grabbing to one of colonial administration.[38] While most of these works were about Muslims from the Ottoman Empire, North America provided a convenient site for imagining the dynamics of intermarriage as a form of colonial rule even as its fate as a British colony was beginning to be in question by the time of the publication of *The Female American* in the late 1760s. Wheeler notes that in all of these novels, it is Christianity that proves to be the most significant difference between the intercultural couples and not skin colour. Unca Eliza's father's objection to marrying her mother was not that she was an Indian, but rather that she was a "Pagan." We are told that "[t]hough a complexion so different, as that of the princess from an European, cannot but at first disgust, yet by degrees my father grew insensible to the difference" (41). Her religion, however, could not be overlooked. In each intermarriage novel of the period, the high-ranking non-European woman becomes a Christian before her marriage to the European. Thus, "[t]he consent of non-Europeans to this formative trope of British national identity enacts an unproblematic change of their religious and cultural affiliation: each time, their assimilation is successful."[39] In the case of Unca Eliza, a product of intermarriage, she is raised Christian and so she does not suffer for her complexion, which is only significant in other novels prior to the main characters' Christian conversions. It is, in fact, her in-betweenness that makes her appealing when she visits Britain: "My tawny complexion, and the oddity of my dress, attracted every one's attention, for my mother used to dress me in a kind of mixed habit, neither perfectly in the Indian, nor yet in the European taste, either of fine linen, or a rich silk. I never wore a cap; but my lank black hair was adorned with diamonds and flowers" (49). Her hybrid appearance is celebrated in Britain, and her fashion is a visible sign of her colonial origins, perfectly combined in the metropolis to visualize the fantasy of transcultural desirability.

While hybridity could in many instances be menacing to colonial rule, Unca Eliza's liminal status is not only aesthetically appealing in London, but is also shown to be beneficial in converting the Indians. Anne McClintock argues that "the staging of symbolic disorder by the privileged can merely preempt challenges by those who do not possess the power to stage ambiguity with comparable license or authority."

She suggests that "mimicry and cross-dressing" can be "a technique not of colonial subversion, but of surveillance."[40] The colonial agent knows that "passing 'down' the cultural hierarchy is permissible; passing 'up' is not," and there is therefore an "other side of mimicry: the colonial who passes as Other the better to govern."[41] This kind of "passing" is one of the "privilege[s] of whiteness" in colonial discourse, and the threat of hybridity becomes a tool in deflating colonial resistance.[42] While Unca Eliza is not strictly white, her upbringing and cultural identity as a Christian makes her an acceptable British subject in the racial discourse of the period.

Unca Eliza's use of hybridity as a means of aiding her efforts to convert Indians becomes central to the narrative. While on a ship back to England, she is left on a deserted island after she refuses to marry the son of the captain. As Michelle Burnham suggests, the text "critiques the helplessness of women within a coercive marriage market, and it goes on to offer a fantastic alternative to typical female roles within dominant culture."[43] A "female Crusoe," Unca Eliza explores the island, cataloguing its life like a naturalist, and discovers how to survive thanks to an old guide written by a hermit. She effectively assumes white male strategies of survival and exploration, and is largely dependent upon the words and experience of the man who came before her. The guide warns her that Indians come to the island annually to worship at their ancient ruins; she discovers a hollow idol in which she can get and resolves "to ascend into the hollow idol, speak to the Indians from thence, and endeavour to convert them from their idolatry" (83).[44] By speaking to them in their own language, she believes she will "prejudice their minds greatly in favour of what I should say to them," and, should she reveal herself to them, "my tawny complexion would be some recommendation" (84). Thus, while much of her information comes from the old hermit, she proves herself to be more bold and ambitious in spreading Christian doctrine. It is true that the novel presents what Burnham describes as a kind of feminist utopia on the island, but at the same time, as she suggests, this is tempered by the ideology of Christian imperialism.[45]

The hybrid heroine is ultimately successful in converting the Indians by using their own religious artifacts and beliefs, and, before she appears to them, she tells them that "[a] person shall come to you, like yourselves, and that you may be the less fearful or suspicious, that person shall be a woman, who shall live among you as you do" (111). Her method of using ventriloquism through a male idol to address the Indians, and her strategy of exploiting her gender and racial identities to aid in this conversion, are remarkable for the ways in which they subvert and challenge other kinds of missionary or imperialist writing of the period. And yet, in the end the novel resolves in a typical marriage plot, with Unca Eliza marrying her English cousin and deferring to him, though she notes that they "never intended to have any more to do with Europe" (154) and they stay among the Indians. Thus the hybridity of the characters and plot of the text becomes what McClintock calls a "symbolic disorder," creating the ideal conditions of colonial governance. Indeed, the desire for cross-cultural missionaries was reflected in mainstream missionary discourse; a major premise of Eleazar Wheelock's Indian Charity School was the similar goal of sending out Indians to live among and preach to other Indians, and Mohegan preacher Samson Occom toured across England the same year that *The Female American* was printed to raise money for this endeavour.[46]

The Female American represents one strand of British sentimentalism, rooted in missionary efforts and built around pity for Indians rather than admiration. Protestant missionary writing, which by the end of the eighteenth century had been produced for over one hundred and fifty years, was key to shaping representations of Indians, but was also significant for its contribution to the collective shared feeling of sentimentality.[47] These texts and their audience prefigured and shaped the culture of sensibility which began to appropriate the fortitude and authenticity of Indian voices by the end of the century, although the poor Indian of missionary texts, unlike the magnanimous noble savage, is in need of European intervention.[48] Thus the Indian-Briton (or perhaps Briton-Indian) of *The Female American* does not function in a way meant to appropriate the virtues of the Indians, but rather to introduce European virtue among them.

The Secularization of Sentimental Indians

The depiction of cultural interactions with Indians in the following novels and texts show that it is Britons who need the merits of Indians, not the other way around. This is not to suggest that *The Female American* is a singular text that does not reflect prevalent ideologies or sentiments, but that it belongs more to the genre of intermarriage novels which Roxann Wheeler discusses in her article on the subject, and, while it is illuminating for a number of other reasons, it presents a model of hybridity which is less about the specificity of Indians and more about a broader cultural fantasy of conversion and governance.

Representations of Indians in sentimental fiction present an epistemological contradiction; on the one hand, the "poor Indian" was an important aspect in the foundation of the culture of sensibility.[49] On the other hand, in its secular form outside of missionary discourse and in imaginative writing, Indians became the opposing pole to sensibility and fellow-feeling. Intercultural contact thus produced both the sympathy that marked the British, and their desire for the virtues possessed by the objects of pity. The failure of the missionary effort overall led to the perception of the cultural strength of Indians, but the rhetoric of this effort contributed to the melancholic romanticization of their plight. How can it be that missionary works on Indians, which aimed at pity over sympathetic identification, led to the texts which sought to hybridize British people by bringing in the perceived virtues of Indians? That is, how did this process become reversed? The following texts provide some account of this transformation.

The Man of the World and the Impartial Cherokee

Henry Mackenzie's The Man of the World (1773) is in some ways a companion piece to his earlier The Man of Feeling (1771). As Sir Walter Scott notes, "in [The Man of Feeling] he imagined a hero constantly obedient to every emotion of his moral sense; in The Man of the World, he exhibited, on the contrary, a person rushing headlong into guilt and ruin, and spreading misery all around him, by pursuing a selfish and sensual happiness which he expected to obtain in defiance of the moral sense."[50] The novel tracks the villainous Sir Thomas Sindall, who we are told is a "Man of the World," and his relentless pursuit of vice. While at Oxford he corrupts the virtuous Billy Annesly, whose sister Harriet becomes the object of Sir Thomas's lust. In an elaborate scheme to win the favour of the Annesly family, Sir Thomas manipulates Billy into a life of poverty and vice, to the point that the young man is forced to commit a robbery to relieve a gambling debt. Billy is, as Lise Sorensen suggests, a "failed man of feeling,"[51] and he is transported from Britain to the West Indies. His master dies soon after he arrives, after which Billy is enlisted in a regiment as a felon. He notes that he could have used his station and education to his advantage, but he resolves to "[suffer] every part of my punishment" (168). He casts away the marks of cultural distinction, while his suffering improves his physical constitution, and some officers single him out to go on several "Indian expeditions" in America. Others start to resent him as he gains respect for his actions and, after fighting one of his detractors, he is sentenced to 500 lashes. Billy resolves to attempt suicide after the first 100 are administered, but after inadvertently freeing himself from his binds, decides to flee the further injustice of the army to "join the Indians" (173). Mackenzie places his sentimental hero among stoic Indians who still possess the emotional control that Britons can no longer access. While Harley in *The Man of Feeling* ultimately dies pathetically, Billy's passions are shaped and correctly contained by the Indians.[52] Billy comes across a party of Cherokees and shows them the lashes he received from the British fort to convey to them "my friendship to [their] countrymen and hatred to my own" (174). In response, the Indians load him with the burdens of two of their prisoners, a situation which, due to his fresh lashes, is very painful; but he is aware that "fortitude was an indispensable virtue with the Indians" and so he "bore it without wincing" until they are suitably impressed and remove it (175–6). When they reach the Cherokee village, many of the captives are taken in by families and are "adopted ... in place of the relations they had lost" (177). In another demonstration that absorption and annihilation are not far apart in their significance, the remaining prisoners are brutally tortured in a "festival of their revenge." They are careful not to show any signs of pain and instead "they sung, in their rude, yet forcible manner, the glory of their former victories, and the pleasure they had received from the death of their foes" (177). The victims provoke their tormentors when they slow down in their tortures, so that "intenseness of pain might not be wanting in the trial of their fortitude." The elder of the tribe gestures to Billy during particularly brutal moments, to show him the proper way to endure suffering. The next day, he experiences a similar fate when he is tied and stabbed repeatedly, after which his wounds are rubbed with gunpowder. Following this, they "laid quantities of dry gun-powder on different parts of my body, and set fire to them, by which I was burnt in some places to the bone" (179–80). Like Lismahago's punishment at the hands of the Miamis in *Humphry Clinker*, Billy's torture involves the use of distinctly European commodities. His "mangled body" is invaded by the implements of exchange, and he is able to endure this brutal treatment thanks to "a life of hardship" and a "contempt of existence" brought about by his own people.

The Indians approve of his strength and, after healing his wounds, he is adopted by the elder as his son, who "gave me a name, and fastened round my neck a belt of wampum" (181). He is welcomed as a Chero-kee, "to whom shame is more intolerable than the stab of the knife, or the burning of the fire." He lives among them happily, admitting that "scarce any inducement could have tempted me to leave the nation to which [the old man who adopted him] belonged" (182). Cherokee life is a balance between complete freedom from authority and total self-con-trol, a constant pursuit of wants without a wish for their fulfilment or for accumulation. Billy observes, "Certain it is, that I am far from being a single instance, of one who had even attained maturity in Europe, and yet found his mind so accommodated, by the habit of a few years, to Indian manners, as to leave that country with regret" (183). This acknowledgment of the numerous Britons and other Europeans who found themselves among Indians and willingly chose to live among them was a fact that was generally disavowed in fiction of the time. Captivity episodes almost always involved elements of coercion, even in cases where the captives become happy members of the tribe. In this case, Billy must prove himself before he is allowed to join them, show-ing the legitimate alternative that Indian life offered. The Indians may be a less "polished people," but they "[feel] no regret, for the want of those delicate pleasures." It is precisely that polish and delicacy which leads Billy to be corrupted, and he learns more among the Cherokee than during his time at Oxford. The decadent and degraded gentry and the vices of commercial society are presented as the other to the rustic Indians. The Cherokee provide Billy with a new self, renaming him and giving him the confidence to make proper ethical and emotional deci-sions through their profound self-control and personal freedom.

Mackenzie's account of Billy's initiation into the Cherokee world is remarkably similar to Adam Smith's description of savage life in *The Theory of Moral Sentiments*. Indeed, *The Man of the World* was report-edly the only novel in English that Smith owned,[53] and the two men were friends, so it is hardly surprising there should be such similarities. Smith claims that the "magnanimity and self-command" of savages "are almost beyond the conception of Europeans" (399). "The savages in North America," Smith writes, "assume upon all occasions the great-est indifference, and would think themselves degraded if they should ever appear in any respect to be overcome, either by love or grief, or resentment" (399). He describes how the Indian, upon receiving a death sentence after being captured, does not show "any other passion but contempt of his enemies" (401). While he is in the midst of the most brutal bodily tortures, the savage "derides his tormentors, and tells them with how much more ingenuity, he himself had tormented such of their countrymen as had fallen into his hands" (401). As in Mackenzie's novel, Smith also describes the "song of death," which is "a song ... he is to sing when he has fallen into the hands of his enemies, and is expiring under the tortures which they inflict upon him" (402).

Indian songs became popular in Britain beginning in the 1760s; Tim Fulford notes that the death song in particular was seen as "both noble in itself and a form of terrible enquiry – a means that Indians use to test each other's resolution, to probe the determination with which they maintain their identity."[54] Furthermore, "the death song seemed to be an overflow of being into language – an articulation of essential self without the intervention of self-consciousness or pre-meditation."[55] This represented, on the surface, the opposite to the educated, lettered English gentleman, yet, as Fulford rightly points out, "[t]he Indian of the death song ... was not simply the other but the secret twin of the British male reader – the embodiment of his taboo desire."[56] The desire for an authentic expression of selfhood was thus a large part of the British fascination with the death song. In Smith's description, he writes that the Indian "sings this song upon all extraordinary occasions, ... whenever he has a mind to show that he has familiarised his imagination, to the most dreadful misfortunes, and that no human event can daunt his resolution, or alter his purpose" (402). Smith extends his claim and suggests that "[t]he same contempt of death and torture prevails among all other savage nations," and there is not a single African "who does not, in this respect, possess a degree of magnanimity which the soul of his sordid master is scarce capable of conceiving" (402). His admiration of Indians extends to all the other savage "nations of heroes [subjected] ... to the jails of Europe," and is a good example of the ways that some writers sympathized with or positively represented Indians in the hopes of bringing British attention to the abolition of the slave trade. The overpowering strength of the savage's subjectivity shames the cruel Europeans who enslave or conquer them, and the Indian's existence primarily outside the system of chattel slavery makes him an ideal masculine site of identification for Smith.

Robert Goadby, the printer behind *The Life and Adventures of Bampfylde-Moore Carew*, claims in *The Universe Displayed* (1763) that the death song "has something mournful and haughty at the same Time," and describes the gist of most of the songs: "*I am brave and intrepid; I do not fear Death, nor any Kind of Tortures: Those who fear them, are Cowards; they are less than Women: Life is nothing to those that have Courage: May my Enemies be confounded with Despair and Rage: Oh! that I could devour them, and drink their Blood to the last Drop"* (42). This presents a model of masculinity remarkable for its excess, and the unbridled eruption of contempt and audacity embodied by the Indian and his death song exists outside any possible model of polite expression for the British male; faced with his own destruction, the Indian provokes his enemies into torturing him more, giving the appearance that, as Goadby writes, "they take pleasure in being tormented." At the end of his life, the Indian warrior asserts his identity and strength of character over that of those about to take it.

The British fascination with the Indian death song also helped establish the imaginative link between Indians and death that became an important aspect of American colonial ideology in the nineteenth-century expansion of territory at the expense of Indigenous people.[57] Their acceptance, even welcoming, of death could, on an ideological level, be viewed as a dehumanizing or objectifying aspect of violent colonialism. The British male can absorb the fortitude and strength of character exemplified by the death song, while the Indian is given an honourable but inescapable death. This is indicative of the Romantic use of Indians in both the British and American context, and they become abstracted and sentimentalized to the point that the Indian death opens a symbolic space for the white reader to occupy. The brave Indian sacrifices himself for the affective response of the European in this cultural fantasy.

The model of savage fortitude Smith presents does not simply martyr the Indian for the purposes of British subjectivity, but also demonstrates the humanity of non-Europeans and gives reasons to admire them. It is not, however, to be taken as an ideal model of behaviour for the sympathetic citizen. Smith was sceptical of the view of savage life presented by Rousseau in his *Discourse on the Origin and Basis of Inequality Among Men* (1754) and wrote in a 1755 letter to the *Edinburgh Review* that "Mr. Rousseau, intending to paint the savage life as the happiest of any, presents only the indolent side of it to view, which he exhibits indeed with the most beautiful and agreeable colours, in a style, which, tho' laboured and studiously elegant, is every where sufficiently nervous, and sometimes even sublime and pathetic."[58] Smith admits that "[t]he life of a savage, when we take a distant view of it, seems to be a life either of profound indolence, or of great and astonishing adventures; and both these qualities serve to render the description of it agreeable to the imagination." However, this view presupposes the idea that "there is in man no powerful instinct which necessarily determines him to seek society for its own sake." While commercial society may have negatively impacted the virtues of Europeans and their ability to suppress their emotions, it is also the only state of being which can produce sympathy. Indeed, Smith observes in *The Theory of Moral Sentiments* that savage nations cultivate virtues of self-denial rather than those founded upon humanity (397–8), though this is not reason to dominate or oppress them. He argues that "all savages are too much occupied with their own wants and necessities, to give much attention to those of another person" (398–9).

Though Smith did not endorse the life of the savage, his description partially laid the groundwork for the subsequent abstraction of Indigenous people into sentimental objects. The appropriation that occurs in Mackenzie and later Romantic thinkers comes in part from the description of the "impartial spectator," abstracted onto the Indigenous people of North America.[59] Mackenzie puts forth a literalization of Smith's spectator in the form of the Cherokee, who, when coupled with a British man of feeling, can form a subject who gauges appropriate emotional responses and controls their vices.

Mackenzie's Billy leaves the Indians following the death of his adopted father, which "naturally awakened in me the remembrance of a father in England, whose age might now be helpless, and call for the aid of a long-lost son to solace and support it" (187). His Cherokee father's final words are spent critiquing the follies of Europeans, particularly their religious hypocrisy in hoping for an afterlife, and notes when he sees Billy's tears that he still "retained so much of the European." He tells him, "In those tears ... there is no wisdom, for there is no use" (184). This is in stark contrast to Harley in *The Man of Feeling*, who proclaims during one of his numerous outbursts that "there is virtue in these tears; let the fruit of them be virtue" (100). The Indian functions as the impartial spectator in *The Man of the World*, reigning in his adopted son's potentially unruly emotions and urging him to listen to "the spirit within us" as his guide to living rather than self-serving religious doctrine (186). When Billy returns to the people of his birth he admits that he perceives them as representing "fraud, hypocrisy, and sordid baseness," while the Indians possess "honesty, truth, and savage nobleness of soul" (190).

There is a gap between the "poor Indian" of missionary writing and the "noble savage," or perhaps magnanimous savage, as described by Smith and deployed by Mackenzie;[60] one exists solely as an object of pity, while the other is incapable of experiencing sympathy for others and elicits admiration. While both offer critiques of European hypocrisy, they differently participate in the economy of sentiment.[61] In a sense, the bold savage pities, even scorns, the European in the same way as the European pities the poor Indian, and this becomes more prevalent in sentimentalized representations of Indians beginning in the 1770s.

Sentimental accounts of transculturation later in the century are often attempts to re-write and re-imagine the kinds of cultural contact that were represented in earlier "non-fictional" descriptions of the brutality of life for British captives, discussed in the third chapter. These captivity narratives led to the broader British interest in the possibilities of life among the Indians, but as we have seen they present a radically different vision of cultural contact. The texts also have a problem with making sense of Indian violence. While the torture and execution of European bodies represents a critique of British colonial practices, or at least a response to them, the extreme violence is often carried out and described with such excess that it goes beyond any symbolic critique. It becomes, in a sense, meaningless, providing only a pornographic spectacle rather than a metaphor of deeper value. To a certain extent, it is this meaningless violence that fuelled the popularity of these texts; like sentimental writing, the vision of dismembered, suffering British bodies often produced affective responses rather than rational or political ones, and aestheticized colonial violence to the point that these representations threatened to efface its causes. The struggle with the significance of Indian violence is in part what led authors of fiction to take up this violence to produce meaning. In fiction, this violence is rarely so superfluous, particularly in texts containing captivity episodes beginning in the late 1760s.

William Richardson's Sentimental and Cosmopolitan Indians

William Richardson, a Scottish professor and literary scholar, first published his short story "The Indians, A Tale" in 1774 in his collection *Poems, Chiefly Rural*, which was re-printed that year, again in 1776 and 1781, and as *The Cacique of Ontario, A Tale*, in 1786. He would later adapt it for the stage as *The Indians, A Tragedy*, and it was performed at the Theatre-Royal in Richmond and in Glasgow "with considerable applause."[62] Both the *Critical* and the *Monthly* reviews saw some merit in it; the *Critical* found that, despite some tedious language, "more striking marks of originality are to be found in the present publication ...

than in any which for several years past have come under our inspection,"[63] while the *Monthly* less generously maintained that "though not in the first rank of tragedies, [the play] is interesting and pathetic."[64] Richardson was ultimately more acclaimed as a scholar than a writer, but his story was circulated to the point that it was re-printed in America in several magazines. Like fellow Scotsman Mackenzie, Richardson depicts the encounter between British sentimentality and stoic Indians, but his Indians are not quite the same unfeeling, heroic savages we find in Adam Smith.

The story paints a radically different picture of Indian culture than that which appeared in the press of the same time. The 1774 edition begins with the sentimental scene of the weeping Marano, whose name is presumably meant to confuse the reader as to her cultural identity at the outset.[65] The opening sentences also refer to her "snowy arm" and "[h]er blue eyes" (115), thus emphasizing her difference in complexion from "The Indians" of the title, and her hybrid identity. As she speculates with melancholy on the fate of her missing husband Oneyo, his father, the respected elder Ononthio, comes to her side to comfort her. In their ensuing conversation it is revealed that Marano is indeed a Briton who was captured as a child during a raid by the Outagami, who adopted and raised her, but she admits that even still, "at the name of Briton, my bosom glows with peculiar transport" (117). Despite her upbringing among the Indians, she is still able to identify as being British, but, unlike earlier representations of captives, she does not assert this identity above her adoptive family. She admits, "I have heard of European refinements, of costly raiment and lofty palaces; yet to me the simplicity of these rocks and forests seems far more delightful" (118). In the texts from this period, the elevation of savage life does not necessarily diminish the value of being British. This scene contradicts the unfeeling depictions of savagery of the press and periodicals, and opens up a moment of sympathetic identification with the benevolent old man who worries about losing his adopted daughter to her homeland.

The Indians eventually capture the people they believe to be responsible for the presumed death of their beloved Oneyo, and their leader is a bold Briton named Sidney. It turns out that he is Marano's long-lost brother, and she begs that his life be spared as they prepare to torture him. Ononthio immediately offers to adopt him into their tribe, and allow him to "[s]upply the place of the dead," presenting him with a calumet and a girdle of wampum (127). Sidney is not able to comprehend such a rapid shift in relations from enemy to friendship, but the elder tells him, "You reason ... according to the maxims of Europeans, whose external guise is imposing, but whose souls are treacherous and implacable" (127). Ononthio then gives a lengthy speech on the weakness of European justice and retribution, in that it fails to prevent future wrongs and attempts to ruin the offender with infamy. He acknowledges that Indian practices may appear cruel, but argues, "[T]he simple Indian is not inhuman. Our reason may be obscured, but our principles are innocent. Our passions may be excessive, but they are not corrupt" (129). While this is hardly exemplary of Smith's model of stoic self-command, Ononthio displays a level of interiority and self-reflexivity that is equally appealing. He explains to Sidney that the death he was on the brink of suffering was not meant to insult him, but to honour him: "Death is not a misfortune but to the feeble, to those whose lives have dishonoured their memory, who disgrace their nature by unseemly feats, and affront the Almighty with their distrust" (129). There is no contradiction between the torture and execution of a captive and his or her adoption into the tribe, since both are acts of substitution. This text, however, differs from Sussman's observation that both options involve the fear of incorporation; the commercial fear which typifies Smollett's transcultural vision of "the collapsing distinctions between foreign sites of capital accumulation and domestic spaces of consumption"[66] becomes in texts such as this a sentimental desire for appropriation. Adoption is a conceit of romance, but also challenges the culture of inheritance. Among Indians, the adopted Briton is born anew and allowed to rise within their ranks on their own merits.

Following the elder's speech, Sidney is "filled with astonishment and admiration," and asks, "Can I ... who am of a different origin, born of a people whom you have reason to execrate, and the votary of a different religion, can I be adopted into your nation?" (130). Ononthio replies that "the simple, unaffected Indian ... is a stranger to your distinctions." This lack of social distinction is precisely what fuelled the fear of Indian violence in the press, since they treated all enemy combatants equally, but also what made them so fascinating to critics of stratified British society. The Indian explains in a cosmopolitan speech that while human difference exists, it does not mean that people should "hate or contemn the stranger" (130).[67] He denies that Europeans and Indians are of a different religion, since they all reflect "the creating Spirit," and encourages the Briton to "[e]njoy your faith, your freedom, and the love of your country; but give us your friendship and intrepid valour" (131). As in other representations of cultural adoption from the period, Britons can in fact perfect their Britishness by assuming an Indian identity. Sidney's initial response reflects his faulty European values, and though he admires the "elevation of sentiment" and the lack of bigotry and prejudice, he "cannot allow that the uncivilized life of an Indian is preferable to the culture and refinement of Europe" (131). Ononthio argues that refinement does not "better the heart or improve the affections," but in fact dulls sympathy and the "exquisite sensations of youth" over time. He encourages Sidney to "[b]e guiltless – Be an Indian" (132). While Sidney already possesses the virtues that Indians admire, despite being brought up among Europeans, the Indian way of life is elevated as being an unmediated way of experiencing morality and emotional life and of preserving the passions that are deadened by polite society. Not surprisingly, Richardson was a defender of the authenticity of Ossian, and no doubt saw in his own understanding of Indians the immediacy of experience embodied by an oral culture.

After this exchange between the wise old man and the virtuous Briton, a party of Indians return with the news that Oneyo has been slain, and one of them points to Sidney as the man guilty of the killing. There is a call for vengeance from the tribe, but Marano and Ononthio intercede once again on the Briton's behalf. He reveals that he spared the honourable warrior his life, but is unsure what became of him after their encounter. Marano takes her brother and the other captives away from the incensed throng, and Ononthio urges Sidney to not judge his people because they "follow the immediate impulse of nature, and are often extravagant" (136). This, he assures him, will not last, because they are unaware of "latent or lasting enmity" (136). Soon after, Oneyo returns secretly and displays this same impetuousness; he observes Marano in the arms of her brother, who is a stranger to him, and he plans to kill the man. Upon recognizing Sidney as the soldier who had spared his life in battle, however, he decides to take his own life. All is quickly revealed before he can act on his rash plan, the lovers are reunited, and Ononthio welcomes them to the village, where "the day was crowned with rejoicing" (140). While there is no explicit mention of the ultimate fate of the Britons, they presumably stay among the Indians and live out their lives. The numerous editions of this story and the later play suggest its popularity, perhaps influencing fellow Scottish poet Thomas Campbell's more well-known *Gertrude of Wyoming* (1809),[68] and while William Richardson may not be remembered for his literary prowess, his vision of Indians embodying the virtues that Britons should aim for while self-reflexively understanding their own motivations and limitations offers an evident contradiction to the broader press coverage of the 1770s. Ononthio's open invitation to "[b]e an Indian" powerfully articulates the desire for an authentic expression of individuality at the heart of the emerging modern self. Though Richardson's defence of Ossian suggests his alignment with a primitivist critique of the modern, the Indian occupies both the pastoral past and, more importantly, a future possibility; in the epilogue of the subsequent play, Richardson writes, "Th' Indian loves liberty, and will be free: / And so have Britons been, and still will be" (57). Indians may be what Britons once were, but now it is Britons who need to strive to be like the Indians.

Heroic Hybridity in *The Basket-Maker* and William Augustus Bowles

The hybrid Indian-Briton appears again in Irish playwright John O'Keeffe's *The Basket-Maker* (printed in 1790, performed in 1789 at the Hay-Market), and was, O'Keeffe would later claim, inspired by his own encounter with Indians in London in 1782. While he had also seen the Cherokees who visited in 1762,[69] who "wore their own dress, and were objects of great curiosity," he writes that the later delegation "were not so wild in their appearance as the former," and "were accompanied by an Englishman, who had long resided among them, (and on this circumstance, some years after, I partly founded my two-act piece of 'The Basket-Maker')."[70] O'Keeffe showed the men the mechanism of the stage, demonstrating the stage traps and letting them rise up and down on them, and remarked upon the "dignity and composure" with which they conducted themselves. He adds, "I stood close to them, and paid particular attention to the Cherokee-Englishman, whose name was Bowles: he was in the full Cherokee dress, and not to be distinguished from a native. I was told he had been the chief means of introducing civilization and Christian benevolence among them. He is my King Simon in 'The Basket-Maker'."[71] As Helen Carr notes, the Cherokee as O'Keeffe saw them in their later visit had, in fact, largely achieved their present state of "civilization" through their own means, and the suggestion that Bowles had introduced Christianity among them was no doubt meant for the more conservative audience reading his memoirs.[72] There is no mention in the play itself of conversion or civilizing the Indians, nor is it implied at any point.

O'Keeffe's memoirs were written in 1826, years after this encounter. While Carr speculates that the "Cherokee-Englishman" he met could have been Chief Duwa'li Bowles or his Scottish father,[73] there does not appear to be any evidence of a Cherokee delegation in 1782, or of any visit to London by either man. In 1790–1, however, after *The Basket-Maker* was first written and performed, a six-person delegation of Creeks and Cherokees arrived in London. They were led by William Augustus Bowles, the "Ambassador from the United Nations of Creeks and Cherokees to the Court of London." It is most likely that it was this man whom O'Keeffe encountered, and the author's insistence that Bowles is King Simon is a conflation of encounter and inspiration. Bowles claimed to have been appointed by Creek and Cherokee leaders as a negotiator, but he was nonetheless turned away by King George III.[74] However, Bowles had his portrait painted twice, one of which survives. Two members of his group were also painted. The portrait of the Englishman is a further indication that O'Keeffe mistook the dates of his encounter with this hybrid subject who so fascinated him. In the painting, Bowles appears in a costume that, as Stephanie Pratt observes, emphasizes his authority as a leader. His feathered turban, complete with a gemstone, and the wampum and gorget around his neck were, as compared to the paintings of the Native men in his delegation, flamboyant. Pratt suggests that "[t]he credibility of this British-born [*sic*] expatriate is thus mediated through these signs of Indian authority and their emphasis is a necessary strategy in the creation of his identity as a legitimate delegate and commander."[75] Benjamin Baynton's *Authentic memoirs of William Augustus Bowles, Esquire* (1791), offers a curious portrait of the man, which attempts to depict him as a self-made hero.

Given the failure of Bowles's embassy, it seems the biography did not have the desired influence in official circles. The *Critical Review* noted that the author "gives such an improbable account of Mr. Bowles' natural ingenuity respecting different arts and sciences, as cannot impress us with any great opinion of the authenticity of the narrative."[76] Despite this and other inconsistencies, the reviewer believes that Bowles "is a gentleman of great merit, and [we] are happy to think that Great Britain has so faithful and zealous a friend among the Creek Indians." The *Monthly Review* was less kind, suggesting that "[m]emoirs written by nobody, are worthy or nobody's attention; for what assurance can we have that there is a single word of truth in an anonymous publication, for which no one can be found to answer?"[77] Bowles, the writer reminds the audience, "at this time, appears in London in the character of an

Painted by T. Hardy

Engrav'd by J. Grozer

WILLIAM AUGUSTUS BOWLES.

Chief of the Embassy from the Creek & Cherokee Nations.

Published as the Act directs March 26 1791 by T. Hardy No 4 Great Marlborough Street.

Figure 5.2 William Augustus Bowles. Artist: Joseph Grozer after Thomas Hardy, 1791. Mezzotint on paper. National Portrait Gallery, Smithsonian Institution. Used with permission.

Indian Chief," though he "is not an Indian by birth." He summarizes the biography and Bowles's character in the following words: "[B]eing of an unsettled, roving, and enterprizing disposition, [he] attached himself to one of the Indian nations, became enamoured of a savage life, and, which is perhaps more excusable, of a savage *girl*, whom he married." Bowles "is now, by adoption, though not by birth an '*Indian Warrior*'." The author complains that "[w]hat his errand, and that of his companions, is here, the pamphlet does not inform us." Baynton himself admits that he "is altogether ignorant of the nature of Mr. Bowles's embassy," but assumes it "is doubtless a friendly one, and as such he wishes it success" (iv). The *Monthly* author's scepticism about both the authenticity and motivations of Bowles's transculturation is an indication that the relative success of the hybrid as a literary subject beginning in the 1770s was still greeted with ambivalence by the reading public.

Though the *Memoirs* did not receive the critical reception and praise the author no doubt sought as a means of bringing attention to his subject, it offers a significant portrait of a man whose heroic qualities are traced to his merging of Anglo-American and Creek subjectivities. Born in Maryland to "respectable parents," Bowles joined a Loyalist regiment at the outbreak of the Revolutionary War when he was just 13. Like Billy in *The Man of the World*, the young man finds himself wrongfully persecuted by his fellow soldiers. He is dismissed from his commission and, after finding himself destitute, joins a party of Creeks. His time among them quite quickly "had reduced him to the appearance of a savage" (13), but he leaves them after a few months. He ventures off on his own, fashioning a boat "like an Eskimaux," and lives by hunting and fishing, "the sky his canopy, and the earth his bed" (16). He is forced "to seek for resources in himself alone; resources which at some future day were to shield him in the hour of danger, and which alone could complete him for the leader of a brave and gallant nation" (17). While Bowles was introduced to life among the Indians, he teaches himself how to be one. His ambition and individuality are what ultimately lead him to success with the Creeks, but not among Britons. Following a cold year in 1779, he joins a white settlement. His dislike of labour, however, inclines him to re-join the Creeks. This time he remains for two years, and he marries the daughter of one of the chiefs. "His children," the author writes, "were living pledges of their father's fidelity," and he becomes united to the Indians "both from inclination, and the ties of blood" (22–3). Family among the Indians empowers the Britons who take up their ties. Bowles finds a home with the Creeks, and "[h]abit now confirmed his predilection for a state of nature" (23). He joins them in battle, and distinguishes himself as a warrior; he becomes known, as the author writes earlier, as "the Beloved Warrior." He is noteworthy for his love of the British nation, which "is only to be equalled by his affection for those by whom he was adopted" (26). The love for both does not diminish his ties to either, and his patriotism, like his identity, is transnational. He is invited to re-join the British army, though his appearance is "in every respect like a savage warrior" (29), but he is once again jealously pursued by his fellow soldiers. They bring numerous charges against him, including "ungentleman-like behaviour" because he was seen collecting scalps. He does not deny these charges.

The conflict between British standards of behaviour and "barbarous custom" threatens Bowles' re-entry into white society, but the author explains that "at the time now specified, Mr. Bowles was not only naked, like a savage, but was fighting side by side with his brother chiefs, who would have considered his withholding his hand from seizing this distinguished badge of a warrior's bravery, as a mark of pusillanimity, and treated him accordingly" (39–40). Furthermore, he argues, scalping may be "savage," but it is far from "inhuman" if we consider that "the victim is already dead, or senseless, before the scalp is thus torn away" (40). The transcultural subject becomes exempt from British standards of conduct and is given the benefit of moral relativism due to his split identity. Bowles is acquitted, and gets permission to visit his father and then the Creeks. He stays with them for a year, implementing cultural and political changes, reflecting that "he had experienced the worst that civilized men could do to him: from barbarians he had found shelter, in the days of calamity; to them he was perhaps indebted for his existence" (43). Though still only 19, he "had learned to know the animal man, stripped of artificial habits; and he knew him also with his seducing charms of polished manners. The contrast was striking; and the judgment he formed appears to be decisive" (44). That is, he chooses to live with the Creeks, who reward his singularity.

Bowles's heroic individualism, however, does not solely lie with his internalization of Creek cultural values; it is also found in his ability to coalesce both British and Indian methods of self-expression. Accordingly, in a fantasy of social liberty, he forms an acting troop, teaches himself to paint, including manufacturing his own colours as a chemist, and learns the violin and flute. He is a "self-formed hero" (53), who has taken on the "gravity of manners corresponding with those of the nations whose habits he has assumed" (68). Unlike earlier examples in the century of fluid subjects who could cross cultural boundaries, Bowles is self-consciously driven by ambition. He is, among other things, an actor without having seen plays, a painter without knowing art, "a chemist, without even the rudiments of the science," and a "self-taught warrior, instructing savages in tactics" (71). He has the ability of "altering his whole nature, without making him effeminate" (72). While his cultural identity can shift according to his needs and desires, his masculinity is never in question. Unlike previous subjects whose selves are malleable, Bowles is driven by a core subjectivity, an individual who can merge cultures and classes to serve his needs, rather than be shaped externally by them.

The author of the text, Benjamin Baynton, was like Bowles a staunch Loyalist born in the colonies whose sense of a British identity was not troubled by persecution following the Revolutionary War. His celebration of Bowles as a transcultural hero is in part due to his own experience as a fractured subject, and to the understanding that ties between Indians and whites did not diminish the value of either one. The *Memoirs* are no doubt filled with hyperbole, but clearly Bowles's charismatic and hybrid presence, preserved in a portrait, affected many who actually encountered the young man on his mission to London. Certainly O'Keeffe carried the memory for many years.

To return, then, to *The Basket-Maker*, retroactively inspired by the striking young white man in Indian dress that O'Keeffe had encountered in London, we can see once again a heroic figure whose allegiances are untroubled by cross-cultural adoption. Simon Rochefort, the supposed model of Bowles, is a Frenchman who has become king of the Iroquois. The trajectory of the hybrid in Indian society in these British texts is always one of ascendancy. King Simon first appears onstage "in regal Indian dress," and reveals that he owned a tract of land in Canada, but was dispossessed of it by a new Governor. Left with only a marshy parcel of land, he entrusted his son to the care of a poor basket-maker and left to join the Iroquois. He distinguished himself in their war against the Huron, and they subsequently made him their king. The plot primarily revolves around his determination to regain his land from the decadent governor Count Pepin and to reunite with his son, William, now a basket-maker himself. Basket-making was, significantly, a cross-cultural activity; while it was a trade that was known in Britain, and was to a certain extent synonymous with virtuous and humble hard labour and little reward,[78] baskets were also at this time known as important objects of Indian manufacture.[79] Given O'Keeffe's familiarity with and approval of Cook's voyages,[80] it is reasonable to speculate that he had taken in some of the ethnographic displays of West Coast Native objects, including many baskets, brought back to Britain following Cook's fateful third voyage and was exploiting the ethnic ambiguity of the profession. William functions on the periphery of both Indian and European colonial culture. His trade, as well as the culture of the Indians, is set in contrast to the easy life of Count Pepin, the arrogant and indulgent gentleman.

King Simon plans to have his Indians kidnap Pepin and force him to surrender the land he took from him. Though his plan is botched by a series of misunderstandings, in the end the Count is chastened and forced by the Indians to become William's servant. He at first refuses, arguing that people like William "are low vulgar bourgeois, a different species from us, they are born only to make and weave, ... and contribute to the ease of us noblemen" (359). He later appears on stage "in a Bear skin, his hair still in dress," comically caught between stations and identities, and he laments, "I find a gentleman is a cursed bad trade; I've served my time to it, and now here's my occupation" (368). His humility following the intervention of the Indians indicates that he will be reformed through his transculturation.

Yet O'Keeffe burlesques the Indian practice of adopting white captives near the end of the play when the foolish English servant Wattle is saved from being burned alive by King Simon's faithful ally Chichikou. The Iroquois man interrupts some of his brethren who are about to execute the hapless Englishman by declaring in pidgin English, "By custom of country, when relation killed in battle, we have a right to make prisoner relation in him room – I do claim his life, and take this man in place of my brother, that was kill in our last battle against Huron Nation" (370). Wattle is overjoyed, and Chichikou tells him, "You have now every right, privilege, name, goods, house, and all dat did belong to my dead brother, Kickapows, de warrior." Wattle quickly tries to exploit this situation when he discovers he is entitled to all the dead warrior's possessions. He claims more than the man was owed, but is quickly put in his place when the Indians try to begin to collect the man's debts as well, including an ear (371–2). Wattle is the only explicitly English character in the play, and his disingenuous adoption is put in contrast to the merited rise of King Simon among the same tribe. Earlier in the play, Wattle, who is a deserter from the army, longs for his homeland over the wild forests of French colonial country: "Oh, sweet London! I wish I was this moment sitting in the stocks, at

Bethnel-green" (339). His inability to accommodate himself to his situation leads to his failure as a transculturated individual, and he carries forward the lessons of the metropolis rather than the periphery. His failure also suggests that the Indian's virtues are only available to the elite man, not the impoverished scoundrel. By contrast, in the end, the Marquis de Champlain declares to the now humbled Pepin, who vows to change, "And Count, when return'd to the gay world, tell the proud accomplish'd man of fashion, that the best master of manners, is a wild savage." To this King Simon adds, "And the truest schools for civilization, are the forests of America" (375).

The problematic nature of the hybrid subject, however, is made clear in the ending of the play; King Simon regains his land and the Count is reformed, but no mention is made of the Indians' struggle or reward.[81] The text does contain strong anti-colonial critiques; the first song, omitted from some later anthologized versions of the play, has King Simon singing about British colonialism, despite the ostensibly French setting. He first evokes the Roman conquest of Britain, in which the Briton "now a godlike name, / Was savage then by Caesar call'd" (1). They fought for freedom, and "[p]oor Indians are but Britons now, / And we the Romans of the day." O'Keeffe draws attention to the parallels and ironies of British colonial action in the context of their own history. He asks, "Why from his wood the Indians drive, / And why usurp his native fields? / Unknown, unknowing let him live, / In all the sweets that freedom yields" (2). This song makes the sentiments of King Simon clear in relation to colonial conquest, and yet when the Iroquois Sokoki directly asks him, "But what right had King in Europe, to grant our land here in America?," the question goes conspicuously unanswered. The Indians cannot access the justice and freedom of the hybridized European, whose own struggles usurp the Indigenous people's legitimate claims for redress.

Hermsprong and Masculine Reform

Robert Bage's Hermsprong (1796), like The Female American, has received increased scholarly attention over the last several years.[82] Bage's novel is informed by the radical political culture brewing in Britain in the wake of the French Revolution and, like O'Keeffe as well as earlier French writers, his use of the Indian is largely meant to provide a critique of the decadence and arbitrary authority of the gentry. As in The Man of the World, Bage's protagonist returns to Britain following his time among the Indians and carries forward the lessons learned by his cultural adoption. He appears suddenly in the book to rescue the virtuous Caroline Campinet, the daughter of the arrogant and corrupt Lord Grondale, and her aunt as their carriage is being driven to the edge of a cliff (78). This intervention introduces him as an ideal masculine subject, who, in addition to a remarkable capacity for feats of strength, carries "an unstudied, unimitated ease" that "seems his own" (89). He is valued not for his rank or title but his individuality and his "manly" nature. Hermsprong revives the young woman and converses with her about the perils of unmerited fortune after she reveals her familial identity. She praises the stranger's profound philosophy, and wonders how it could be natural that one so young could be so wise. He assures her that it must be natural, "since it was of the sons of nature I learned it" (80). This is the first allusion to his origins, which are slowly revealed in the book during his clashes with the decadent gentry and polite society.

I will focus primarily on these origins; while they come much later in the text and comprise a relatively brief section, they are meant to account for the broader critique which Hermsprong offers throughout the novel in his encounters with elite English culture and people with unmerited titles, such as Lord Grondale. Bage's description of the young man's upbringing among the "Nawdoessie" Indians[83] near Michillimackinac, like the description of Indian life in *The Female American*, does not rely on ethnographic specificity. Indeed, the novel lacks the broader descriptions of Indian life and culture found in most novels with Indian episodes, however fictionalized or stolen directly from other histories they may be, and depicts the Nawdoessie as polite and tolerant, yet tenacious in their beliefs. While the episode among the Indians is short, and is not described until the third volume, it is nonetheless an important section since the novel is predicated on the hybrid origins of the virtuous young man.

Hermsprong's European parents fled for North America following a series of family disgraces that saw them disowned from their elite families, and marry in Philadelphia. Following a mysterious Catholic threat against him and "the quarrels then arising between America and her mother country," Hermsprong's father gives up his dream of lecturing in philosophy or heading an academy. Pursued by networks of corrupt continental European power and newer eruptions of British colonial conflict, the couple are left with little options within their existing world. During this time a friend in the fur trade introduces Hermsprong's father to the son of a Nawdoessie chief. As he was "fond of seeing man in a less civilized state," he converses with the Indian. He realizes that through the chief's son "he might find an asylum, gratify his ardent desire to know man, assist his friend's business, and employ himself to advantage" (248). He therefore sets out to join the Nawdoessie, and like other Europeans before him, including Billy in *The Man of the World*, Hermsprong's father resolves to join the Indians to escape the persecutions or limitations of the European world. However, he makes his commercial interests equally important to his other motivations, and the benefits of embedding himself among the Nawdoessie extend beyond his desire to enrich his philosophical understanding of man. Indian life and commercial interests are compatible in this novel, not each other's opposites.

He is well received by his Indian hosts when he arrives, and the chief, Lontac, is pleased when he learns their language. The chief tells the gathering of head men from all the villages that they will build a large wigwam for the European man, so they can store "all the good things we want from the European people"; he adds, "When we return from hunting he will buy our skins. So we shall have powder and guns, cloth to warm us in winter, and rum to cheer us" (249). The relationship between Hermsprong's father and the Indians is fashioned around exchange, in which Hermsprong's family supplies material objects while the Nawdoessie provide a cultural refuge from the European world. The influx of European goods, however, betrays this appearance of cultural purity. Indeed, the Europeans themselves seek out alternatives to the natural existence among the Indians, and Hermsprong notes that they brought with them "our books, our music, our instruments of drawing, and every thing that could be supposed to alleviate the solitude my mother had pictured to herself." These remnants of European culture prove to be unnecessary, however, as the people are "civil and attentive," and there is "novelty in the scene" (249). Even Hermsprong's father, the man of letters, finds it "difficult to procure leisure for the studies and amusements he most liked," since he is so occupied by their adoptive hosts.

Ultimately life among the Nawdoessie proves to be a masculine and patriarchal space, where the young Hermsprong thrives while his French mother, a "zealous catholic," increasingly resents the polite but uncompromising Indians. She attempts to convert members of the tribe they live among to assuage her guilt over her own perceived transgressions of faith. She begins her missionary efforts with Lodiquashow, the wife of the leader, Lontac. She soon finds that the Indian woman defers too much to the opinion of her husband, and is unable to persuade her to adopt the Catholic faith. Hermsprong's mother decides to wait a further two months, mastering the Nawdoessie language and building the courage to approach the "venerable chief" himself in an attempt to proselytize. While the chief finds it to be "an inversion of order, that [he] should lend his ear to a woman for instruction," at the same time Hermsprong notes that "there is in these people a politeness derived from education ... which qualifies them for patient hearers, to a degree I have never observed in more polished nations" (250). Elsewhere in the novel, Hermsprong endorses the ideas of Mary Wollstonecraft, yet the subservience of Indian women is not critiqued in the book.[84] The subjectivity and physical prowess of Indian men is meant to correct the effeminacy and degeneration of the European gentry, and their tolerance for the ideas of others contrasts with the paranoid, anti-Jacobin political climate of England during the French Revolution. But their distilled masculinity is seemingly incompatible with women's rights, even though they challenge the corrupt European social order and present a much more desirable alternative to a failing English culture. It is only in hybrid form, through Hermsprong, that this natural masculinity and tolerance can provide a space for women and carry forward the virtuous and noble aspects of the Nawdoessie.

Hermsprong's mother fails in converting the Indians, and the chief notes that "[i]t is better to believe than contradict" the religious beliefs of others. Exasperated by their tolerance, Hermsprong's mother complains to her husband that she despises the Indians and "shall never be easy amongst them." He tells her that he himself despised them until he "found them equals in knowledge of many things of which I believed them ignorant; and my superiors in the virtues of friendship, hospitality, and integrity" (251–2). The Indians possess the values which the gentry in the novel lack, and they are clearly not in need of religious intervention like those in *The Female American*. Hermsprong's father adds that his wife will be comfortable among them as long as she "[doesn't] think of converting them." While the critique of the missionary impulse is somewhat tempered by its depiction as Catholic and feminine, the point that it is Europeans, and not Indians, who need reforming is a central concern in this episode. Indians are comfortable with who they are without class or religion, and they privilege liberty and individual merit over all values.

Unlike his mother, Hermsprong thrives among the Indians, and his only barrier to becoming an equal to his brethren is likely due to "the sedentary portion of my life, spent with my father in learning languages, in mathematics, in I know not what" (252). As a result of his father's attachment to Europe, Hermsprong claims he is "superficial," which makes him "resemble the generality of young Englishmen" (253). The value of Indian life is that it is "calculated to render man robust, and inure him to labour and fatigue," creating an ideal, rational masculinity in the young man. His internalization of this upbringing suggests that it produces a greater individuality, separating him from the "generality," and the emphasis on physical development is a corrective to the European decline of manual labour and self-sufficiency. Despite the patriarchal culture under which he is raised, however, Hermsprong does not share the value of timidity in women; he tells the English women gathered to listen to the story of his youth that they should "acquire minds to reason, understandings to judge," and this can govern their "propriety of action" (253). Thus, while he does not judge their subordination of women, he breaks from the Indians who raised him in this regard thanks to the tolerance and individual thinking they helped instil in him.

Hermsprong ultimately leaves the Indians following the death of his father and returns to France with his mother. His connection to the tribe is, significantly, through patrilineal ties. While he does not become a king among the Indians, he is eventually able to marry a noblewoman and restore his family name in Britain thanks to his intercultural identity.[85] He turns out to be Sir Charles Campinet, the rightful Lord Grondale and son of the current lord's elder brother. Once again, hybridity serves the European but does little for the Indians who shaped him, and while Bage offers a radical critique of British society in some ways, it is in the end a vision of masculine reform rather than revolution.[86]

Conclusion

In tracking the representations of Indians towards the end of the century, it is striking that, particularly in the 1770s, never had the poles between fear and desire grown so far apart. While this polarity existed before and for long after, and indeed continues to, it is this same time that witnessed the emergence of the hybrid figure who appropriated aspects of Indian culture. The Indian was a source of anxiety that challenged dominant discourses of British cultural superiority, and while this was already the case prior to the final quarter of the eighteenth century, earlier modes of self-imagining did not seek to willingly take on this thrilling subjectivity. In the press, Indians were the wedge that threatened to split the trans-Atlantic British self with their inhuman barbarity, but in imaginative literature, they were a source of the re-unification of this subject, providing an important role in the foundation of the modern self. By internalising the Indian, the self becomes modern, a cosmopolitan, masculine, and individualistic subject. Paul Gilroy suggests that modernity begins in the "constitutive relationships with outsiders that both found and temper a self-conscious sense of western civilization."[87] In the case of the Indian, this relationship is distinctly paradoxical, resulting in a modernity that both rejects and appropriates the outsider. Actual Native people, however, were effectively excluded from the new discourses of liberty and human rights which encounters and conflicts with them helped shape. In both British and American discourse, they became powerful symbols, but the complexities of Native cultures were written out of this history.

6 Native North American Material Culture in the British Imaginary

Around his manly Neck shone the beauteous Beads of *Wampum*, composed of shining Shells of variously reflecting Hues; his arms were ornamented with the same Decorations; around his Middle yet a broader Belt held in its varying Girt his fatal War-ax, and his pointed Ponyard; across his Shoulders hung his Bow and Quiver for the Chace; his Arms for War were the Fire-arms of Europe.

– John Shebbeare, *Lydia, or, Filial Piety* (1755)

Representations of Indians in the eighteenth century, as in John Shebbeare's description of his idealized Iroquois man, are often largely dependent upon their invocation of materiality; the numerous appearances of wampum, tomahawks, feathers, calumets, scalping knives, and so forth, are fundamental to the vocabulary of Indianness, and the well-known phrases from treaty negotiations, such as "bury the hatchet," "boil the (war) kettle," and "brighten the chain," deploy objects of exchange as metaphorical diplomatic acts. Indeed, part of the humour in Smollett's depiction of the foolish Duke of Newcastle in *Humphry Clinker* is not only his complete lack of geographical understanding but his ignorance of this material vocabulary, proclaiming, "Let [the Five Nations] have plenty of blankets, and stinkubus,[1] and wampum; and your excellency won't fail to scour the kettle, and boil the chain, and bury the tree, and plant the hatchet – Ha, ha, ha!"[2] Richard Owen Cambridge, writing in *The World* in 1754, observed that the new fashionable words in English would doubtless emerge from North America, and he provides a sample of "a letter from one of our colonies" to prepare the reader for this influx of novel language:

The *Chippoways* and *Orundaks* are still very troublesome. Last week they *scalped* one of our Indians: but the *Six nations* continue firm; and at a meeting of *Sachems* it was determined *to take up the hatchet*, and *make the war-kettle boil*. The French desired to *smoak the calumet of peace*; but the *half-king* would not consent. They offered the *speech-belt*, but it was refused. Our Governour has received an account of their proceedings, together with *a string of wampum*, and *a bundle of skins to brighten the chain*.[3]

He claims that "no man will be fit to appear in company" unless he can "ornament his discourse with those jewels," and while the piece is meant to mock the fashion for using exotic words to demonstrate worldliness, it also highlights the correlation between the phrases from the Indians and material things. This final chapter will argue that this vocabulary emerges from an actual body of objects, and that like the literary trope of the Indian, this material functioned as a uniquely double-sided site of disavowal and appropriation. The material culture from North America that appeared in Britain presents a parallel narrative to Indians in literature. For example, Indian weaponry contained within it the transcultural fears and desires of the British subject in much the same way as the cruel savage of the captivity narrative, while collecting itself became a form of appropriation for some soldiers and antiquarians alike during the same period that produced hybrids such as Hermsprong and William Augustus Bowles. Indeed, Indian objects would come to shape historical narratives in the paintings of Benjamin West.[4] Thus, in closing with this chapter, I hope to show that the kinds of relationships and contradictions fostered by Indians in literature can also be viewed from the perspective of the history of British interactions with Indigenous objects.

This chapter is in part informed by "thing theory," which has spawned a robust body of scholarship in eighteenth-century studies for its interest in the ways that relationships between people and objects mediated the changing world. As Bill Brown writes, "the thing really names less an object than a particular subject-object relation."[5] Arjun Appadurai similarly argues that "[w]e have to follow the things themselves, for their meanings are inscribed in their forms, their uses, their trajectories"; it is, after all, "the things-in-motion that illuminate their human and social context."[6] Thus in the case of Indigenous material culture, tracing its circulation from sites of both domination and exchange, looking at both its manufacture and subsequent representative value, we can understand the broader "social life" of the objects and their import to British representations of the Indian.

From both an Indigenous and a European perspective, material culture was a central mediator for understanding and interpreting the other from the time of first contact; in most Iroquoian languages, the word for the Dutch is *Kristoni* or "metal-workers," while the word for "Europeans" more broadly is *Asseroni*, which translates as "ax-or knife-makers."[7] There is little ambiguity in this terminology and, as Joseph Roach notes, ethnohistory in this case shows us how "Native American languages record the symbolic inventiveness of the material relationships between Iroquoia and northern Europe at this historic juncture."[8] There are numerous examples of the centrality of material exchange with Europeans and its importance to Native societies; in a well-known passage from the Jesuit relations, an Algonquin chief boasts to the French that "his body was hatchets; he meant that the preservation of his person and of his Nation was the preservation of the hatchets, the kettles, and all the trade of the French, for the Hurons."[9] European goods here become the vocabulary of embodied political power, and the eruption of Pontiac's Rebellion over a century later in 1763 came about in part due to Native dissatisfaction with the English reluctance to give gifts to the nations around Detroit following the Seven Years' War.[10] Many scholars now understand the Indigenous appropriation of European goods as a political decision and articulation of symbolic power, and not, as Europeans frequently assumed, proof of the inherent superiority of their goods.[11] Indeed, in a speech by Onondaga chief Canassatego during treaty negotiations with British officials in 1744, widely reprinted in Britain beginning with the 1747 edition of Cadwallader Colden's *The History of the Five Indian Nations*, the chief notes that the English claim

> we should have perished if they had not come into the country and furnished us with Strowds[12] and Hatchets, and Guns, and other Things necessary for the Support of Life; but we always gave them to understand that they were mistaken, that we lived before they came amongst us, and as well, or better, if we may believe what our Forefathers have told us. We had then Room enough, and Plenty of Deer, which was easily caught; and tho' we had not Knives, Hatchets, or Guns, such as we have now, yet we had Knives of Stone, and Hatchets of Stone, and Bows and Arrows, and those served our Uses as well then as the *English* ones do now. (105)

Canassatego reminds the British that while his people may have adopted European goods into their lives, they would gladly give them back if it meant reclaiming the inheritance of their ancestors. The much

despised Tory gadfly and physician Shebbeare would re-write Canassatego into the virtuous Iroquois character "Cannassatego" in *Lydia,
or Filial Piety* (1755) described in the epigraph above, who laments the
arrival of Europeans, the "faithless Invaders," and views his people
"wrapt in *European* Manufactures, as Men bearing the Badge of Slavery" (7). Within a few years, these sentiments that Shebbeare projects
onto the Indian would spread in the colonies through the teaching of
Lenape prophet Neolin.[13] Just as Neolin rejected all European wares
with particular focus on the destructive trade in alcohol,[14] Cannassatego swears off "that enebriating Liquor, which totally deprives
Humanity of Reason" and "had never clothed himself but in the
Skins of those Beasts which he had slain with his own Hands" (7). That
the imagined cultural tenacity of Indians by writers like Shebbeare,
hardly a radical, would be mirrored in actual anti-colonial resistance
indicates the imaginary and real importance of material exchange. But
this contested side of the exchange, the Native appropriation of British goods through treaty negotiations, the fur trade, and other sites,
has been well explored by anthropologists and historians.[15] What is less
clear in this historical relationship are the ways in which Native material culture was perceived in Britain and how it informed British conceptions of Native people and of their own cultural moment.[16]

While the British did not appropriate Indian objects in the same way
or on the same scale, they too came to define the other and their relationship with them through material culture. In 1777, during the American Revolutionary War and some thirty years following Canassatego's
rousing words about the prevalence of British axes and knives in the
colonies, William Pitt the elder gave a speech in the House of Lords
to address the use of Indian allies to fight against colonists: "[N]ow we
had *sullied* and *tarnished* the arms of Britain for ever," Pitt declared, "by
employing Savages in our service, by drawing them up in a British line,
and *mixing* the *scalping knife* and *tomahawk* with the *sword* and *firelock*."[17]
This is odd for a European, an *Asseroni*, a knife and ax maker, to define
the savagery of the other through the very things that he supplied
them with; how could this use of Indians bearing British manufactures
become "a contamination, a pollution of our national character"(490)?
In Shebbeare's book, the fictional Cannassatego declares that

the very Garments which we wear are Testimonies of the Truth, of how
small Account an *Indian* Chief, and his Exploits, is deemed amongst [the
British]; these Coverings, if these Men may be believed, are the Productions

of the lowest People, the Price of Metal dug from the Bowels of the Earth, the Toil of six Days only, by Hands which never wield the Ax, or meet their Foes in Battle; these are the Purchase of an *Indian* Warrior's Arm, his Fame, his Family, his Being; and his Country. (10–11)

For him too the degenerate nature of the other is in their material culture, in similar objects for the "Indian trade" that Pitt uses to depict Indian savagery. But Canassatego draws attention to the production of these goods, a site continually effaced in the literature of the period but never difficult to find if we look to the material record and see the stamps of British cutlers on tomahawks and scalping knives.

Yet by the 1760s the scalping knife and tomahawk had become synonymous with the cruelty of Indians, easy shorthand to distinguish what one writer later described as "striking proofs of British valour, opposed to tomahawk cruelty."[18] This association is dramatized in Benjamin West's 1768 painting *General Johnson Saving a Wounded French Officer from the Tomahawk of a North American Indian*, in which Sir William Johnson humanely intervenes to save a wounded French enemy from what is clearly a weapon of European manufacture. This picture is further complicated with the knowledge that Johnson himself had requested 10,000 such tomahawks in 1765 for treaty negotiations, to be manufactured in Birmingham and Sheffield and worth £875.[19] By 1777, there were near daily accounts in the British press of some new outrage committed by Indians, nearly always embodied by the tomahawk and the scalping knife. Even a cursory look reveals examples such as this from the *London Evening Post*: "How [is] … the use of the tomahawk and the scalping knife, which indiscriminately butcher the innocent with the guilty, (sparing neither age nor sex) to be justified before God or Man?" Another newspaper approvingly tells of some gentlemen at a dinner who toast their meal by declaring, "May those who employ *Savages*, in acts of cruelty, fall by the Tomahawk." And a New Years resolution poem in the *Post* for 13–15 January 1778 reads in part, "Cease Britain, cease the horrid strife, / The bloody contest now give o'er, / No longer use the Scalping Knife, / The Tomahawk employ no more."

How did it come to be that the same objects which in the colonies represented British trade and mechanical superiority were representative in Britain of the inhumanity and utter savagery of the Indian? Perhaps even more perplexing, how is it that British soldiers and travellers could trade with different Native groups and bring back these British-made hatchets and knives and display them as examples of

Figure 6.1 General Johnson Saving a Wounded French Officer from the
Tomahawk of a North American Indian. Artist: Benjamin West, c. 1768. Oil on
canvas. Derby Museum and Art Gallery. Used with permission.

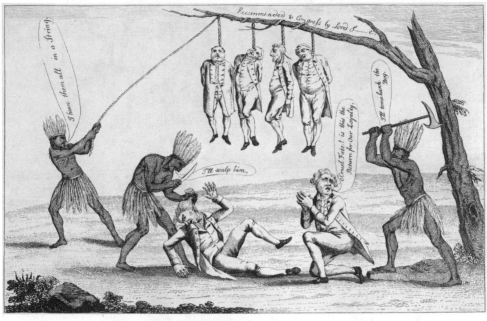

Figure 6.2 The savages let loose, or, The cruel fate of the loyalists, 1783. Etching. Lewis Walpole Library. Used with permission.

Indian curiosities? Early pipe tomahawks in the British Museum and other collections were made in England in the eighteenth century, and brought back in the same period.[20] Sarah Stone painted a knife in 1780 for the auction of the contents of the Leverian Museum, and while the ornamental quillwork is Northeastern Indigenous, likely Huron, the blade clearly shows the marks of a British cutler.

Were the people who collected and viewed items such as these unaware of the provenance of this material, or were there other cultural forces at work that led to British manufactures being mistaken for ethnographic items and symbols of savagery? As late as 1841, painter George Catlin was frustrated by what he perceived as the cultural impurity of Native nations as he painted them and gathered ethnographic objects, and proclaimed that

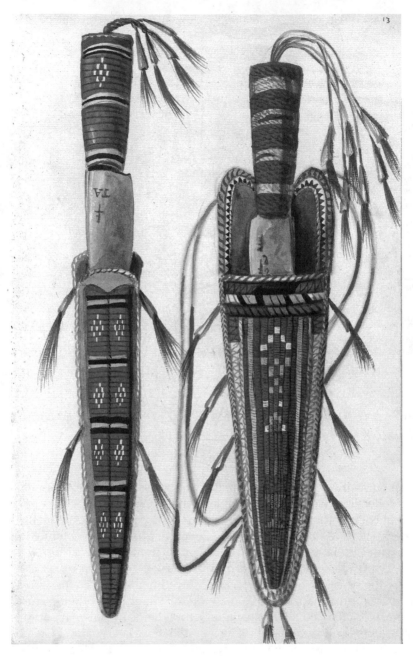

Figure 6.3 Illustration of Woodlands knife from the Leverian Museum. Artist: Sarah Stone, 1780. Watercolour. British Museum. Used with permission.

If I ... should ever cross the Atlantic with my collection, a curious enigma would be solved for the English people, who may enquire for a scalping-knife, when they find that every one in my Collection (and hear also, that nearly every one that is to be seen in the Indian country, to the Rocky Mountains and the Pacific Ocean) bears on its blade the impress of G.R., which they will doubtless understand.[21]

Yet objects such as these in Catlin's collection already were in Britain and did not seem to influence British awareness of their own involvement in making them. Any reference to the European part in manufacturing the weapons fundamental to depictions of Indian cruelty is nearly impossible to find outside of letters between colonial officials; Henry Timberlake observes in his memoirs of 1765 that the "tommahawkes" used by the Cherokee by mid-century were "all made by Europeans,"[22] though his work had little impact at the time. The fact that neither Burke nor Pitt mentions this trade in their speeches before Parliament suggests that the material connection to such a troubling reality could be difficult to articulate or even conceive, but I will return to these weapons and their surprising provenance below.

I will here take a step back to the beginning of this side of the material relationship, to track, however provisionally, the emergence of fragments of the so-called New World in Europe. The history of North American material culture in Europe cannot be separated from the physical processes of empire and the expropriation of colonial wealth that, beginning in the late fifteenth century, gave rise in part to European modernity. The transatlantic movement of resources, profits, artifacts, and people was in turn shaped by, and gave shape to, what has been variously described as the "Indian Atlantic" and, more recently, the "Red Atlantic."[23] This re-naming and re-imagining of an historical process has been in part meant to emphasize the importance of Indigenous peoples of the Americas in the transatlantic world, and nowhere is this paradigm more fruitful and more fraught than in looking at the collections of cultural objects, sacred and otherwise, that were brought to Europe in a variety of circumstances starting in the early modern period.

Early European Collecting of American Objects

If the influx of European goods into the Americas over the next few centuries beginning with Columbus undoubtedly had its effects on Native societies, so too did the appearance of "Americana" in Europe.

Silvia Spitta claims that "indigenous objects would literally overcome Europe's ability to order things," suggesting that Foucault's narrative of the epistemological shifts in the early modern period are incomplete without considering the effects of the "misplaced objects" arriving from the Americas. "For what work could misplaced objects do," asks Spitta, "other than signal the destruction of indigenous cultures and at the same time throw the thinking of early modern Europe into question?"[24] For Renaissance Europe, the objects of the "New World" produced a sense of wonder that can be troubling for its erasure of the colonial violence that allowed these wondrous things to cross the Atlantic. Wonder is also, however, ambiguous as a discourse. Thus in 1520, while visiting Brussels, Albrecht Dürer observed the first of the objects sent back by Cortés to Charles V from "the new golden land" of Mexico and he "marvelled at the subtle *ingenia* of men in foreign lands" while declaring these "wonderful things" to be "much more beautiful to behold than prodigies."[25] Stephen Greenblatt reminds us that it would be disingenuous to ignore the "relations of power and wealth that are encoded in the artist's response," but it would at the same time perhaps be even worse to reduce Dürer's reaction to those objects he viewed in Brussels as a celebration or pure expression of these relations.[26] Dürer declares that "[a]ll the days of my life I have seen nothing that has gladdened my heart so much as these things," and this sense of wonder at material culture from the Americas would continue in Europe for at least two more centuries.[27]

Yet while wonder may offer a new kind of epistemology through encounters with profound otherness, it also would become an ordering principle in an emerging form of collection and display in the early modern period, the curiosity cabinet. The *kunst-* or *wunderkammer*, as these cabinets were known in German-speaking countries, displayed singular objects from the natural world alongside works of art, classical sculpture, and machines.[28] While their organization, often baffling to later eyes, was based more on singularity and curiosity rather than the taxonomies of later Enlightenment collections, they nonetheless offered a meditation on the relation between nature and culture and were not simply a random, purely aesthetic experience.[29] The precise role of "exotica" in these collections was shifting and not always clear, but foreign objects were almost always crucial to the completion of any display. In the surviving inventories of early *kunstkammern*, the most common descriptive term for non-European items is "Indian," and though it is often impossible to tell what culture is meant to be the originator,[30] there were indeed many items from the Americas.[31] The position of these exotic artificial curiosities in collections was ambiguous, like the discourse of curiosity and wonder itself;[32] Horst Bredekamp notes that *exotica* in early modern cabinets existed outside of the classificatory schemes of collectors and antiquarians, somewhere between the natural and artificial worlds.[33] In 1565, the first theorist on museums, Samuel Quiccheberg, proposed five principal sections around which to organize collections[34] and placed "Indian" objects in two of them, suggesting that they could not be accommodated to one vision within the microcosm.[35] Similarly, as Dürer rhapsodises over Cortés's spoils in his journal, reflecting on the value and rarity of these Indigenous things, he ends by proclaiming, "Indeed I cannot express all that I thought there." For the early modern European, New World objects were a challenge to fit into the classical world view, and ways of seeing the world had to be modified.

While cabinets were sites of speculative learning to a certain extent, they also produced knowledge, and the slippage that saw many non-European objects labelled as "Indian" carried forward into the Renaissance iconography of all foreign or "non-civilized" cultures, which was influenced by these collected curiosities.[36] Featherwork in particular frequently evoked this early modern vision of exoticism in visual culture, and geographical distance collapsed under the rubric of otherness. Thus if we recall the "naked Indian" riding an elephant in William D'Avenant's court masque *The Temple of Love* (1635), the cabinet is brought to life in his adornment in the "tire and bases of several-coloured feathers, representing the Indian monarchy."[37] The masque, like the cabinet itself, integrates otherness into its metaphorical vision of the world just as it effaces non-European specificity. But before this time, pageants on the continent would deploy objects themselves to produce spectacles of encounter. Rulers would attempt to appropriate the wonder held by the material culture of the New World.[38] Archduke Ferdinand II took feathers from a pre-Columbian headdress and placed them in his helmet worn during his second marriage,[39] while Duke Friedrich of Württemberg himself played the Queen of America in a carnival in 1599, complete with American weapons from his cabinet.[40] In Rouen, France, in 1550, two Brazilian villages were recreated on the banks of the Seine for the entrance of Henri II, complete with foliage, monkeys, parrots, hundreds of naked French people acting as Indians, and over 50 actual Indigenous people. The villages were then burned to the ground as the various actors staged a mock battle with each other. This display of the Americas in Europe, both joyful and apocalyptic, was certainly the largest of its kind in the period.[41] What is striking is that while the vast body of material culture obviously shaped existing epistemological views, at the same time there was little desire to understand it in any terms outside of its curiosity or rarity. Objects of the Americas were chosen solely on aesthetic terms to this point, not necessarily because their place of origin held a special interest.[42]

Early British Collections

Britain lagged behind many continental countries in collecting, and while it was influenced by the iconography of foreignness shaped by "feathered Indians," as seen in D'Avenant's masque for the court of Charles I, its rulers did not maintain cabinets which were meant to establish microcosms of the known world.[43] The vast royal cabinets of dynasties such as the Habsburgs had no counterpart in Britain, and British collecting in its infancy was done by private men, often with the help of elite masters or benefactors. It was done with seemingly less methodology than on the continent, and took place, as Arthur MacGregor suggests, "lower down the social scale."[44] Interest in objects from the Americas did not become widespread until the period following the English Civil War, with the rise in anti-Spanish sentiments and the English translation of texts on the colonization of the "New World," particularly the writing of Dominican friar Bartolomé de las Casas.[45] Prior to this time, Sir Walter Cope, who began as a gentleman usher but rose to be a powerful administrator, was among the first to establish a widely admired cabinet in Britain.[46] In 1599, the Swiss traveller Thomas Platter visited his collection. Cope personally showed Platter through his cabinet, and the visitor's account lists objects such as "[a]n Indian stone axe, like a thunder-bolt," pieces of featherwork, and a "long narrow Indian canoe, with the oars and sliding planks, hung from the ceiling of this room."[47] Platter notes that "[t]here are also other people in London interested in curios, but this gentleman is superior to them all for the strange objects, because of the Indian voyage he carried out with such zeal."[48] While Platter sees items such as "an embalmed child," "a unicorn's tail" a "flying rhinoceros," and many other "queer foreign objects," it is the objects from the Americas that most strike him. Like Dürer marveling at the collections in Brussels some eighty years earlier, it is not the prodigies but the productions of Indians that most captivates the Swiss. Unlike the large variety of objects in early modern continental Europe, items once possessed by Indians were at this time still rare in Britain, and, for an aspirational gentleman like Cope, they were an effective means of distinction. When some "Virginians" arrived in England in 1603 in the midst of the plague, Cope entertained them, and there is a good chance that his canoe, suspended in the rarified space of his cabinet's ceiling, was put to use by these men as they rowed on the Thames.[49] The audience, given the grim circumstance in London, was no doubt diminished as compared to other such similar spectacles of Indian visitation, and these unnamed men vanished from the record after their appearance. They are absent from the listings of subsequent English voyages back to the Americas, so they perhaps succumbed to the deadly disease ravaging their captors.[50]

Collecting after Cope remained a primarily private pursuit, notwithstanding Francis Bacon's call in 1605 for a "substantial and severe collection of the Heteroclites or Irregulars of nature" which rejects "fables and popular errors."[51] Platter's description of a pelican in Cope's cabinet, likely from the collector himself, asserts that it "kills its young, and afterwards tears open its breast and bathes them in its own blood, until they have come to life," which presumably indicates a cavalier attitude to such high-minded concerns for empirical study. However, Bacon's vision of collecting, more importantly, insisted on the importance of ethnography for new knowledge; he argues in *Novum organum* (1620) that "[i]t would disgrace us, now that the wide spaces of the material globe, the lands and seas, have been broached and explored, if the limits of the intellectual globe should be set by the narrow discoveries of the ancients."[52] Ethnographic objects represented a world not known to the classical mind, and presented for Bacon an opportunity to provide, as Alain Schnapp suggests, "continuity between the discovery of the material world and the laws of human intelligence."[53] A reliance on antiquity represented a continual repetition, a struggle over memory and tradition that threatened the advancement of science and learning.

While Cope was part of the early wave of collecting in Britain, one of his admirers was John Tradescant the elder, a gardener to various noblemen at the beginning of the seventeenth century who would have a more important role to play in the institutionalization of collections into the forms that are recognizable today. Tradescant began collecting specimens through travel in Europe and North Africa and connections with the powerful men for whom he worked, including Cope, and following the assassination of his employer the Duke of Buckingham in 1628, he bought a house and established his museum known as "The Ark" at Lambeth.[54] While it was his collection of botany that brought him fame, Tradescant also boasted numerous "Indian" objects. These were presumably increased following a voyage by his son John Tradescant the younger to Virginia in 1637. The younger Tradescant took over from his father following his death in 1638, and the collection would eventually fall into the hands of solicitor, astrologer, and antiquary Elias Ashmole after the younger died in 1662. Ashmole had helped compile the catalogue for the Tradescants' collection, the *Musaeum Tradescantianum*, which was printed in 1656 and became the first museum catalogue in Britain.[55] He would later inherit the collection, rather dubiously according to some,[56] and donate it to Oxford under his own name. This would become the Ashmolean Museum, which opened as Europe's first public museum in 1683. The catalogue contains numerous objects from the Americas, and, significantly, they often appear using the North American Indigenous terms, which marks the start of a shift in British understandings of North American material culture. These include "A Canow & Picture of an Indian with his Bow and Dart," under "Variety of Rarities" (42), the "Tamahacks, 6 sorts," under "Warlike Instruments" (46), "*Pohatan*, King of *Virginia*'s habit all embroidered with shells, or Roanoke," in "Garments, Vestures, Habits, Ornaments" (47), "Virginian purses imbroidered [*sic*] with Roanoake," and "Black Indian girdles made of Wampam peek, the best sort" (51). There are also numerous "match-coat" (47), a recently Anglicized word from the Algonquin *matchkore*. While the word "Indian" is still ambiguously used in some instances, this level of specificity for North American objects is a new development. It suggests a more sophisticated relationship with Indians, mediated by both material and cultural exchange, and a greater shift from the aesthetic appreciation of *exotica* to its ethnographic value. While the feathered items predominately from Mexico and South America had informed exotic iconography from their position in earlier European cabinets, the visibility and vocabulary of North American collections began to redefine the iconography of the "Indian" to what is still today a familiar form. As Eugenio Donato notes, this form of collecting "is the result of an uncritical belief in the notion that ordering and classifying, that is to say, the spatial juxtaposition of fragments, can produce a representational understanding of the world."[57]

Nehemiah Grew's catalogue of the Royal Society, *Musaeum Regalis Societatis* (1681), similarly contains ethnographically specific details about North American Indians. The entry on "Several sorts of *Indian* MONEY, called WAMPAMPEAGE," describes the objects in detail, both in material and design, and goes on to explain the different values of individual pieces (370). He notes that strings of wampum "pass among the *Indians*, in their usual Commerse, as *Silver* and *Gold* amongst us," though observes that this string money, "being loose, is not so currant." He nonetheless breaks down their equivalent value, from the white single strings at five shillings per fathom, all the way up to the woven girdles "sometimes worn as their richest Ornaments; but chiefly used in great Payments, esteemed their Noblest Presents, and laid up as their Treasure." Grew attempts to rationally categorize all aspects of the collection. He explains that in his description of the objects from other cultures, "instead of medling with Mystick, Mythologick, or Hieroglyphick matters; or relating Stories of Men who were great Riders, or Women that were bold and feared not Horses; as some others have done: I thought it much more proper, To Remarque some of the Uses and Reasons of Things" (v). The curiosity that typifies an encounter with a cabinet of wonders, unrestrained by rational history or context, is reigned in by Grew's text. Fellow Royal Society member Robert Hooke would use stronger language, proclaiming that "the use of such a Collection is not for the Divertisement, and Wonder, and Gazing, as 'tis for the most part thought and esteemed, and like Pictures for Children to admire and be pleased with, but for the serious and diligent study of the most able Proficient in Natural Philosophy."[58] Such goals, however, were easier said than put into practice. Indeed, the source of much of the collection came from the purchase of Robert Hubert's cabinet of natural curiosities, which was assembled on principles of rarity and wonder and displayed as a public spectacle at his "Musick House."[59]

Like Ashmole's account of the Tradescant collection, the Royal Society's catalogue sought to make the mutable contents of its repository transcendent or, as Michael C.W. Hunter writes, it "reified the collection in book-form so that its fame spread even more widely than it did from travellers' reports."[60] German traveller Zacharias Conrad von Uffenbach, who visited the Repository in 1710, wrote, "Both in Germany and elsewhere an exalted idea of this Society has been formed, both of it and of the collections they have in their Museum" thanks in large part to "the fine description of the Museum by Grew."[61] Von Uffenbach's reaction to the collection in material form, now widely cited, reveals the extent to which the Society achieved its aim of a collection worthy of "serious and diligent study"; he writes that while there are present "the finest instruments and other arts (which Grew describes)," they are "not only in no sort of order or tidiness but covered with dust, filth, and coal-smoke, and many of them broken and utterly ruined."[62] Because they have only known the collection in textual form, von Uffenbach remarks that "foreigners have just grounds for amazement when they hear how wretchedly all is now ordered."[63] He does not mention any of the ethnographic collection, but we can assume that it too sat in mouldering neglect. By the time the Society's collection was donated to the British Museum in 1781, much of it ruined by "time and dirt" as the repository's keeper observed in the 1760s, it seems the little that remained was natural history specimens and not the more fragile "artificial curiosities."[64]

Thus while the actual collection itself disintegrated to dust, the North American objects survived in print, in Grew's widely read text. Indeed, this is a pattern throughout the period in Britain, with many catalogues listing objects that are lost to history. In Yorkshire, Ralph Thoresby's Musaeum Thoresbyanum also contained a wealth of North American Indian material and attracted a steady stream of visitors in its own right. One visitor from London saw it as superior even to the Ashmolean, proclaiming in the guest book, "Oxford be silent, I this Truth must write, / Leeds hath for Rarities outdone thee quite."[65] Thoresby had been a voracious collector and maintained regular correspondence with Royal Society members, particularly Hans Sloane, even penning some reports for the Society's *Philosophical Transactions* himself. His catalogue appeared in his *Ducatus Leodiensis: or, the topography of the ancient and populous town and parish of Leedes* (1715), his principal work. In the catalogue for his museum, he cites Grew's text often as an authoritative source and gives detailed descriptions of his objects, including their materials, origins, uses, and the person from whom he acquired them. The vocabulary for Indian objects was still provisional, so the tomahawk is variously known as a "*Tomahaw*" and a "*Tamahauke*," while wampum is often referred to, and understood as, "shell money" in various denominations. Thoresby attempts to provide context to his objects, gesturing to the importance of the written catalogue in noting that he has some Indian things that "are not mentioned by any Author I have met with" (428). Some of his items remain difficult to interpret due to their seeming singularity to Thoresby's collection; he lists one object as an "Indian periwig" made of feathers, complete with comb, while his "*Assonagh* or *Escocheon*" used "at the Funeral of the Princess *Eliz. Sonam*, Sole-Daughter and Heir Apparent of *Ann Sonam*, a converted *Indian* Queen in *Maryland*" (484), describes both an unknown object and a seemingly untraceable historical character. Upon his death, some of the valuable contents of the museum were brought to Thoresby's son's house in Stoke Newington, but most of it lay "in a garret like a Heap of Rubbish" until the elements rendered it "like a Dunghill."[66] As such we are not likely to ever know the contents of Thoresby's collection, only its textual legacy.[67]

For those following in the legacy of Hooke and the "new philosophy," the subjective experience of wonder had to be displaced when encountering Indian objects, and increasingly there were efforts to understand this growing body of material in culturally comparative terms. In this attempt, Western epistemologies could be frustrated, as when one writer, in discussing the 1710 visit to London by the "Four Indian Kings," members of the Haudenossaune or Iroquois confederacy, writes that the calumet, which is their "method of making peace ... is the most mysterious thing in the World, for it is us'd in all their important Transactions; however, it is nothing else but a large Tobacco-Pipe."[68] A periodical essay in *The Connoisseur* later in the century has a country gentleman obsessed with current affairs proclaim, "I am a great admirer of the Indian oratory; and I dare say old Hendrick the Sachem would have made a good figure in the House of Commons. There is something very elegant in the *Covenant-Belt*; but pray what a pox are those damned *Strings of Wampum?* I cannot find any account of them in Chambers's Dictionary."[69] While this is obviously written with tongue in cheek, the elusive meaning behind such objects could lead to reductive interpretations of Indigenous cultures. In *The Spectator* no. 56 from 4 May 1711, one week following the essay on the Four Indian Kings, Joseph Addison writes that North American Indigenous people believe that everything has a soul, including "inanimate things, [such] as stocks and stones," and "all the works of art, as of knives, boats, looking-glasses" (408–9). As a result of this belief, "they always place by the corpse of their dead friend a bow and arrows, that he may make use of the souls of them in the other world, as he did of their wooden bodies in this" (409). Addison goes on to tell the story of Marraton and Yaratilda, in which, like Orpheus, the Indian Marraton visits the land of the dead to see his beloved wife. On his journey, he encounters various spirits engaged in both work and play, and observes multitudes of them "employing themselves upon ingenious handicrafts with the souls of *departed utensils*, for that is the name which in the Indian language they give their tools when they are burnt or broken" (411). According to Addison, Indians imbue the world of objects with a fetishistic and sacred quality that may appear absurd, but he notes that "our European philosophers have maintained several notions altogether as improbable" (409). While Addison ends, typically, on a note of shared, if not condescending, humanity, fetishism increasingly became the interpretation of the relationship between Indians and their goods alongside a similar anxiety in Britain over the rise in consumerism.[70]

Perhaps most representative of this was wampum, which British writers described variously as money, as a special kind of gift, as writing, and simply as ornament. Even Scottish Enlightenment thinkers such as Hugh Blair and James Beattie admitted to not knowing exactly how it functioned in their treatises on writing and language.[71] Like the Incan *quipos*, which mystified Europeans as some form of secret knowledge or "language to the eyes" in Horace Walpole's phrase,[72] wampum existed somewhere between competing regimes of value. And the blurring of the distinction between commerce and written memory was troubling to a society witnessing the commodification of culture itself. This anxiety is manifested in *Memoirs of the life and adventures of Tsonnonthouan*, which, as discussed in a previous chapter, tells the story of an Indian continually searching for a new object to worship as his god or manitou while reflecting on the interchangeability of commercial writing in the wake of the popularity of *Tristram Shandy*. This critique articulates the ideology that underlies claims by moralists such as the Archdeacon of Lincoln, John Gordon, who wrote in 1762, "There was a time, when the weakness of men was such, that every thing was to be transacted by tokens, symbols, and pledges. What is the Calamet and Wampum among the Indians at this day, but a proof, that they are now in a state, in which all mankind once were?"[73] Gordon's real critique is of the contemporary desire for ornament and "external form," or the "deviations from simplicity" evident in followers of fashion, and he sees in these metaphorical objects a dangerous attachment to transitory things.

And what about the actual display of Indian objects in places such as the British Museum, Don Saltero's Coffeehouse in Chelsea, or Thoresby's Museum in Leeds? According to catalogues and guidebooks they occupied significant space on display, but it is difficult to know how the public received such objects. Angela Todd argues that Saltero's collection, established in the late seventeenth century by a former servant of Sloane's, "recapitulated British nationalist, religious, and Orientalist ideologies,"[74] while Troy Bickham claims that "Indian primitiveness was an inescapable message to visitors of almost any major exhibition" of Native material culture in the eighteenth century.[75] He cites an account of the Leverian Museum in 1782, which describes how the visitor is transported by the exhibits and "sees the Indian rejoiced at, and dancing to, the monotonous sound of his tom tom; he sighs to recollect the prevalent power of fear and superstition over the human mind, when he views the rude deformity of an idol carved with a flint, by a hand incapable of imitating the outline of nature, and that works only that it may worship."[76] It is without question that a display such as this one in Ashton Lever's Holophusicon at Leicester Square achieved some of its effect by diminishing non-European cultures and their material advancements, yet this same collection of Indian objects included a "[r]eal tomahawk, and tobacco-pipe in one," an object no doubt of European manufacture. And while the European origins of this tomahawk may have been hidden from the author of the guide, he nonetheless admires the "curiously carved" weapons he observes, and notes that these foreign objects "make his active fancy travel from pole to pole through torrid and through frigid zones." He himself becomes subject to the curious power of the objects, and admits that "he looks at the vast volumes of actual information, that every where surround him, and is indeterminate where to begin, or on which to fix his attention most." This hardly sounds like the assertion of a hegemonic gaze on the primitive other, and resonates more with Dürer's early modern wonder over men in far-away lands than a confident articulation of British superiority. Indeed, he is implicated in the Indian ceremony, rejoicing over the fetish objects that surround him.

Elsewhere, Indian objects helped shape historical narratives. The painter Benjamin West possessed a collection of Native North American items in his London studio, a number of which survive in the British Museum.[77] He used these objects to lend authenticity to his paintings of colonial scenes and idealized Indians, most famously in The Death of Wolfe (1770). West's contemplative Indian, an embodiment of a philosophical noble savage, was based on a Native soapstone pipe in the artist's possession. The iconography of the Indian in West's paintings is in very clear ways shaped by the North American items that he owned, and Native objects, while not integrated into the material lives of British people like steel and iron among Indigenous nations in North America, helped bridge the divide that The Death of Wolfe addressed between the non-specific classical setting of baroque history and modernity.[78] In this sense we can see this work, a new approach to historical painting, as a transcultural document, and West's pipe and other Native items connect rather than separate so-called primitivism and the European.

Figure 6.4 The Death of General Wolfe. Artist: William Woollett after
Benjamin West, 1776. Line-engraving with etching. Yale Center for British Art,
Paul Mellon Collection. Used with permission.

Indeed, the Indian in the painting is wearing a knife from West's studio that is likely made of Sheffield steel,[79] and his rifle and tomahawk,
European goods with Indian ornamentation, physically connect him to
the body of the dying Wolfe.[80]

Even before the widespread availability of such transcultural items
in Britain, Indian objects in collections could become something altogether different from an assertion of ethnographic difference. As we
have seen in the cases of Thoresby and of the Royal Society, British
collecting in the period focused more on the cataloguing of objects for
posterity than on the actual display and preservation of these things.
While foreign visitors were dismayed by the conditions of objects in

Figure 6.5 Smoking Pipe from Benjamin West's studio. Made by North-east Peoples, c. 1600–1750. Carved soapstone. British Museum. Used with permission.

British collections, subject to damp in repositories and ruinous tobacco smoke in coffeehouses, they were at the same time impressed by the catalogues. Marjorie Swann describes this "impulse to textualize collections" as revealing "the interrelationships of material and literary culture,"[81] and it is significant that the item that perfectly exemplifies the textual impulse and the collapse of text and object is from a North American Indian. Swann draws attention to a peculiar North American spoon in Sloane's possession, one which would later become part of the founding collection of the British Museum in 1753. This item is inscribed with the story of its own provenance, and on it is written in ink:

Anno 1702 An Indian Spoon [made of] the Brest bone of a Pinguin made by Papenau an Indian whose Squaw had both her Legs gangrend & rotted off to her knees and was cured by bathing in balsam water. [M]ade by Winthrop esq. New England[.] The method was thus[:] he Ordered

two Oxe Bladers to be filled wi his Rare Balsamick Liquor made warme
and the stumps put into the Bladers wth the Water was kept comfortably
Blood warme, and the Leggs were perfectly cured in a few days time.

This is the earliest North American object whose maker is named,
but more significant is its transformation from artifact to narrative. It
is forever tied to the story of John Winthrop and his clever cure, more
so than the craft of Papenau or cultural context of his people, and the
object cannot be perceived outside of its singular history.[82] This spoon is
the catalogue entry made flesh, and the collector's story supersedes the
thing itself. The Indian object is once again appropriated for European
self-imagining, but the story of technological superiority inscribed
upon it equally suggests the importance of its transcultural value.

Conclusion

In this context we can return to the tomahawk and scalping knife; if
the other Indian objects become fetishes because of the limits of knowledge or the fear of commodities becoming a new system of value, while
others are appropriated into historical narrative, why do these British
goods come to represent what looks on the surface to be such a profound otherness? In describing the actions of Indian allies in his celebrated speech in Parliament discussed earlier, Edmund Burke claimed
that to use Indians "was merely to be cruel ourselves in their persons,
and to become chargeable with all the odious and impotent barbarities, which they would certainly commit, whenever they were called
into action" (521). He precisely articulates what these objects embody,
though perhaps without knowing their material specificities. They
become saddled with the violence of colonialism and the profoundly
disturbing prospect of the violent separation of the transatlantic British subject. One newspaper in 1777 described this paranoia as "the
Tomahawk and Scalping knife fever," while Richard Tickell, lampoon-
ing parliamentary discord over the use of Indians, calls the weapons
"[S]atanic instruments of death."[83] Their fearful power grew from their
reflection of self, and as such they had to be disavowed. Yet even this
disavowal would be reversed.

Just as in the case of the literary Indian, things began to change following the Revolutionary War, and narratives began to shift. Scotsman Peter Williamson, whose transculturation following a supposed
six month captivity among the Lenape has already been discussed at

Figure 6.6 Sir John Caldwell. Anonymous, c. 1780. Oil on canvas. The National Museums, Liverpool. Used with permission.

length, claims in a remarkable biographical revision in 1789 that "from his infancy, [he] was brought up with … Savages, and taught nothing else but the use of the tomahawk and scalping knife." When he died in Edinburgh in 1799, his body was interred, according to a newspaper report, "in the full panoply of a Delaware Indian Chief." An anti-Jacobin periodical named itself *The Tomahawk* in the 1790s because, it asserted, "THE TOMAHAWK is not an instrument of a dastardly nature, like the Italian stiletto, but is a manly weapon, used by manly nations; and boldly thrown, in the broad face of day, at the foes of their freedom." And other British men used their collections of Native weaponry and clothing acquired during the Revolutionary War to display a kind of aristocratic masculinity that served as a corrective to the debauched or effeminate image of the gentry prevalent at the time.[84] Sir John Caldwell had himself painted wearing full regalia comprising various Native cultures, constructing an identity that relied on the perceived fierceness of Woodland warriors.[85] Prominently featured in this appropriation, in this collection of disparate fragments displayed as a fictional totality on his body, of course, is his tomahawk, no longer terrorizing the British psyche, and back in the hands of an ax-maker, but still obscured from its origins and networks of exchange.

Conclusion: "Pen-and-Ink Work"

As the case of Indigenous material culture indicates, by the 1790s the contradictions of the Indian in the British imagination were still unresolved. Indeed, if anything they were magnified by the mass production of supposedly primitive materials such as tomahawks and scalping knives in British steel mills, further entangling European modernity and notions of North American savagery. British attempts to appropriate the iconographic symbols of Indianness were, however unknowingly, troubled by the transcultural origins of some of those objects. This appropriative gesture, as in Sir John Caldwell's portrait, embodies the ability of the Indian to be both a consolation to colonialist culture, recalling Vizenor's description of the Indian in dominant cultural imaginings, and a disruption to that culture. While Caldwell attempts to display his own cosmopolitan masculinity by domesticating the Indian,[1] he does so while brandishing a European-made tomahawk that threatens to collapse the distinctions between civility and savagery that he is trying to maintain. Ultimately, however, as Beth Fowkes Tobin suggests, the decontextualization of various tribal cultures into a form of souvenir gives Caldwell power, and he emerges from the painting as the "only true subject."[2] The same can be said of all representations of Indians and their cultural materials in British texts by the end of the eighteenth century; they perform important functions, but ultimately become fragments adorning a modern subject or discourse they helped to shape. This does not diminish their importance, but is rather a reminder of the inherent gap in representational power.

With this in mind, it is necessary to approach European representations with an awareness of their more troubling aspects, particularly their role in attempting to erase Indigenous voices from the historical record. In treaty negotiations at Lancaster, Pennsylvania in 1744, mentioned in the previous chapter, Haudenosaunee leader Canassatego complained that his people are "liable to many other Inconveniences since the *English* came amongst us, and particularly from that Pen-and-Ink Work that is going on at the Table (*pointing to the Secretary*)."[3] For him, British incursions onto their traditional territory were explicitly tied to the exploitation of ambiguities in the language and intent of treaties.[4] Native people viewed agreements with other nations as living acts in need of continual regeneration rather than permanent inscriptions recorded by one clerk and at the mercy of human error or self-interest. Our only account of this transaction, of course, is from the very hand chastened by the Iroquois spokesman, while the Indigenous epistemologies and cultural practices that informed treaty negotiations were seen by the British as transitory and ceremonial as compared to the written account. Yet even after Canassatego's protest over the duplicitous European practice of writing, in which he cites specific examples of the loss of land endured by his people, the British colonial representatives would insist that

> This Treaty ... is what we must rely on, and, being in Writing, is more certain than your Memory. That is the Way the white People have of preserving Transactions of every Kind, and transmitting them down to their Childrens Children for ever, and all Disputes among them are settled by this faithful kind of Evidence, and must be the Rule between the Great King and you. (122)

European writing was the promise of eternal certainty at the expense of Indigenous voices, an enduring text that also performed an act of erasure. This book has focused on the "Pen-and-Ink Work" on the secretary's table, so to speak, or the privileged medium of European negotiation, and has attempted to unravel "this faithful kind of Evidence" as a site of continual slippage. Indeed, the eighteenth century is a productive site in which to discuss and analyse representations of Indians because, in Britain at least, there was no uniform agreement about them. There are, of course, tropes that were regularly deployed, but they do not form a discursive force comparable to, for example, orientalism.[5] Because of this lack of authoritative power, and the ability to elude definition by writers of philosophy, natural history, and fiction, the figure of the Indian possessed a singular rhetorical power in the period. By looking to this earlier discursive formation, I attempt to draw attention to the subsequent mobilization of these tropes in later, and indeed current, cultural contexts. It is my hope that, in eighteenth-century studies, the ongoing recovery of colonialist texts in both pedagogy and scholarship begins to address more available works representing Native people outside of Early American studies. These texts will make the field engage with the political in new and vibrant ways complementary to the important work of postcolonial scholars. While many works were no doubt peripheral even in their own time, the vast body of texts featuring Indians deserves scholarly attention for their insight into not only the colonial past and present of North America, but for their negotiation of the modern world.

Despite the contradictory body of knowledge about Indians in the period, the real fate of Native populations is much more clear; in both the emerging American state and the British colonies which would later become Canada, Indigenous people were subject to harmful, sometimes genocidal, policies and practices whose effects continue to be felt today.[6] As Marshall and Williams note, even the images of Indians which attempted to celebrate or fetishize them ultimately "proved powerless to protect [them]," since the attempt to erase North American Indigenous people from history "was a belief supported by interest, not merely by sentiment."[7] In Britain, the conflict between settlers and Native people was obviously experienced quite differently, and the romanticization of Indians towards the end of the century was largely self-generating, without the input of new accounts of frontier encounters. It is noteworthy that British fictional texts would then cross the Atlantic and inform the sentimental Indians who appeared in nineteenth-century American texts, despite the very real brutality of westward expansion and displacement.[8] Once again, sentiment would prove ineffective against interest.

Given the current circumstance of Native people in North America, where racism, a lack of autonomy, land rights, and other issues are distinct realities, it is important to consider the political efficacy of scholarship of this kind. These images, after all, have had the power to effect historical process, and there is a valid concern that revisiting these often stereotypical representations can reinforce or reiterate the one-sided nature of colonialist texts. I hope that ultimately this work can speak for itself on this issue, but it is worth discussing the validity of such an approach. As I suggest in the introduction, this book does not seek sites of "authentic" voice and representation, but is rather meant to turn the gaze back on the people who constructed this discourse.

In this way it becomes possible to see the entanglements and contingencies which inform the modern self, and to expose the fiction of not only the "Indian," but also the fiction of a coherent and autonomous subject. Western modernity as we know it has not been empowering for most Native populations, and it is important to understand how it is built upon the instrumentalization of Indians in the service of its self-imaging. In this way we can contest the narrative authority of colonialist culture, which continues to exist for Native people in very tangible ways, and work towards a more inclusive modernity.

Notes

Introduction

1 This stadial theory would become more pronounced in the latter half of the century. See, for example, William Robertson's *The History of America* (1777) for an extended look at the "perils and hardships of the savage state" (2.46).

2 See Berkhofer, *The White Man's Indian*, Pearce, *Savagism and Civilization*, Deloria, *Playing Indian*, Francis, *The Imaginary Indian*, and Bataille, *Native American presentations*.

3 Two notable exceptions of literary studies that engage in British texts from the period are Stevens, *The Poor Indians*, and Fulford, *Romantic Indians*. See also Flint, *The Transatlantic Indian*, which covers some late-eighteenth century texts. Bissell, *The American Indian in English Literature of the Eighteenth Century*, is somewhat outdated and more bibliographic than analytical. See also note 5 below.

4 Stephanie Pratt notes that in terms of contact between European and Native people, the eighteenth century lacks the "glamour of the two founding moments," and falls somewhere between the "excitement of European discovery and curiosity in the New World" during the sixteenth century, and the "mystique of the westward-moving frontier as the United States of America came into being" during the nineteenth century; Pratt, *American Indians in British Art*, 4.

5 Bickham, *Savages Within the Empire*, 9, 13; Marshall and Williams, *The Great Map of Mankind*, 203; Bissell, *The American Indian*, 212.

6 See, for example, Bellin, *The Demon of the Continent*, and Sayre, *Les Sauvages Américains*.

7 Nancy Armstrong and Leonard Tennenhouse, it should be noted, claim that Mary Rowlandson's narrative influenced Samuel Richardson's *Pamela*, and captivity more broadly influenced English culture. Armstrong and Tennenhouse, *The Imaginary Puritan*, 202–3.

8 This dates back at least to Pearce, who writes that "The Indian became important for the English mind, not for what he was in and of himself, but rather for what he showed civilized men they were not and must not be" (*Savagism and Civilization*, 5). See also Bellin, *The Demon of the Continent*, 2.

9 Vizenor, *Manifest Manners*, 11.

10 On the subject of Native visitors to Britain, see Vaughan, *Transatlantic Encounters*, Fullager, *The Savage Visit*, and Thrush, *Indigenous London*.

11 I am referring to Pratt's influential use of the term in *Imperial Eyes*.

12 Qtd. in Brown, *Fables of Modernity*, 9.

13 Wilson, *The Island Race*, 30–1.

14 For the role of other figures of alterity in shaping modernity, see Gilroy, *The Black Atlantic*, Brown, *Fables of Modernity*, and Felski, *The Gender of Modernity*.

15 Foucault, "Nietzche, Genealogy, History," 76.

16 Ibid., 81.

17 Ibid., 95.

18 Qtd. in Byrd, *The Transit of Empire*, xxxiii.

19 Ibid., xxxii. For a broader discussion of the issue of postcolonial theory and Indigenous Critical theory, see ibid., xxxi–xxxix.

20 For a discussion of this subject in the context of Canadian literature, see Moss, *Is Canada Postcolonial?*

21 Stevens, "Transatlanticism Now," 95. For important studies that have helped lay the groundwork of transatlantic literary studies, see Gilroy, *The Black Atlantic*, and Roach, *Cities of the Dead*.

22 Weaver, *The Red Atlantic*, 17.

23 Armitage, "Three Concepts of Atlantic History," 23.

24 See especially Wahrman, *The Making of the Modern Self*, but also Wheeler, *The Complexion of Race*, Hudson, "From 'Nation' to 'Race'," and Laqueur, *Making Sex*.

25 See Goldie, *Fear and Temptation*, 13–14, and Deloria, *Playing Indian*, 1–10.

26 Stewart, *On Longing*, 156.

27 Brown, *Fables of Modernity*, 15.

28 Ibid.

29 Ibid.

1 Indians and the Construction of Britishness in the Early Eighteenth Century

1 For visits prior to 1710, see Vaughan, *Transatlantic Encounters*, 1–112.
2 Duncan, *Scott's Shadow*, 248. See also Pincus, *1688: The First Modern Revolution*.
3 See Todorov, *The Conquest of America*, Hart, *Representing the New World*, and Greenblatt, *Marvelous Possessions*.
4 Account is in Woodfield, *English Musicians in the Age of Exploration*, 108–9.
5 His focus is on Spanish writing, but see Pagden, *The Fall of Natural Man*.
6 For a look at the influence of America on British literature, in particular on the role of British failures to colonise it during the early modern period, see Knapp, *An Empire Nowhere*. See also Rome, *The English Embrace of the American Indians*.
7 See Harris, *Indography*.
8 D'Avenant, *The Temple of Love*, 287.
9 For a study of representations of non-Europeans during this period and their reflection of the early modern world view, see Barbour, *Before Orientalism*.
10 On Locke, see Arneil, *John Locke and America*.
11 See Stevens, *The Poor Indians*, 1–33.
12 Casas, *A Short Account of the Destruction of the Indies*, xlii.
13 See Stevens, *The Poor Indians*.
14 Some scholars, including Berkhoefer, suggest that the British did not in fact celebrate this discourse of the noble savage, nor did it achieve any kind of popularity in British texts as compared to the French. Further to this, Ter Ellingson argues that there never was a widely accepted construction of the "noble savage" by Rousseau or anyone else in the period. See Ellingson, *The Myth of the Noble Savage*, and Berkhofer, *The White Man's Indian*.
15 Dryden, *The Conquest of Granada*, Act I, ll. 207–10.
16 Dryden, "Religio Laici," ll. 175–9.
17 Ibid., ll. 185, 188–9.
18 Stevens, *The Poor Indians*, 126.
19 Ibid., 121.
20 Ibid., 124–5.
21 Ibid., 48.
22 As Stevens suggests, Rowlandson "seared the transatlantic English imagination with images of brutal savages." Stevens, *The Poor Indians*, 179.
23 See Colley, *Captives*, 1–22.

24 Ibid., 151.
25 Ockanikon, *A true account*, 3. Stevens suggests that this account nonetheless "reinforce[s] a discourse of benevolent domination." Stevens, *The Poor Indians*, 186–7.
26 Behn, *Oroonoko*, 76–7.
27 Ibid., 77, 122.
28 See, for example, Molineux, "False Gifts/Exotic Fictions," 467–9. For a discussion of the Indians in Behn's *The Widow Ranter*, see Viconsi, "A Degenerate Race."
29 Dennis explains that the actual name is "Agnie," but he uses Angie "for the sake of the better sound." Dennis, *Liberty Asserted*, x.
30 This is quoted by Voltaire; see Voltaire, "Proposal," 123.
31 Anonymous, *The Life of Mr. John Dennis*, 22–3.
32 Cibber, *The Lives of the Poets*, 221–2.
33 Frohock, *Heroes of Empire*, 48–9.
34 Ibid., 24.
35 Ibid., 24–5.
36 For more discussion of this sexualized body and land, see McClintock, *Imperial Leather*, 24–31.
37 Frohock, *Heroes of Empire*, 50, 45.
38 Pratt, *Imperial Eyes*, 7.
39 Pincus, *1688: The First Modern Revolution*, 12.
40 For greater details on this visit, including many of the works produced at the time, see Garratt, *Four Indian Kings*, and Bond, *Queen Anne's American Kings*.
41 See Vaughan, *Transatlantic Encounters*.
42 Anonymous, *The Four Kings of Canada*, 7. For a detailed analysis of these paintings, see Pratt, *American Indians in British Art, 1700–1840*, 35–9, and Pratt, "The Four 'Indian Kings'," 22–35. See also Muller, "From Palace to Longhouse," 26–49.
43 They were, as Eric Hinderaker claims in a mild overstatement, "a miscellaneous collection of young and relatively powerless anglophiles, among whom four of the five tribes of the Iroquois confederacy went unrepresented." Hinderaker, "The 'Four Indian Kings'," 491.
44 Vaughan, *Transatlantic Encounters*, 121.
45 Brown, *Fables of Modernity*, 137.
46 Hinderaker, "The 'Four Indian Kings'," 489–90.
47 Kersey, "Addison's Indian," 266; see also Colley, *Britons*, 1–54.
48 Swift, *The Journal to Stella*, 111.
49 Anonymous, *The Four Kings of Canada*, 4.

50 McGregor, *The Noble Savage in the New World Garden*, 18–19.

51 Kersey, "Addison's Indian," 269.

52 Colley, *Britons*, 11–54.

53 Scholars have debated the extent to which the Mohock terror was real or created by the press; see Guthrie, "'No Truth, or Very Little in the Whole Story'?," 33–56.

54 Wahrman, *The Making of the Modern Self*, and Wheeler, *The Complexion of Race*.

55 Hinderaker, "The 'Four Indian Kings'," 488–9.

56 Genest, *Some Account of the English Stage*," vol. 2, 451–2; see also Roach, *Cities of the Dead*, 119–78.

57 Pratt, "Four Indian Kings," 35 n. 10. See also Richter, "'Some of Them ... Would Always have a Minister with Them'," 471–84.

58 Colley, *Captives*, 164.

59 Qtd. in Vaughan, *Transatlantic Encounters*, 129.

60 Qtd. Hinderaker, "The 'Four Indian Kings'," 524.

61 Ibid., 526.

62 Hulme, *Colonial Encounters*, 141. Mary Dearborn argues that the Pocahontas story is among the "single most important metaphor[s] of female ethnic identity" (*Pocahontas's Daughters*, 97).

63 Hendricks, "Civility, Barbarism, and Aphra Behn's *The Widow Ranter*," 236–7.

64 For a compilation of various versions, see Felsenstein, *English Trader, Indian Maid*.

65 Felsenstein, *English Trader, Indian Maid*, 74.

66 Horejsi, "'A Counterpart to the Ephesian Matron'," 205.

67 Brown, *Ends of Empire*, 119, 112.

68 Hulme, *Colonial Encounters*, 239.

69 Blanchard, "Richard Steele's West Indian Plantation."

70 Bissell, *The American Indian in English Literature of the Eighteenth Century*, 216.

71 Hulme, *Colonial Encounters*, 253–4.

72 Qtd. in Brown, *Fables*, 9.

73 See Whitney, *Primitivism and the Idea of Progress in English Popular Literature of the Eighteenth Century*.

74 See also Horejsi, "A Counterpart to the Ephesian Matron'," 203–6.

75 Anonymous [Boswell], "An Account of the Chief of the Mohock Indians," 339.

76 Their precise relationship is somewhat disputed; see Vaughan, *Transatlantic Encounters*, 220–32, and Pratt, "The Four Indian Kings," 57–67.

2 The Indian as Cultural Critic: Shaping the British Self

1 Miller, *Art and Nature*, v. Cibber was at this time married to Susanna Maria Cibber, born Arne, sister to Thomas Arne and daughter of the upholsterer in Covent Garden with whom the four Indian Kings stayed in 1710.

2 This had more to do with factors outside of the merits of the play itself; there was a perfect storm of public protest against the licensing act and ill will aimed at Miller following his previous play, *The Coffee-House*. See Kern, *Dramatic Satire*, 56.

3 For a discussion of Carew's relationship to broader representations and understandings of gypsies in the period, see Houghton-Walker, *Representations*, 49–51.

4 For a description of the typically "characterless" representation of novels in the period, see Lynch, *The Economy of Character*, 80–119.

5 Rousseau witnessed the success of the play in Paris, though he attributed it not so much to a desire for the audience to imitate the virtuous Indian as to their enjoying the "new and unusual ideas" of nature being represented. See Cro, "Classical Antiquity," 413.

6 See Deloria, *Playing Indian*.

7 See Wheeler, *The Complexion of Race*, 1–48.

8 See, for example, Castro, "Stripped," 104–36.

9 See also Belmein in Charlotte Lennox's *The Life of Harriot Stuart* (1750), who disguises himself as a Mohawk to capture the protagonist. He is "so altered by his Indian dress, that it was impossible to know him" (104), and his villainy is heightened by his hybrid dress.

10 Thompson, *The Making of the English Working Class*, Watt, *The Rise of the Novel*, Colley, *Britons: Forging the Nation*, and Wahrman, *The Making of the Modern Self*. See also Mascuch, *Origins of the Individualist Self*, and Porter et al., *Rewriting the Self*.

11 Brown, *Fables of Modernity*, and Aravamudan, *Tropicopolitans*.

12 Wahrman, *The Making of the Modern Self*, 198. Wahrman has been criticized for his insistence on the rather sudden shift from the older form to modern identity, not to mention the many instances of identity which do not follow his chronology; but I find his description of each period convincing enough as a broader framework through which to see personal identity.

13 Taylor, *Sources of the Self*, 390.

14 Mascuch, *Origins of the Individualist Self*, 8.

15 As Berkhofer notes, "the Noble Savage really pointed to the possibility of progress by civilized man if left free and untrammeled by outworn institutions" (*The White Man's Indian*, 76).

16 See Wahrman, *The Making of the Modern Self*, 259, and Lynch, *The Economy of Character*. Lynch notes that "[i]n several respects, pretenders, old and young, represent the paradigmatic subject of the narratives of social circulation" (90).

17 Stevenson suggests that "for a century, his was one of the most famous names in Britain" (*The Real History of Tom Jones*, 125–6).

18 See Tavor Bannet, *Transatlantic Stories*, 94–8.

19 Wahrman notes that "one could readily sketch the contours of the *ancien régime* of identity … through the public images of its notable gallery of impostors" (259). See also Hug, *Impostures in Early Modern England.*

20 *The Gentleman's Magazine*, no. V (May 1731): 218.

21 Hug, *Impostures*, 6.

22 Tavor Bannet notes, however, that extracts from the text in periodicals often framed the protagonist in a negative light. *Transatlantic Stories*, 94–5.

23 Bannet, 95. On Carew and his title, see Lynch, *The Economy of Character*, 91.

24 Sorenssen, "Vulgar Tongues," 445.

25 Qtd. in Houghton-Walker, *Representations*, 50.

26 See Houghton-Walker, *Representations*.

27 For a study of the lives of transported criminals, see Morgan and Rushton, *Eighteenth-Century Criminal Transportation*.

28 Barrell notes that colonial space in Carew's account "is produced entirely as an economic rather than as a social space, or as a space in which social exchange is presumed to be entirely a function of commercial exchange." Barrell, "Afterword," 237.

29 See Berson, "The Memoirs of Bampfylde Moore Carew."

30 Houghton-Walker, *Representions*, 51.

31 See the discussion of Burke's speech on Indian warfare below.

32 Sandberg, "Beyond Encounters," 7.

33 Well-known Mohawk leader Hendrick was also said to have a similar set of clothes from the king, though the plausibility of this is disputed. Shannon, "Dressing for Success," 14. See also Hinderaker, *The Two Hendricks*, 160.

34 Wilson, "Empire, Gender, and Modernity," 16.

35 Paul Goring notes that politeness, long associated with the culture of eighteenth-century Britain, "could never achieve any settled or secure hegemony," and it was challenged even within the culture by "frenzied Methodist preachers" and others. Goring, *The Rhetoric of Sensibility*, 25.

36 Sorensen, "Vulgar Tongues," 445.

37 Houghton-Walker, *Representions*, 23–4.

38 Wahrman, *The Making of the Modern Self*, 158.

39 Castle, *Masquerade and Civilization*, 2.

40 Ibid., 4. For a discussion of the ways in which masquerades were potentially less liberating for women, see Craft-Fairchild, *Masquerade and Gender*.

41 For an account of his visit, see Vaughan, *Transatlantic Encounters*, 151–62.
See also Alther, *"Tombo-Chiqui,"* 412. For a balanced assessment of the man
and an attempt to debunk the myths around him, see Sweet, "Will the Real
Tomochichi Please Come Forward?"

42 See also Fullagar, *The Savage Visit*.

43 *The Critical Review*, vol. 5 (March 1758): 206. Cleland and Smollett were
friends, so the positive review is not surprising; see Donoghue, *The Fame
Machine*, 127.

44 For a history of Jewish peddlers and hawkers in eighteenth-century Britain, see Endelman, *The Jews of Georgian England*, 166–91.

45 Nussbaum, *Torrid Zones*, 16.

46 Ibid., 15.

47 Garrick, *The Private Correspondence of David Garrick*, 59.

48 Berkhofer, *The White Man's Indian*, 76.

49 Qtd. in Cro, "Classical Antiquity," 413.

50 Brown, *Fables of Modernity*, 14.

51 Ibid., 180.

52 Pratt, *Imperial Eyes*, 6.

53 Cornu notes that Johnson's argument in this instance is to show that the
choice of this white woman to live among Indians "argues no virtues in the
savage life," but showed instead that she had "surrendered her humanity
and had thus impeached the testimony of her action." Cornu, "The Historical Authenticity," 358.

54 Smith, *An historical account*.

55 Snader notes that British writers took little interest in captive women in
both fact and fiction, whereas early American writers keenly explored this
possibility. Snader, *Caught Between Worlds*, 183.

56 Snader suggests authors attempt to show the "failure of adoption to effect
permanent changes in British character." Snader, *Caught*, 173–5.

57 For a non-academic biography of Williamson that does not question the
veracity of his tale, see Skelton, *Indian Peter*.

58 For an earlier account of a transculturated British subject among Central
American Indians, who is somewhat untroubled by the effects of his time
among the Indians, see Lionel Wafer's *A new voyage and description of the
Isthmus of America* (1699).

59 Sussman, "Lismahago's," 603.

60 For an historical account of adoption and torture practices among north-
east Native nations, see Haefeli et al., *Captors and Captives*, 45–163.

61 Sussman, "Lismahago's," 598.
62 Ibid., 602. For a discussion of violent depictions of military life and conflict in other contexts, see McNeil, *The Grotesque Depiction*.
63 Shannon, "King of the Indians," 23, 33–4.
64 These include *Some considerations on the present state of affairs* (1758) and *A brief account of the war in North America* (1760).
65 According to Shannon, it is "the first image of a British subject dressed in Indian clothing published on either side of the Atlantic." While this is not strictly true, if we consider theatrical images such as Anne Bracegirdle dressed as "the Indian Queen" Semernia for her role in Aphra Behn's *The Widdow Ranter*, it is still significant. Shannon, "King of the Indians," 27.
66 See ibid.
67 Ibid.
68 The pipe-tomahawk was itself a transcultural object, symbolic of both war and peace for both Indigenous people and Britons; see Shannon, "Queequeg's Tomahawk," 589–633, and also chapter below.
69 Shannon, "King of the Indians," 7.
70 Barchas, *Graphic Design*, 30.
71 See Blewett, *The Illustration of Robinson Crusoe*, 29–30.
72 Barchas, *Graphic Design*, 47.
73 Ibid., 59.
74 Nolan, "Peter Williamson in America," 23.
75 Shannon, "King of the Indians," 29.
76 Ibid., 27–9.
77 Martin was self-educated, but nonetheless opened a school were he taught a variety of subjects. He sought entry into the Royal Society to increase his credibility, but was not admitted. Millburn. "Martin, Benjamin (*bap.* 1705, *d.* 1782)."
78 For an account of Baron Dieskau's career and context of capture, see Steele, *Betrayals*, 41–54.
79 Among Walker's admirers was Horace Walpole, who wished the artist would tackle more ambitious subjects because of his obvious talent. Worms, "Walker, Anthony (1726–1765)."
80 Shannon, "King of the Indians," 29.
81 See Leslie Tobias Olsen. "A tale of two Indians." The John Carter Brown Library. June 2008. Brown University. 26 November 2010. [http://www.brown.edu/Facilities/John_Carter_Brown_Library/I%20found%20it%20JCB/June08.html].
82 Colley, *Captives*, 192.
83 Shannon, "King of the Indians," 44.

84 For many instances of whites living among Native people, see Axtell, *White Indians*.

85 Wahrman, *The Making of the Modern Self*, 214–15.

86 See Hinderaker, *The Two Hendricks*.

87 Qtd. in Shannon, "Dressing," 14.

88 *Gentleman's and London Magazine*, Vol. XXIV (September 1755): 457.

89 See especially Douglas, "Britannia's Rule and the It-Narrator," Kibbie, "Circulating Anti-Semitism," Martinez, "From Peruvian Gold to British Guinea," and Borque, "Cultural Currency."

90 *Critical Review*, May 1760, 419.

91 Qtd. in Taylor, Alan, *The Divided Ground*, 48.

92 For a biography of Johnson which includes this and other personal stories, see O'Toole, *White Savage*.

93 Furthermore, as Tim Fulford suggests in relation to Smollett's depiction of conflict in the colonies in *Humphry Clinker*, "[c]olonial war … is more grotesque than epic" (*Romantic Indians*, 108).

94 See Martinez, "From Peruvian Gold to British Guinea," 189.

95 Page references to Oxford edition.

96 Sussman, "Lismahago's," 603.

97 Wallace, *Imperial Characters*, 100.

98 Fulford, *Romantic Indians*, 108.

99 Ibid., 110.

3 Captivity Narratives and Colonialism

1 Césaire, *Discourse on Colonialism*, 41.

2 Rutherfurd's narrative did not appear in print until 1958 (see below).

3 Slotkin, *Regeneration Through Violence*, 94–5.

4 For a brief overview of this scholarship, see Goodman, "Money Answers All Things," n. 1.

5 Colley, *Captives*, 140.

6 See Cutter, "The Female Indian Killer Memorialized," 10–26. The New Hampshire Historical Store also carries a "bobblehead" with "A Mother's Revenge" inscribed on its base.

7 Burnham, *Captivity and Sentiment*, 4.

8 For works that focus on non-Puritan eighteenth-century narratives, see Colley, *Captives*, and Joe Snader, *Caught Between Worlds*.

9 This dismissal of later narratives goes back some time; see Pearce, "The Significances of the Captivity Narrative," 1–20. Pearce insists that "[t]he first, and greatest, of the captivity narratives are simple, direct religious

documents," whereas in the later narratives, "the propagandist value ... became more and more apparent" (2–3). He writes that later narratives came almost exclusively to serve as propaganda in order to "register as much hatred of the French and Indians as possible" (6), and maintains that depictions of Indian cruelty, as in Peter Williamson's *French and Indian Cruelty* (1757), are merely "vulgar, fictional, and pathological" (9). Vaughan and Clark, in their influential collection of narratives, maintain that later captivity narratives of the eighteenth century evolved into "ornate and often fictionalized accounts that catered to more secular and less serious tastes." See Vaughan and Clark, *Puritans Among the Indians*, 3.

10 See Bannet, *Transatlantic Stories*, 61–3, and Ebersole, *Captured by Texts*, 19.

11 Derounian, "Publication," 247.

12 White, *The Middle Ground*, 237.

13 Colley, *Captives*, 161.

14 See Nolan, "Peter Williamson in America," 23–9.

15 Williamson, *French and Indian Cruelty* (1757), 22.

16 Ibid., 46.

17 Colley, *Captives*, 182–5.

18 Williamson, *French and Indian Cruelty*, 48.

19 Steele claims the work is "a clever piece of purposeful literature," though other historians such as Brumwell treat it as at least a potentially true account. See Steele, *Setting All the Captives Free*, 410–11, and Brumwell, *Redcoats*, 170.

20 This includes men born in the colonies who strongly identified themselves as British; as Philip D. Morgan suggests, "[f]or exiles, Britishness became a reality abroad in ways it never did at home" (45). See Morgan, "Encounters," 42–78. It is worth noting that the texts printed only in the colonies, such as Eastburn's, generally have more religious aspirations than those by Grace, Saunders, Kirk, and Williamson.

21 For the privileging of the importance of the passive female as protagonist, see especially Slotkin, *Regeneration*, and Toulouse, *The Captive's Position*.

22 Rutherfurd, *Narrative of a Captivity*, 259.

23 Foucault, *Discipline and Punish*, 43.

24 Quoted in Mitchell, "The Violence of Sympathy," 321–41.

25 Williamson, *French and Indian Cruelty*, 46.

26 See Snader, *Caught Between Worlds*, 97.

27 Mary Rowlandson, *The soveraignty & goodness of God* (1682).

28 See Colley, *Britons*; "Britishness and Otherness."

29 Smith, *An historical account*, 29.

30 For an account of British missionizing efforts and the manipulation of public affect, see Stevens, *The Poor Indians*.

31 Axtell, "The White Indians," 326.

32 Rutherfurd, *Narrative*, 232.

33 Williamson, *French and Indian Cruelty*, 12.

34 Brown, *A Plain Narrative*, 15.

35 Ebersole, *Captured by Texts*, 195.

36 Anne McClintock argues that "the staging of symbolic disorder by the privileged can merely preempt challenges by those who do not possess the power to stage ambiguity with comparable license or authority." She suggests that "mimicry and cross-dressing" can be "a technique not of colonial subversion, but of surveillance"; the colonial agent knows that "passing 'down' the cultural hierarchy is permissible; passing 'up' is not," and there is therefore an "other side of mimicry: the colonial who passes as Other the better to govern." I would argue that this is emphatically not occurring in these captivity narratives. See McClintock, *Imperial Leather*, 69–70.

37 Grace, *The history of the life and sufferings of Henry Grace*, 15–16.

38 Rutherfurd, *Narrative*, 237.

39 Bhabha, *The Location of Culture*, 86.

40 Qtd. in Vizenor, *Manifest Manners*, 13.

41 Smethurst, *A narrative*, 12–13.

42 Fleming, *A Narrative of Suffering and Deliverance*, 13–14.

43 Robert Eastburn, *A faithful narrative*, 13.

44 Rutherfurd, *Narrative*, 246.

45 Deloria, *Playing Indian*, 32.

46 For early American narratives of transculturation, see, for example, Smith, *An account of the remarkable occurrences in the life and travels of Col. James Smith* (1799) and Seaver, *A narrative of the life of Mrs. Mary Jemison* (1824). For a discussion of captivity narratives published during and after the American Revolution, see Colley, *Captives*, 203–38, and Denn, "Captivity Narratives of the American Revolution," 575–82.

47 Goldie, *Fear and Temptation*, 16.

48 Quoted in Axtell, "The White Indians," 335.

49 Pratt, *Imperial Eyes*, 185.

50 Williamson, *French and Indian Cruelty*, 35.

51 Rutherfurd, *Narrative*, 274.

52 Snader, *Caught Between Worlds*, 103.

53 Saunders, *The Horrid Cruelty of the Indians*, 19, 16.

54 Grace, *History*, 55.

55 Eastburn, *A faithful narrative*, 31, 42.

56 Grace, *History*, 56.

57 Ibid., 42.

58 Williamson, *French and Indian Cruelty*, 103.

59 Williamson, *French and Indian Cruelty*, 5th ed., 118–19.

60 Williamson, *The trial of divorce*, xxiii–xxiv. See also Colley, *Captives*, 190–2.

61 Quoted in Nolan, "Peter Williamson," 28.

62 Colley records that "[i]n just two months, October and November 1758, over sixty American colonists captured … were shipped from New France to England, where they were fed and clothed for several months before finally being transported home." Colley, *Captives*, 173.

63 Jean Lowry, *A Journal of the Captivity of Jean Lowry*, 17.

64 Nelson, *New Jersey Biographical and Genealogical Notes*, 97.

65 Eastburn, *A faithful narrative*, 40.

66 Grace, *History*, 13, and Rutherfurd, *Narrative*, 232, 6–7, 17.

67 Colley, "Going Native, Telling Tales," 170–93, 192.

68 McClintock, *Imperial Leather*, 72.

69 Smith, *Decolonizing Methodologies*, 34.

4 Novel Indians: *Tsonnonthouan* and the Commodification of Culture

1 Bissell, *American Indian*, 96.

2 There has historically been very little critical discussion of this book; James R. Foster complained in 1953 that "the attention paid to Tsonnonthouan by modern scholarship is not very flattering" (348), and this is still the case. See Foster, "A Forgotten Noble Savage," 348–59. The authorship is difficult to track, but Foster suggests it could be Charles Johnstone, author of *Chrysal; or, The Adventures of a Guinea* (1760); another possibility, based on an attribution in a gentleman's book catalogue and a shared sense of humour, is satirist Archibald Campbell, whose *Lexiphanes* (1767), a satire on Dr Johnson, had the same bookseller as *Tsonnonthouan*. Another catalogue lists the author as "Dr. Kenrick," presumably referring to the infamous pamphleteer and playwright William Kenrick; however, based on stylistic differences, this seems less likely.

3 Weston, "The Noble Primitive," 59–71.

4 Ibid., 66–7. John Shebbeare, *Lydia, or Filial Piety*, 4 vols. (London: J. Scott, 1755).

5 See Brown, *Fables of Modernity*, 177–220. Cleland's Tombo-Chiqui, as discussed in chapter 2, is a notable exception. For a slightly different view of noble savages as bourgeois critique, see White, *Tropics of Discourse*, 183–96.

6 See Fulford, *Romantic Indians*, 30–4, 101–19, and Weston, "The Noble Primitive," 68. See also Ellingson, *The Myth of the Novel Savage*, in which the very premise that the British believed in the "noble savage" is denied.

7 Bakhtin, *Problems of Dostoevsky's Poetics*, 114–19. See also Weinbrot, *Menippean Satire Reconsidered*, 6–7.

8 Weston, "The Noble Primitive," 67 and Bakhtin, *Problems*, 114.

9 Charlevoix, *Letters*, 113.

10 Weston, "The Noble Primitive," 67.

11 Examples include Johnstone's *Chrysal* and anonymously written texts such as *The Memoirs and Interesting Adventures of an Embroidered Waistcoat* (1751), *The Adventures of a Corkskrew* (1775), and *The Adventures of a Watch!* (1788). See Blackwell, ed., *The Secret Life of Things*.

12 Douglas, "Britannia's Rule," 149.

13 McKendrick et al., *The Birth of a Consumer Society*, 9.

14 Pratt, "From Cannassatego to Outalissi," 60.

15 *The Adventurer*, vol. 1, no. 67 (London: J. Payne, 1753): 397–402. Hereafter cited in the text by page number.

16 *Tsonnonthouan* appeared just months after the Treaty of Paris ended the Seven Years' War in Europe and its North American offshoot, the French and Indian War. This ceded large portions of North America to the English, which forced the British government and its people to deal with Native populations more closely than they ever had. This lack of experience led, within a matter of months, to Pontiac's Rebellion, a widespread Indigenous resistance to failed British policy that would last for three years. The Royal Proclamation of 1763, meant to slow white settler incursions into Native land, failed to end the rebellion. See Bickham, *Savages Within the Empire*, 113–33.

17 Walpole, *The Letters of Horace Walpole*, 402–3.

18 Phillips and Idiens, "A Casket," 23.

19 For a discussion of the significance of the sentimental Indian to British culture, and Colden's contribution to it, see Fulford, *Romantic Indians*, 41.

20 Publication noted in *Gentleman's Magazine* XXXIII (1763): 259, *London Magazine* XXX (1763): 452, though the title is misspelled. *Critical Review* XV (May 1763): 378–88. *Monthly Review* XXVIII (June 1763): 492–3. *British Magazine* IV (May 1763): 257–9. It is possible, according to Foster, that Smollett wrote the favourable review in the *Critical*. See also Spector, "Smollett's Use of *Tsonnonthouan*," 112–13.

21 *British Magazine* IV (May 1763): 257–9.

22 A heavily abridged and cleaned-up French edition was printed in 1778 and a more faithful translation was printed in 1787 in Basel. See Foster, "A Forgotten Noble Savage," 348, 350–1. There is a 1974 Garland facsimile edition of the original novel.

23 Foster, "A Forgotten Noble Savage," 350.

24 Brown, *Fables of Modernity*, 142.
25 Ibid., 137.
26 Bosch, *Labyrinth of Digressions*, 12, 56.
27 Keymer, *Sterne, the Moderns, and the Novel*, 61.
28 Bosch, *Labyrinths*, 12–13.
29 Sabin et al., *A Dictionary*, 556. It is worth noting that neither the *Monthly* nor the *Critical* compared *Tsonnonthouan* to *Tristram Shandy*, favourably or otherwise. The *Critical* praises it as having a design which is "altogether *sui generis*," and this "originality" distinguishes it from "those flimsy productions which appear every day, under the name of adventures, memoirs, or romances," but are "a sorry imitation of some successful pattern, supported by borrowed features, and pilfered scenes" (378). The review immediately before *Tsonnonthouan* in the *Critical* is of comedic actor George Alexander Steven's *The Dramatic History of Master Edward, Miss Ann, Mrs. Llwhuddwhydd, and Others*, which is described as a "hodge-podge, without head or tail," whose "irregularity" can "certainly be compared even with the celebrated *Life and Opinions of Tristram Shandy*, a book which seems to have given rise to this, and many other monstrous productions" (373).
30 Charlevoix, *Journal*, 48.
31 Foster notes that details on the killing of bears, corrupt medicine men, inept European doctors, and the meaning of dreams come directly from Lebeau's *Avantures*, while the contemporary piece in the *Critical* observed that the "game of the platter" and other details came from Charlevoix. Foster, "A Forgotten Noble Savage," 352, 385.
32 *Monthly Review* XXVIII (June 1763): 492.
33 *Monthly Review* XXIII (December 1760): 425.
34 As cited in the previous chapter, see Taylor, *Sources of the Self*, Wahrman, *The Making of the Modern Self*, and Colley, *Britons*. For the role of consumption on subjectivity, see McKendrick et al., *The Birth of a Consumer Society*, Brewer and Porter, eds., *Consumption and the World of Goods*, and Sussman, *Consuming Anxieties*.
35 Sussman, *Consuming*, 84.
36 McKendrick et al., *The Birth*, 11.
37 Charlevoix, *Letters*, 250–1.
38 Preston, "Smollett," 232.
39 Bosch, *Labyrinths*, 133.
40 Given the rarity of the name in the period, and that Goldsmith was likely familiar with *Tsonnonthouan* because of its appearance in the *British Magazine*, it seems reasonable to speculate that Goldsmtih's Diggory in *She Stoops to Conquer* at the least borrows his name from Bunce.

41 Beverley, *History*, 16.
42 Mancall, *Deadly Medicine*, 43.
43 Thomson, *An enquiry*, 75–6.
44 No copies of this text from New York have been located, if it in fact ever existed.
45 Quoted in Mancall, *Deadly Medicine*, 116.
46 See Sussman, *Consuming Anxieties*.
47 Occom, *Collecting Writings*, 193.
48 Colley, *Britons*, 1–100.
49 *A Brief Narrative of the Indian Charity-School*, 8.
50 Beverley, *The History and Present State of Virginia*, 63–4.
51 Mancall, *Deadly Medicine*, 24.
52 Walpole, *Letters*, 455.
53 Mancall, *Deadly Medicine*, 54.
54 Charlevoix, *Journal*, 219–20.
55 Thomson, *Enquiry*, 76.
56 Sussman, *Consuming Anxieties*, 85.
57 See also Fulford, *Romantic Indians*, 20.
58 *Critical* XV, 388, 383; *Monthly* XXVIII, 492.
59 See Stevens, *The Poor Indians*.
60 Ibid., 11–12, 125.
61 Dartmouth College, *About the Native American Program*. http://www.dartmouth.edu/~nap/about/ (accessed 1 May 2009). For letters written by Occom during his unhappy time in Britain, in which he frets over the poverty of his family and his rebellious son back home, see Occom, *The Collected Writings*, 76–85.
62 Hodgkins, *Reforming Empire*.
63 *Monthly* XXVIII, 492.
64 Brown, "Reading Race and Gender," 426.
65 Sussman, *Consuming Anxieties*, 88.

5 Becoming Indians: Sentiment and the Hybrid British Subject

1 See, for example, Wheeler, *The Complexion of Race*, 291–302.
2 See Deloria, *Playing Indian*.
3 Again, on adoption and torture as fear of incorporation, see Sussman, "Lismahago's."
4 Bergland, *The National Uncanny*.
5 Bergland, *The National Uncanny*, 9, 48.
6 Deloria, *Playing Indian*, and Goldie, *Fear and Temptation*, 13.

7 See Suleri, *The Rhetoric of English India*, 49–74.

8 As Fulford notes, "Indians, in British accounts, were often shaped by the complexities of imperial politics outside, as well as inside, America." He argues, not unlike Bergland but in a different context, that Indians were "uncanny figures because they suggested that at the heart of the British self was a kinship with the foreign, a kinship that Britons wanted to explore but were frightened to acknowledge." See Fulford, *Romantic Indians*, 31–2.

9 Richard Slotkin argues that the shared trait in European representations of relations between British colonists and Indians, whether positive or negative, is "the association of the Indian with the forces of the unconscious, the suppressed drives and desires that undergulf the intellect." Slotkin, *Regeneration Through Violence*, 205.

10 For a compelling discussion of Britons dressed as Indians, and vice versa, in paintings, see Tobin, *Picturing Imperial Power*, 81–109.

11 Celia Brickman argues that modern psychoanalysis is similarly predicated on colonial ideas of otherness and regression: "[T]he abjected past from which the psychoanalytic subject is believed to have emerged includes the maternal (infantile) past, the evolutionary (racial) past of humankind, the social (racial/ethnic group structure) past, and the cultural (religio-symbolic) past. Domination and subordination were the political relations of primitivity; enthrallment was the psychology of primitivity; religion was the ideology of primitivity; disgust and repugnance were the emotional affects provoked by primitivity; and non-white was the skin color of primitivity." See *Aboriginal Populations*, 171.

12 Bhabha, *The Location of Culture*, 82.

13 Ibid., 86.

14 Tim Fulford argues that "[i]t is not too much to say that Romanticism would not have taken the form it did without the complex and ambiguous image of Indians that so intrigued both the writers and their readers." See *Romantic Indians*, 12.

15 Rosaldo, "Imperialist Nostalgia," 107–22. See also Sayre, *The Indian Chief*, 5.

16 As Fulford notes, Ponteach is "the first fully-fleshed Native American hero in English literature," possessing "authority, dignity, honesty, wisdom, and a strong sense of political justice." *Romantic Indians*, 21.

17 Bickham, *Savages*, 65–112.

18 Ibid., 61.

19 Ibid., 62, 63.

20 *The Scots Magazine*, vol. 40 (October 1778): 523. For another account of the speech, see O'Neill, *Edmund Burke and the Conservative Logic of Empire*, 73–5.

21 Bickham, *Savages*, 70.
22 Adair, *History*, 379.
23 Ibid., 379.
24 On Brant's 1776 visit, see Vaughan, *Transatlantic Encounters*, 225–30.
25 The story first appeared at the height of the popular success of so-called propagandist captivity narratives, in *The Royal Magazine* 5 (July 1761): 27–9. Upon Kellet's death at Bath in 1788, *The British Mercury*, among other periodicals, reported that this story even fooled the Abbé Raynal, who published it in his works. *The British Mercury* 31 (July 28) 154–5.
26 While it is more in the nineteenth-century context, Colin G. Calloway explores the similar experiences and representations of Indians and Highlanders in the British empire. See *White People, Indians, and Highlanders*.
27 For a discussion of sympathy and violence, see Bersani, "Representation and Its Discontents," 145–62.
28 This image became synonymous with Indian captivity beginning at least with W.R. Chetwood's *The voyages, dangerous adventures and imminent escapes of Captain Richard Falconer* (London: T. Jauncy, 1720). The frontispiece of the text depicts the protagonist in this exact position. See Snader, *Caught Between Worlds*, 185, fig. 8.
29 Qtd. in Fenton, *The Great Law and the Longhouse*, 389.
30 For an exploration of the rise of the family unit and domestic space, see McKeon, *The Secret History of Domesticity*, 110–61.
31 Wahrman, *The Making of the Modern Self*, 233.
32 Little is known about who the anonymous author was, or even if she was in fact a woman. In all likelihood, however, the author was female, possibly from the colonies. See Michelle Burnham's introduction to the text, 22–4.
33 Kalata Vaccaro, "'Recollection ... sets my busy imagination to work'," 134.
34 See Smith-Rosenberg, *This Violent Empire*, 207–49.
35 For a history of the Pocahontas story in the American context, see Tilton, *Pocahontas*.
36 See, for example, Benjamin West's portrait of Colonel Guy Johnson.
37 Stevens, *Poor Indians*, 2.
38 Wheeler, "Desire," 316.
39 Ibid.
40 McClintock, *Imperial Leather*, 69.
41 Ibid., 70.
42 Ibid.
43 Introduction to *The Female American*, 16.

44 These Indians are, presumably, not meant to be Indigenous to the Caribbean but from somewhere near Virginia, based on their shared language with Unca. This non-specificity is typical of the Indians in this novel. However, on British representations of Indigenous Caribbean peoples, see Hulme, *Colonial Encounters*.

45 *The Female American*, 21.

46 See Fields, "Samson Occom," 14–20.

47 Stevens, *Poor Indians*, 6–7.

48 Ibid., 19.

49 Ibid.

50 Mackenzie, *Miscellaneous Works*, iv.

51 Sorensen, "Savages," 75.

52 As Sorensen argues, "[i]f *The Man of Feeling* represents the decline of the ambiguous discourse of sensibility, *The Man of the World* seems to pick up this dead-end, remodelling a passionate man of feeling by giving him the heroic qualities associated with stoical Indians." Sorensen, "Savages," 84.

53 John Rae notes that Smith cared little for the popular form of the novel, and did not own any Fielding, Richardson, or Smollett. See Rae, *Life of Adam Smith*, 348.

54 Fulford, *Romantic Indians*, 145.

55 Ibid.

56 Ibid.

57 See Bergland, *The National Uncanny*, 1–24, and Stevens, *The Poor Indians*, 160–94.

58 *The Edinburgh Review* (July 1755): 131–5.

59 Sorensen suggests that in both Smith and Mackenzie, the stoical Indian presents "an attractive, if highly ambivalent, alternative to the modern passionate self." Sorensen, "Savages," 74. Maureen Harkin notes that "[t]he vision of discipline and self-denial offered by the figure of the impartial spectator clearly offers something of a parallel to the self-control of the savage." Harkin, "Adam Smith's Missing History," 442.

60 Ellingson dismisses the notion that the "noble savage" was a concept of the eighteenth century, and suggests that Mackenzie's seeming reference to it is "specifically identified as a construction of the imagination rather than as reality, and the context is not that of an idealization of the savage." The extent to which the latter is true can be debated, but my point is not that it is a concept of absolute idealization. Ellingson, *The Myth of the Noble Savage*, 5.

61 See Stevens, *The Poor Indians*, 19.

62 *The Monthly Mirror* (May 1806): 293.

63 *Critical Review* (January 1791): 203.

64 *Monthly Review* (April 1791): 430.

65 Her name could also be a reference to "Morano," the black pirate in John Gay's *Polly* who is in fact a Briton in racial drag. Her name is spelled "Maraino" in the play.

66 Sussman, "Lismahago's," 598–9.

67 For a study of the rise of human rights discourse in the eighteenth-century novel, see Hunt, *Inventing Human Rights*, 35–69.

68 Hutchings, *Romantic Ecologies*, 114.

69 See Vaughan, *Transatlantic Encounters*, 165–75.

70 O'Keeffe, *Recollections*, 45–6.

71 Ibid., 46.

72 Carr, "And the truest schools," 148.

73 Ibid., 153 n. 44.

74 Pratt, "Representatives," 113.

75 Ibid., 115. Baynton, however, claims that Bowles was in fact born in Maryland.

76 *Critical Review* (January 1791): 238.

77 *Monthly Review* (April 1791): 356.

78 See, for example, the basket-maker in Thomas Day's *The History of Sandford and Merton* (London, 1783) and "The basket-maker, an original fragment," in *The Village Orphan: A Tale for Youth* (London, 1797). Robinson Crusoe also manufactures baskets, recalling watching the craft as a child and helping the basket-makers in the town of his father.

79 In the nineteenth century, baskets rather than tomahawks often became iconic of Indian identity, as in depictions of Huron-Wendats. Phillips, *Trading Identities*, 137.

80 O'Keeffe wrote a pantomime called *Omai, or A Trip Around the World* (1785), about the Pacific islander brought to London by Cook. See Carr, "And the truest schools," 147.

81 As Carr notes, "it is the good fortune of the Indianised European, not of the Indians, that ends the story" (ibid., 151).

82 Like *The Female American*, part of this increased attention is owing to a well-edited Broadview edition. While Bage's novels were respected in their time, interest waned until the later twentieth century with, as Gary Kelly notes, "the renewed attention to political and ideological aspects of literature." See Kelly, "Bage, Robert (1728?–1801)."

83 Santee Sioux people.

84 See Carr, "And the truest schools," 144.

85 Fulford notes that "[t]he only good aristocrat, Bage suggests, is an Indianised one, a hybrid of true civilization and Native American savagery, a man that neither culture could have produced alone." Fulford, *Romantic Indians*, 114.

86 For a different Jacobin vision of Indians and the corrupt gentry, see Smith,
   The Old Manor House. The character Orlando returns from his Iroquois
   captivity as a spectral, damaged figure, but is still able to secure a wealthy
   inheritance. Wolf-hunter, the Indian who saved Orlando from his cruel
   brothers, is forgotten upon the Englishman's return to Britain.
87 Qtd. in Wilson, *The Island Race*, 31.

6 Native North American Material Culture in the British Imaginary

1 "Bad liquor, esp. adulterated spirits." *OED*.
2 Smollett, *Humphry Clinker*, 240–1.
3 *The World*, no. 102 (1754): 285–6.
4 In addition to the paintings addressed in this chapter, see also Rigal,
   "Framing the Fabric," for a discussion of *Penn's Treaty with the Indians* and
   the role of material culture.
5 Brown, "Thing Theory," 4.
6 Appadurai, "Introduction," 5.
7 Roach, *Cities of the Dead*, 120.
8 Ibid. See also Laurier Turgeon: "[T]he object was the means by which the
   Amerindian conceived and assessed the other, at least in initial contacts
   with the European." Turgeon, "The Tale of the Kettle," 1–29.
9 Schiavo, Jr, and Salvucci, eds. *Iroquois Wars I*, 117.
10 See Middleton, *Pontiac's War*, 20–1.
11 See Turgeon, "The Tale of the Kettle." See also Richter, *Trade, Land, Power*, 60–1;
   both authors note the word should be "appropriation," not "acculturation."
12 "A blanket manufactured for barter or sale in trading with North American
   Indians." *OED*.
13 Neolin would in turn inspire Pontiac, who adopted his moral code; see
   White, *The Middle Ground*, 284.
14 Ibid., 283.
15 Turgeon, "The Tale of the Kettle," and Richter, *Trade, Land, Power*, 13–41.
16 Bickham has done some work in looking at North American material culture;
   see especially "'A Conviction of the Reality of Things'," 29–47. He does not,
   however, see more than an assertion of European superiority in its display.
17 *The Parliamentary History of England*, vol. XIX, 489–90.
18 *Observer*, issue 439, Sunday, 18 May 1800.
19 Woodward, "The Metal Tomahawk," 9.
20 Acquisition dates are uncertain for many, but see Am1987,Q.13,
   Am,Dc.72.a-b; British Museum catalogue.
21 Catlin, *Manners*, 236.

22 Timberlake, *Memoirs*, 51–2.

23 See Fulford and Hutchings, *Native Americans*, and Jace Weaver, *The Red Atlantic*.

24 Spitta, *Misplaced Objects*, 5.

25 Qtd. in Greenblatt, "Resonance and Wonder," 31.

26 Ibid., 31–2.

27 See Evans and Marr, eds. *Curiosity and Wonder*.

28 There are numerous studies on such collections, but see especially Bredekamp, *The Lure of Antiquity*, 27. For a look at a similar tradition specifically in England, see Arnold, *Cabinets for the Curious*.

29 For a look at the shift from Renaissance to Enlightenment epistemologies, and the corresponding role of wonder and wonders, see Daston and Park, *Wonders and the Order of Nature*, and Evans and Marr, eds. *Curiosity and Wonder*.

30 Bujok, "Ethnographica," 19. See also Feest, "European Collecting," 3, and Bredekamp, *The Lure of Antiquity*, 35.

31 Yaya, "Wonders of America," 173–88.

32 Benedict, *Curiosity*, 1–23.

33 Bredekamp, *The Lure of Antiquity*, 28.

34 For a brief description of these categories, see Bubenik, *Reframing Albrecht Dürer*, 52.

35 Bredekamp, *The Lure of Antiquity*, 34.

36 Yaya, "Wonders," 177.

37 D'Avenant, *The Temple of Love*, 287. It is also worth remembering Aphra Behn's well-known gift of feathers from Surinam, used in *The Indian Queen* and *The Indian Emperor*, both discussed in chapter 1.

38 Yaya, "Wonders," 177. See also Daston and Park, *Wonders*, 158.

39 Mason, *Infelicities*, 83.

40 Yaya, "Wonders," 178.

41 For an account, see Wintroub, "Civilizing the Savage," 465–94.

42 Yaya, "Wonders," 181, and Feest, "European Collecting," 4–5.

43 For a detailed look at the origins of British collecting, see Arnold, *Cabinets for the Curious*.

44 MacGregor, "The Cabinet of Curiosities," 147.

45 See Maltby, *The Black Legend in England*. For a look at different authors' deployment of Las Casas, particularly Defoe, see Runnell, "Defoe and the Black Legend," 13–28.

46 In the decades following his death, Cope's cabinet was remembered in at least two very similar bawdy songs by Sir John Mennes and Alexander Brome. Mennes would write in "The Fart censured in the Parliament House" (1655), "Sir *Walter Cope* said, this Fart 'twas let, / Might well have broke ope his privy Cabinet," while Brome's "Upon the Parliament Fart" (1662) similarly jests,

"Quoth Sir *Walter Cope* 'twas so readily let, / I would it were sweet enough for my Cabinet." Variations of the verse were published into the eighteenth century.

47 Pearce, *The Collector's Voice*, 23–4.

48 Ibid., 24.

49 Vaughan, *Transatlantic Encounters*, 43.

50 Ibid., 44.

51 Qtd. in Burns, *An Age of Wonders*, 63.

52 Qtd. in Swann, *Curiosities and Texts*, 59.

53 Schnapp, "Ancient Europe and Native Americans," 60.

54 MacGregor, ed., *Tradescant's Rarities*.

55 On its composition see Swann, *Curiosities and Texts*, 38–42.

56 See Altick, *The Shows of London*, 12.

57 Qtd. in Stewart, *On Longing*, 162.

58 Qtd. in Swann, *Curiosities and Texts*, 4.

59 See Altick, *The Shows of London*, 13. For greater background on Hubert and the Royal Society, see Hunter, *Establishing the New Science*, 129–36.

60 Hunter, *Establishing*, 123.

61 Von Uffenbach, *London in 1710*, 98.

62 Ibid., 98. Also qtd. in Altick, *The Shows of London*, 14.

63 Von Uffenbach, *London in 1710*, 98.

64 Thomas, "Compiling 'God's great book [of] universal nature'," 2.

65 Brears, "Ralph Thoresby," 215.

66 Ibid.

67 For a look at what definitively survives from Thoresby's original collection, see Connell and Boyd, "Material from the 'Musaeum' of Ralph Thoresby (1658–1725)," 31–40.

68 Anonymous, *The Four Kings of Canada*, 36; this description is taken, however, from Beverley, *The History and Present State of Virginia* (1705), 20–1, which in turn borrowed it from Hennepin.

69 *The Connoisseur* no. 76 (Thursday, 10 July 1755): 41.

70 For his part, Timberlake interpreted the Cherokee practice of burial along-side possessions as "probably introduced to prevent avarice, and, by preventing hereditary acquisitions, make merit the sole means of acquiring power, honour, and riches." See Timberlake, *The Memoirs of Lieut. Henry Timberlake*, 68.

71 Blair claims wampum to be related to the "speaking by action" as used by Old Testament prophets, but only suggests that it is used to "declare their meaning" as much as speech without specifying how (Blair, *Lectures* vol. 1, 108); Beattie compares wampum to quipos, and notes it is "said to express, I know not how, the particulars of the transaction" (Beattie, *The Theory of Language*, 113).

72 Walpole, *Letters* vol. 7, 489.
73 Gordon, *Occasional Thoughts*, 44–5.
74 Todd, "Your Humble Servant Shows Himself," 132.
75 Bickham, *Savages*, 43.
76 *The European Magazine, and London Review* vol. 1 (January 1782): 21.
77 See King, "Woodlands Artifacts from the Studio of Benjamin West," 34–47.
78 See Green Fryd, "Rereading the Indian," 78–83.
79 King, *First Peoples*, 69.
80 Green Fryd, "Rereading the Indian," 74.
81 Swann, *Curiosities and Texts*, 9.
82 See Arnold, *Cabinets for the Curious*, 88–9.
83 *London Evening Post* (18–20 December 1777) and Tickell, *Anticipation* (1778), 64.
84 Tobin, "Wampum Belts," 692–3.
85 For a further discussion of this portrait, see also Tobin, *Picturing Imperial Power*, 84–91.

Conclusion

1 In replicating the Indian warrior, Tobin suggests, Caldwell projects "an illusion of Indianness, but it is an Indianness rendered powerless by its incoherence." *Picturing Imperial Power*, 85.
2 Ibid., 86.
3 Colden, *History of the Five Indian Nations* (1747), 105.
4 Perhaps the most notorious instance of this in the eighteenth century is the 1737 Walking Purchase; on this treaty and the role of writing, see Shoemaker, *A Strange Likeness*, 61–4.
5 Though orientalism itself, as some critics note, was also lacking in consistent authoritative power in the eighteenth century. See Zuroski Jenkins, *A Taste for China*.
6 For a valuable overview of colonization across the Americas beginning in 1492, see Wright, *Stolen Contents*. For a look at the Canadian residential school system, whose legacy is very much present today, see Milloy, *A National Crime*.
7 Marshall and Williams, *The Great Map of Mankind*, 221–2.
8 Kate Flint notes the British origins of the trope of the "dying Indian," for example, in *The Transatlantic Indian*, 34–40.

Bibliography

Primary

Adair, James. *The History of the American Indians*. London: Edward and Charles Dilly, 1775.

Addison, Joseph, and Richard Steele. *The Spectator*. 8 vols. London: S. Buckley, 1712.

Anonymous. *A Brief Narrative of the Indian Charity-School*. London: J. & W. Oliver, 1766.

Anonymous. *The four kings of Canada. Being a succinct account of the four Indian princes lately arriv'd from North America*. London: John Baker, 1710.

Anonymous. *The Life of Mr. John Dennis, the Renowned Critick. In Which Are Likewise Some Observations on Most of the Poets and Criticks, His Contemporaries. Not Written by Mr. Curll*. London: Printed for J. Roberts in Warwick-Lane, 1734.

Anonymous. *Modern midnight conversation, or matrimonial dialogues*. London: T. Evans, 1775.

Anonymous. *Memoirs of the life and adventures of Tsonnonthouan, a king of the Indian nation called Roundheads*. 2 vols. London: printed for the editor: and sold by J. Knox, 1763.

Anonymous. *A new moral system of geography: containing an account of the different nations, ancient and modern*. 6 vols. London: printed for G. Riley, 1792.

Anonymous. *The trial: or, the history of Charles Horton, Esq*. Dublin: H. Saunders et al., 1772.

Ashmole, Elias. *Musaeum Tradescantianum*. London: John Grimond, 1656.

Bage, Robert. *Hermsprong; or, Man as He is Not*. 1796. Edited by Pamela Perkins. Peterborough, ON: Broadview Press, 2002.

Baynton, Benjamin. *Authentic memoirs of William Augustus Bowles, Esquire*. London: R. Faulder, 1791.

Beattie, James. *The Theory of Language In Two Parts. Part I. Of the Origin and General Nature of Speech. Part II. Of Universal Grammar. A New ed.* London: Printed for A. Strahan, 1788.

Behn, Aphra. *Oroonoko, The Rover, and other Works*. 1688. New York: Penguin, 1992.

Beverley, Robert. *The History and Present State of Virginia in Four Parts*. London: Printed for R. Parker, at the Unicorn, under the Piazza's of the Royal-Exchange, 1705.

Blair, Hugh. *A Critical Dissertation on the Poems of Ossian, the son of Fingal*. London: T. Becket and P.A. De Hondt, 1763.

– *Lectures on rhetoric and belle lettres*. London: printed for W. Strahan, 1783.

Brown, Thomas. *A Plain Narrative*. 1760. Vol. 8. New York: Garland, 1975.

Burke, Edmund. "Commons on employing the Indians." *The Scots Magazine* 40 (October 1778): 521–77.

– *A Philosophical Enquiry into the Origin of Our Ideas of the Sublime and Beautiful*. 1757. *The Writings & Speeches of Edmund Burke*. Vol. 1, 67–262. New York: Cosimo, 2008.

Charlevoix, Pierre-François-Xavier de. *Journal of a voyage to North-America*. Vol. 2. London: R. & J. Dodsley, 1761.

– *Letters to the Dutchess of Lesdiguieres*. London: R. Goadby, 1763.

Cibber, Theophilus, and Robert Shiells. *The Lives of the Poets of Great Britain and Ireland, to the Time of Dean Swift*. Vol. 4. London: R. Griffiths, 1753.

Colden, Cadwallader. *The history of the five Indian nations of Canada, which are dependent on the province of New-York in America*. Third edition. London: Lockyer Davis, 1755.

D'Avenant, William. *The Temple of Love*. 1634. New York: Russell & Russell Inc, 1964.

Dennis, John. *Liberty Asserted: A tragedy*. London: George Strahan, 1704.

Dryden, John. *The Conquest of Granada by the Spaniards*. London: Henry Herringman, 1672.

– *The Indian Emperor, or the Conquest of Mexico by the Spaniards*. London: Henry Herringman, 1667.

– "Religio Laici." In *The Poems of John Dryden*, edited by John Sargeaunt, 93–106. London: Oxford University Press, 1913.

Dryden, John, and Sir Robert Howard. *The Indian Queen*. London: Henry Herringman, 1665.

Eastburn, Robert. *A faithful narrative, of the many dangers and sufferings, as well as wonderful deliverances of Robert Eastburn, during his late captivity among the Indians*. Philadelphia: Printed by William Dunlap, 1758.

Fleming, William. *A Narrative of Suffering and Deliverance*, 1756. New York: Garland, 1975.

Garrick, David. *The Private Correspondence of David Garrick*. Vol. 1. London: Colburn and Bentley, 1831.

Goadby, Robert. *An apology for the life of Bampfylde-Moore Carew*. Sherborne: R. Goadby, 1749.

– *The universe displayed; or, a survey of the wonderful works of creation, and of the various customs and inventions of men*. London: W. Owen & R. Goadby, 1763.

Gordon, John. *Occasional Thoughts on the Study and Character of Classical Authors, on the Course of Litterature [sic], and the Present Plan of a Learned Education*. London: Printed for J. Richardson, 1762.

Grace, Henry. *The history of the life and sufferings of Henry Grace*. Reading: Printed for the author, 1764.

Great Britain. *The Parliamentary History of England from the Earliest Period to the Year 1803*. Vol. XIX. London: T.C. Hansard, 1814.

Grew, Nehemiah. *Musaeum Regalis Societatis, Or, A Catalogue & Description of the Natural and Artificial Rarities Belonging to the Royal Society and Preserved at Gresham Colledge*. London: Printed by W. Rawlins, for the Author, 1681.

Hawling, Francis. *A miscellany of original poems on various subjects*. London: printed for S. Austen, 1751.

Jerningham, Edward. "The Indian Chief." In *Fugitive Poetical Pieces*, 25–7. London: J. Robson, 1778.

Johnstone, Charles. *Chrysal; or, The Adventures of a Guinea*. Dublin: Dillon Chamberlaine, 1760.

Johnson, Samuel. *The Adventurer* 1.67. London: J. Payne, 1753. 397–402.

– *Idler* 41 (20 January 1759), 81 (3 November 1759).

Kellet, Alexander. *A Pocket of Prose and Verse*. 1778. Vol. 11. New York: Garland, 1975.

Lahontan, Baron de. *New voyages to North America*. 2 vols. London: H. Banwicke, 1703.

Las Casas, Bartolomé de, and Nigel Griffin. *A Short Account of the Destruction of the Indies*. London: Penguin, 1992.

Lowry, Jean. *A Journal of the Captivity of Jean Lowry*. 1760. New York: Garland, 1975.

Mackenzie, Henry. *The Man of the World*. Vols. I–II. London: W. Strahan & T. Cadell, 1773.

– *The Miscellaneous Works of Henry Mackenzie Esq. in Three Volumes*. Vol. 1. London: R. Tullis, 1806.

Miller, James. *Art and Nature: A Comedy*. London: J. Watts, 1738.

Occom, Samson. *The Collected Writings of Samson Occom, Mohegan: Leadership and Literature in Eighteenth-Century Native America*. Edited by Joanna Brooks. Oxford: Oxford University Press, 2006.

Ockanikon. *A true account of the dying words of Ockanickon, an Indian King*. London: Benjamin Clark, 1682.

O'Keeffe, John. *Recollections of the Life of John O'Keeffe, Written by Himself*. Vol. II. London: Henry Colburn, 1826.

Oldmixon, John. *The British Empire in America*. London: printed for John Nicholson, Benjamin Tooke, Richard Parker and Ralph Smith, 1708.

Pope, Alexander. "*Alexander Pope to Sarah Churchill, duchess of Marlborough [née Jenyns]: Saturday, 26 August 1741.*" In *Electronic Enlightenment Correspondence*, edited by Robert McNamee et al. Vers. 2.5. University of Oxford. 2014. Accessed 16 December 2015.

– *The Major Works*. Edited by Pat Rogers. Oxford: Oxford University Press, 2006.

Rogers, Robert. *Ponteach: or the savages of America. A tragedy*. London: J. Millan, 1766.

Robertson, William. *The history of America*. Dublin: Price, Whitestone, et al., 1777.

Rowlandson, Mary. *The soveraignty & goodness of God, together with the faithfulness of his promises displayed; being a narrative of the captivity and restauration of Mrs. Mary Rowlandson*. Cambridge: Samuel Green, 1682.

– *A true history of the captivity & restoration of Mrs. Mary Rowlandson*. London: Joseph Poole, 1682.

Rutherfurd, John. "Narrative of a Captivity." In *The Siege of Detroit in 1763*, edited by Milton Quaife. Chicago: R.R. Donnelley, 1958.

Seaver, James E. *A narrative of the life of Mrs. Mary Jemison*. Canandaigua [N.Y.]: J.D. Bemis, 1824.

Shebbeare, John. *Lydia, or Filial Piety*. 4 vols. London: J. Scott, 1755.

Smethurst, Gamaliel. *A narrative of an extraordinary escape out of the hands of the Indians, in the Gulph of St. Lawrence*. London: printed for the author and sold by J. Bew and A. Grant, 1774.

Smith, Adam. *The Theory of Moral Sentiments*. London: A. Millar, 1759.

Smith, Charlotte. *The Old Manor House*. Edited by Jacqueline M. Labbe. Peterborough, ON: Broadview Press, 2005.

Smith, James *An account of the remarkable occurrences in the life and travels of Col. James Smith during his captivity with the Indians*. Lexington: J. Bradford, 1799.

Smith, William. *An historical account of the expedition against the Ohio Indians, in the year MDCCLXIV. under the command of Henry Bouquet*. London: T. Jefferies, 1766.

Smollett, Tobias. *The Expedition of Humphry Clinker*. 1771. Oxford: Oxford University Press, 1984.

Swift, Jonathan. *The Journal to Stella*. Teddington: Echo Library, 2007.

Thomson, Charles. *An enquiry into the causes of the alienation of the Delaware and Shawanese Indians from the British interest*. London: J. Wilkie, 1759.

Thoresby, Ralph. *Ducatus Leodiensis Or, the Topography of the Ancient and Populous Town and Parish of Leedes, and Parts Adjacent in the West-Riding of the County of York. With The Pedegrees of Many of the Nobility and Gentry, and Other Matters Relating to Those Parts*. London: Printed for Maurice Atkins, and Sold by Edward Nutt at the Middle-Temple Gate in Fleet-Street, 1715.

Tickell, Richard. *Anticipation: containing the substance of His M---------y's most gracious speech to both H------s of P----l-----t*. London: T. Becket, 1778.

Timberlake, Henry. *The Memoirs of Lieut. Henry Timberlake (who Accompanied the Three Cherokee Indians to England in the Year 1762) Containing Whatever He Observed Remarkable ... during His Travels to and from That Nation ... Also the Principal Occurrences during Their Residence*. London: Printed for the Author and Sold by J. Ridley, 1765.

Voltaire, "Proposal for a Letter About the English." 1728. In *Philosophical Letters or, Letters Regarding the English Nation*, edited by John Leigh, 123–30. Hackett Publishing: Indianapolis, 2007.

Von Uffenbach, Zacharias Conrad. *London in 1710*. Translated and edited by W.H. Quarrell and Margaret Mare. London: Faber & Faber Ltd., 1934.

Wafer, Lionel. *A new voyage and description of the Isthmus of America*. London: Printed for James Knapton, 1699.

Walpole, Horace. *The Letters of Horace Walpole, Earl of Orford*. Edited by Peter Cunningham. London: R. Bentley, 1858.

Wesley, Samuel. *Georgia, a poem. Tomo chichi, an ode. A copy of verses on Mr. Oglethorpe's second voyage to Georgia*. London: J. Roberts, 1736.

Williamson, Peter. *French and Indian Cruelty; Exemplified in the Life and Various Vicissitudes of Fortune of Peter Williamson*. 5th ed. 1762. Intro. Michael Fry. Bristol, UK: Thoemmes Press, 1996.

– *French and Indian Cruelty*. 1st and 3rd eds. 1757, 1758. Vol. 9. New York: Garland, 1975.

– *The trial of divorce, at the instance of Peter Williamson*. Edinburgh: Printed for and sold by the booksellers in Edinburgh, 1789.

Secondary

Alther, Thomas L. "*Tombo-Chiqui: Or, The American Savage*: John Cleland's Noble Savage Satire." *American Indian Quarterly* 9.4 (Autumn 1985): 411–20.

Altick, Richard. *The Shows of London*. Cambridge, MA: Harvard University Press, 1978.

Armitage, David. "Three Concepts of Atlantic History." In *The British Atlantic World, 1500–1800*, 2nd ed., edited by David Armitage and Michael J. Braddick, 13–32. New York: Palgrave Macmillan, 2009.

Armstrong, Nancy, and Leonard Tennenhouse. *The Imaginary Puritan: Literature, Intellectual Labor, and the Origins of Personal Life*. Los Angeles: University of California Press, 1992.

Appadurai, Arjun. "Introduction: commodities and the politics of value." In *The Social Life of Things: Commodities in Cultural Perspective*, edited by Arjun Appadurai, 3–63. Cambridge: Cambridge University Press, 1986.

Aravamudan, Srinivas. *Tropicopolitans: Colonialism and Agency, 1688–1804*. Durham, NC: Duke University Press, 1999.

Arneil, Barbara. *John Locke and America: The Defense of English Colonialism*. Oxford: Oxford University Press, 1996.

Arnold, Ken. *Cabinets for the Curious: Looking Back at Early English Museums*. Burlington: Ashgate, 2006.

Axtell, James. "The White Indians of Colonial America." In *American Encounters: Natives and Newcomers from European Contact to Indian Removal, 1500–1850*, edited by Peter C. Mancall and James H. Merrell, 324–50. New York: Routledge, 2000.

– *White Indians of Colonial America*. Fairfield: Ye Galleon Press, 1979.

Bakhtin, Mikhail. *Problems of Dostoevsky's Poetics*. Translated by Caryl Emerson. Minneapolis: University of Minnesota Press, 1984.

Bannet, Eve Tavor. *Transatlantic Stories and the History of Reading, 1720–1810: Migrant Fictions*. Cambridge: Cambridge University Press, 2011.

Barbour, Richmond. *Before Orientalism: London's Theatre of the East, 1576–1626*. Cambridge: Cambridge University Press, 2003.

Barchas, Janine. *Graphic Design, Print Culture, and the Eighteenth-Century Novel*. Cambridge: Cambridge University Press, 2003.

Barrell, John. "Afterword: Moving Stories, Still Lives." In *The Country and the City Revisited: England and the Politics of Culture, 1550–1850*, edited by Donna Landry, Gerald MacLean, Joseph P. Ward, 231–50. Cambridge: Cambridge University Press, 1999.

Bataille, Gretchen M., ed. *Native American Representations: First Encounters, Distorted Images, and Literary Appropriations*. London: University of Nebraska Press, 2001.

Bellin, Joshua David. *The Demon of the Continent: Indians and the Shaping of American Literature*. Philadelphia: University of Pennsylvania Press, 2001.

Bellin, Joshua David, and Laura L. Mielke, eds. *Native Acts: Indian Performance, 1603–1832*. Lincoln, NE: University of Nebraska Press, 2011.

Bergland, Renée L. *The National Uncanny: Indian Ghosts and American Subjects*. Hanover, NH: University Press of New England, 2000.

Berkhofer, Robert F. *The White Man's Indian: Images of the American Indian from Columbus to the Present*. New York: Knopf, 1978.

Bersani, Leo. "Representation and Its Discontents." In *Allegory and Representation: Essays from the English Institute*, edited by Stephen Greenblatt, 145–62. Baltimore: Johns Hopkins University Press, 1981.

Berson, Joel S. "The Memoirs of Bampfylde-Moore Carew: Additional Plagiaries and Dateable Events." *Notes and Queries* 54.4 (December 2007): 456–64.

Bhabha, Homi K. *The Location of Culture*. New York: Routledge, 1994.

Bickham, Troy. "'A Conviction of the Reality of Things': Material Culture, North American Indians and Empire in Eighteenth-Century Britain." *Eighteenth-Century Studies* 39.1 (Fall 2005): 29–47.

– *Savages Within the Empire: Representations of American Indians in Eighteenth-Century Britain*. Oxford: Clarendon Press, 2005.

Bissell, Benjamin. *The American Indian in English Literature of the Eighteenth Century*. Hamden, CT: Archon Books, 1968.

Blackwell, Mark, ed. *The Secret Life of Things: Animals, Objects, and It-narratives in Eighteenth-Century England*. Cranbury, NJ: Rosemount Publishing, 2007.

Blanchard, Rae. "Richard Steele's West Indian Plantation." *Modern Philology* 39.3 (February 1942): 281–5.

Blewett, David. *The Illustration of Robinson Crusoe, 1719–1920*. Gerrards Cross: C. Smythe, 1995.

Bond, Richmond P. *Queen Anne's American Kings*. New York: Octagon Books, 1974.

Borque, Kevin. "Cultural Currency: *Chrysal, or The Adventures of a Guinea*, and the Material Shape of Eighteenth-Century Celebrity." In *Eighteenth-Century Thing Theory in a Global Context*, edited by Ileana Baird and Christina Ionescu, 49–68. Farnham, UK, 2013.

Bosch, René. *Labyrinth of Digressions: Tristram Shandy as Perceived and Influenced By Sterne's Early Imitators*. Translated by Piet Verhoeff. New York: Rodopi, 2007.

Brears, P.C.D. "Ralph Thoresby, A Museum Visitor in Stuart England." *Journal of the History of Collections* 1.2 (1989): 213–24.

Bredekamp, Horst. *The Lure of Antiquity and the Cult of the Machine: The Kunstkammer and the Evolution of Nature, Art and Technology*. Translated by Allison Brown. Princeton: Markus Wiener Publishers, 1995.

Breen, T.H. "An Empire of Goods: The Anglicization of Colonial America, 1690–1776." *Journal of British Studies* 25.4 (October 1986): 467–99.

Brewer, John, and Roy Porter, eds. *Consumption and the World of Goods.* London: Routledge, 1993.

Brickman, Celia. *Aboriginal Populations in the Mind: Race and Primitivity in Psychoanalysis.* New York: Columbia University Press, 2003.

Brown, Bill. "Thing Theory." *Critical Inquiry* 28.1 (Autumn 2001): 1–22.

Brown, Laura. *Ends of Empire: Women and Ideology in Early Eighteenth-century English Literature.* Ithaca: Cornell University Press, 1993.

– *Fables of Modernity: Literature and Culture in the English Eighteenth Century.* Ithaca: Cornell University Press, 2001.

– "Reading Race and Gender: Jonathan Swift." *Eighteenth-Century Studies* 23.4 (Summer 1990): 425–43.

Brumwell, Stephen. *Redcoats: The British Soldier and War in the Americas, 1755–1763.* Cambridge: Cambridge University Press, 2002.

Bubenik, Andrea. *Reframing Albrecht Dürer: The Appropriation of Art, 1528–1700.* Burlington: Ashgate, 2013.

Bujok, Elke. "Ethnographica in Early Modern *Kunstkammern* and Their Perception." *Journal of the History of Collections* 21.1 (2009): 17–32.

Burnham, Michelle. *Captivity and Sentiment: Cultural Exchange in American Literature, 1682–1861.* Hanover: University Press of New England, 1997.

Burns, William E. *An Age of Wonders: Prodigies, Politics, and Providence in England, 1657–1727.* Manchester, UK: Manchester University Press, 2002.

Byrd, Jodi A. *The Transit of Empire: Indigenous Critiques of Colonialism.* Minneapolis: University of Minnesota Press, 2011.

Calloway, Colin G. *Pen & Ink Witchcraft: Treaties and Treaty Making in American Indian History.* Oxford: Oxford University Press, 2013.

– *White People, Indians, and Highlanders: Tribal People and Colonial Encounters in Scotland and America.* Oxford: Oxford University Press, 2008.

Carr, Helen. "'And the truest schools for civilization are the forests of America': John O'Keefe's *The Basket-Maker* and Robert Bage's *Hermsprong.*" In *Native Americans and Anglo-American Culture, 1750–1850: The Indian Atlantic,* edited by Tim Fulford and Kevin Hutchings, 136–54. Cambridge: Cambridge University Press, 2009.

Castle, Terry. *Masquerade and Civilization: The Carnivalesque in Eighteenth-Century English Culture and Fiction.* Stanford: Stanford University Press, 1986.

Castro, Wendy Lucas. "Stripped: Clothing and Identity in Colonial Captivity Narratives." *Early American Studies: An Interdisciplinary Journal* 6.1 (2008): 104–36.

Catlin, George. *The Manners, Customs and Condition of the North American Indians: Written during Eight Years' Travel amongst the Wildest Tribes of Indians in North America, 1832–39.* London: Published by the Author at the Egyptian Hall, 1841.

Césaire, Aimé. *Discourse on Colonialism.* 1950. Translated by Joan Pinkham. New York: MR, 1972.

Colley, Linda. "Britishness and Otherness: An Argument." *Journal of British Studies* 31.4 (October 1992): 309–29.

– *Britons: Forging the Nation, 1707–1837.* New Haven: Yale University Press, 1992.

– *Captives: Britain, Empire and the World, 1600–1850.* New York: Pantheon Books, 2002.

– "Going Native, Telling Tales: Captivity, Collaborations, and Empire." *Past and Present* 168 (August 2000): 170–93.

Connell, D.P., and M.J. Boyd. "Material from the 'Musaeum' of Ralph Thoresby (1658–1725) Preserved at Burton Constable Hall, East Yorkshire." *Journal of the History of Collections* 10.1 (1998): 31–40.

Cornu, Donald. "The Historical Authenticity Of Dr. Johnson's 'Speaking Cat'." *The Review of English Studies* 2.8 (1951): 358–70.

Craft-Fairchild, Catherine. *Masquerade and Gender: Disguise and Female Identity in Eighteenth-Century Fictions by Women.* University Park, PA: Pennsylvania State University Press, 1993.

Cro, Stelio. "Classical Antiquity, America, and the Myth of the Noble Savage." In *The Classical Tradition and the Americas*, vol. 1, edited by Wolfgang Haase, 379–418. Berlin: Walter de Gruyter & Co., 1993.

Cutter, Barbara. "The Female Indian Killer Memorialized: Hannah Duston and the Nineteenth-Century Feminization of American Violence." *Journal of Women's History* 20.2 (Summer 2008): 10–26.

Daston, Lorraine, and Katharine Park. *Wonders and the Order of Nature, 1150–1750.* New York: Zone Books, 1998.

Dearborn, Mary V. *Pocahontas's Daughters: Gender and Ethnicity in American Culture.* New York: Oxford University Press, 1986.

Deloria, Philip Joseph. *Playing Indian.* New Haven: Yale University Press, 1998.

Denn, Robert J. "Captivity Narratives of the American Revolution." *The Journal of American Culture* 2.4 (1980): 575–82.

Derounian, Kathryn Zabelle. "The Publication, Promotion, and Distribution of Mary Rowlandson's Indian Captivity Narrative in the Seventeenth Century." *Early American Literature* 23.3 (1988): 239–61.

Dixon, David. *Never Come to Peace Again: Pontiac's Uprising and the Fate of the British Empire in North America.* Norman: University of Oklahoma Press, 2005.

Donoghue, Frank. *The Fame Machine: Book Reviewing and Eighteenth-Century Literary Careers*. Stanford: Stanford University Press, 1996.

Douglas, Aileen. "Britannia's Rule and the It-Narrator." In *The Secret Life of Things: Animals, Objects, and It-narratives in Eighteenth-Century England*, edited by Mark Blackwell, 147–61. Cranbury, NJ: Rosemount Publishing, 2007.

Dudley, Edward, and Maximillian E. Novak, eds. *The Wild Man Within: An Image in Western Thought from the Renaissance to Romanticism*. Pittsburgh: University of Pittsburgh Press, 1972.

Duncan, Ian. *Scott's Shadow: The Novel in Romantic Edinburgh*. Princeton: Princeton University Press, 2007.

Ebersole, Gary L. *Captured by Texts: Puritan to Postmodern Images of Indian Captivity*. Charlottesville: University Press of Virginia, 1995.

Ellingson, Ter. *The Myth of the Noble Savage*. Berkeley: University of California Press, 2001.

Endelman, Todd M. *The Jews of Georgian England, 1714–1830: Tradition and Change in a Liberal Society*. Ann Arbor: University of Michigan Press, 1999.

Evans, R.J.W., and Alexander Marr, eds. *Curiosity and Wonder from the Renaissance to the Enlightenment*. Burlington: Ashgate, 2006.

Feest, Christian F. "European Collecting of American Indian Artefacts and Art." *Journal of the History of Collections* 5.1 (1993): 1–11.

Felsenstein, Frank. *English Trader, Indian Maid: Representing Gender, Race, and Slavery in the New World: An Inkle and Yarico Reader*. Baltimore: Johns Hopkins University Press, 1999.

Felski, Rita. *The Gender of Modernity*. Cambridge, MA: Harvard University Press, 1995.

Fenton, William N. *The Great Law and the Longhouse: A Political History of the Iroquois Confederacy*. Norman: University of Oklahoma Press, 1998.

Fields, Polly Stevens. "Samson Occom and/In The Missionary's Position: Consideration of a Native-American Preacher in 1770's Colonial America." *The Wordsworth Circle* 32.1 (Winter 2001): 14–20.

Flint, Kate. *The Transatlantic Indian, 1776–1930*. Princeton: Princeton University Press, 2009.

Foster, James R. "A Forgotten Noble Savage, *Tsonnonthouan*." *Modern Language Quarterly* 14 (1953): 348–59.

Foucault, Michel. *Discipline and Punish: The Birth of the Prison*. 1975. Translated by Alan Sheridan. New York: Vintage Books, 1995.

– "Nietzche, Genealogy, History." *The Foucault Reader*, edited by Paul Rabinow, 76–100. New York: Pantheon, 1984.

– *The Order of Things; an Archaeology of the Human Sciences*. New York: Vintage Books, 1994.

Frohock, Richard. *Heroes of Empire: The British Imperial Protagonist in America, 1596–1764*. Newark: University of Delaware Press, 2004.

Fulford, Tim. *Romantic Indians: Native Americans, British Literature, & Transatlantic Culture, 1756–1830*. Oxford: Oxford University Press, 2006.

Fulford, Tim, and Kevin Hutchings, eds. *Native Americans and Anglo-American Culture, 1750–1850: The Indian Atlantic*. Cambridge: Cambridge University Press, 2009.

Fullagar, Kate. *The Savage Visit: New World People and Popular Imperial Culture in Britain, 1710–1795*. Berkeley: University of California Press, 2012.

Garratt, J.G., and Bruce Robertson. *Four Indian Kings*. Ottawa: Public Archives of Canada, 1985.

Genest, John. *Some Account of the English Stage, from the Restoration in 1660 to 1830*. Vol. 2. Bath: Carrington, 1832.

Gilroy, Paul. *The Black Atlantic: Modernity and Double-Consciousness*. Cambridge, MA: Harvard University Press, 1995.

Goldie, Terry. *Fear and Temptation: The Image of the Indigene in Canadian, Australian, and New Zealand Literatures*. Montreal: McGill-Queen's University Press, 1989.

Goodman, Nan. "'Money Answers All Things': Rethinking Economic and Cultural Exchange in the Captivity Narrative of Mary Rowlandson." *American Literary History* 22.1 (Spring 2010): 1–25.

Goring, Paul. *The Rhetoric of Sensibility in Eighteenth-Century Culture*. Cambridge: Cambridge University Press, 2005.

Green Fryd, Vivien. "Rereading the Indian in Benjamin West's 'Death of Wolfe'." *American Art* 9.1 (Spring 1995), 72–85.

Greenblatt, Stephen. *Marvelous Possessions: The Wonder of the New World*. Chicago: University of Chicago Press, 1991.

– "Resonance and Wonder." *Bulletin of the American Academy of Arts and Sciences* 43.4 (January 1990): 31–2.

Gustafson, Sandra M. *Eloquence is Power: Oratory & Performance in Early America*. Chapel Hill: University of North Carolina Press, 2000.

Guthrie, Neil. "'No Truth, or Very Little in the Whole Story'?: A Reassessment of the Mohock Scare of 1712." *Eighteenth-Century Life* 20.2 (1996): 33–56.

Haefeli, Evan, and Kevin Sweeney. *Captors and Captives: The 1704 French and Indian Raid on Deerfield*. Boston: University of Massachusetts Press, 2003.

Harkin, Maureen. "Adam Smith's Missing History: Primitives, Progress, and Problems of Genre." *ELH* 72.2 (2005): 429–51.

Harris, Jonathan Gil, ed. *Indography: Writing the "Indian" in Early Modern England*. New York: Palgrave Macmillan, 2012.

Hart, Jonathan. *Representing the New World: The English and French Uses of the Example of Spain*. New York: Palgrave, 2000.

Hendricks, Margo. "Civility, Barbarism, and Aphra Behn's *The Widow Ranter*." In *Women, "Race," and Writing in the Early Modern Period*, edited by Margo Hendricks and Patricia Parker, 225–39. London: Routledge, 1994.

Hinderaker, Eric. "The 'Four Indian Kings' and the Imaginative Construction of the First British Empire." *The William and Mary Quarterly*, 3rd Ser., 53.3, Indians and Others in Early America (July 1996): 487–526.

– *The Two Hendricks: Unraveling a Mohawk Mystery*. Cambridge, MA: Harvard University Press, 2011.

Hodgkins, Christopher. *Reforming Empire: Protestant Colonialism and Conscience in British Literature*. Columbia, MO: University of Missouri Press, 2002.

Horejsi, Nicole. "'A Counterpart to the Ephesian Matron': Steele's 'Inkle and Yarico' and a Feminist Critique of the Classics." *Eighteenth-Century Studies* 39.2 (2006): 201–6.

Houghton-Walker, Sarah. *Representations of the Gypsy in the Romantic Period*. Oxford: Oxford University Press, 2014.

Howard, Susan K. "Transcultural Adoption in the Eighteenth-Century Transatlantic Novel: Questioning National Identities in Charlotte Lennox's *Euphemia*." In *New Contexts for Eighteenth-Century British Fiction: "Hearts Resolved and Hands Prepared": Essays in Honor of Jerry C. Beasley*, edited by Christopher D. Johnson, 109–26. Lanham, MD: University of Delaware Press, 2011.

Hudson, "From 'Nation' to 'Race': The Origin of Racial Classification in Eighteenth- Century Thought." *Eighteenth-Century Studies* 29.3 (Spring 1996): 247–64.

Hug, Tobias B. *Impostures in Early Modern England: Representations and Perceptions of Fraudulent Identities*. Manchester: Manchester University Press, 2009.

Hulme, Peter. *Colonial Encounters: Europe and the Native Caribbean, 1492–1797*. London: Methuen, 1986.

Hunt, Lynn. *Inventing Human Rights: A History*. New York: Norton, 2007.

Hunter, Michael C.W. *Establishing the New Science: The Experience of the Early Royal Society*. Woodbridge: Boydell Press, 1989.

Hutchings, Kevin. *Romantic Ecologies and Colonial Cultures in the British Atlantic World, 1770–1850*. McGill-Queen's University Press, 2009.

Kalata Vaccaro, Kristianne. "'Recollection … sets my busy imagination to work': Transatlantic Self-Narration, Performance, and Reception in *The Female American*." *Eighteenth-Century Fiction* 20.2 (Winter 2007–8): 127–50.

Kelly, Gary. "Bage, Robert (1728?–1801)." *Oxford Dictionary of National Biography*. Oxford University Press, 2004; online ed., May 2006. Accessed 30 November 2010.

Kern, Jean B. *Dramatic Satire in the Age of Walpole, 1720–1750*. Ames: Iowa State University Press, 1976.

Kersey, Mel. "Addison's Indian, Blackwell's Bard and the voice of Ossian." *History of European Ideas* 31.2 (2005): 265–75.

Keymer, Thomas. *Sterne, the Moderns, and the Novel*. New York: Oxford University Press, 2002.

Kibbie, Ann Louise. "Circulating Anti-Semitism: Charles Johnstone's *Chrysal*." In *The Secret Life of Things: Animals, Objects, and It-narratives in Eighteenth-Century England*, edited by Mark Blackwell, 242–64. Cranbury, NJ: Rosemount Publishing, 2007.

King, J.C.H. *First Peoples, First Contacts: Native Peoples of North America*. London: British Museum Press, 1999.

– "Woodlands Artifacts from the Studio of Benjamin West 1738–1820." *American Indian Art Magazine* 17.1 (Winter 1991): 34–47.

Knapp, Jeffrey. *An Empire Nowhere: England, America, and Literature from Utopia to The Tempest*. Berkeley: University of California Press, 1992.

Laqueur, Thomas. *Making Sex: Body and Gender from the Greeks to Freud*. Cambridge, MA: Harvard University Press, 1992.

Lynch, Deidre. *The Economy of Character: Novels, Market Culture, and the Business of Inner Meaning*. Chicago: University of Chicago Press, 1998.

MacGregor, Arthur. "The Cabinet of Curiosities in Seventeenth-Century Britain." In *The Origins of Museums: The Cabinet of Curiosities in Sixteenth-And Seventeenth-Century Europe*, edited by Oliver Impey and Arthur MacGregor, 201–15. Oxford: Clarendon Press, 1985.

– ed. *Tradescant's Rarities: Essays on the Foundation of the Ashmolean Museum 1683, with a Catalogue of the Surviving Early Collections*. Oxford: Oxford University Press, 1983.

Maltby, William T. *The Black Legend in England*. Durham, NC: Duke University Press, 1971.

Mancall, Peter C. *Deadly Medicine: Indians and Alcohol in Early America*. Ithaca: Cornell University Press, 1995.

Marshall, P.J., and Glyndwr Williams. *The Great Map of Mankind: British Perceptions of the World in the Age of Enlightenment*. London: J.M. Dent & Sons, 1982.

Martinez, Mauricio. "From Peruvian Gold to British Guinea: Tropicopolitanism and Myth of Origin in Charles Johnstone's *Chrysal*." In *Eighteenth-Century Thing Theory in a Global Context*, edited by Ileana Baird and Christina Ionescu. Farnham, UK: Ashgate, 2013. 171–90.

Mascuch, Michael. *Origins of the Individualist Self: Autobiography and Self-Identity in England, 1591–1791*. Stanford: Stanford University Press, 1996.

Mason, Peter. *Infelicities: Representations of the Exotic*. Baltimore: Johns Hopkins University Press, 1998.

McGregor, Gaile. *The Noble Savage in the New World Garden: Notes toward a Syntactics of Place*. Toronto: University of Toronto Press, 1988.

McKendrick, Neil, John Brewer, and John Harold Plumb. *The Birth of a Consumer Society*. Bloomington: Indiana University Press, 1982.

McKeon, Michael. *The Secret History of Domesticity: Public, Private, and the Division of Knowledge*. Baltimore: Johns Hopkins University Press, 2005.

McKlintock, Anne. *Imperial Leather: Race, Gender, and Sexuality in the Colonial Contest*. New York: Routledge, 1995.

McNeil, David. *The Grotesque Depiction of War and the Military in Eighteenth-Century English Fiction*. Newark: University of Delaware Press, 1990.

Middleton, Richard. *Pontiac's War: Its Causes, Course and Consequences*. New York: Routledge, 2007.

Millburn, John R. "Martin, Benjamin (*bap.* 1705, *d.* 1782)." *Oxford Dictionary of National Biography*. Oxford: Oxford University Press, 2004; online ed., May 2006. Accessed 26 November 2010.

Millory, John S. *A National Crime: The Canadian Government and the Residential School System, 1879–1986*. Winnipeg, MB: University of Manitoba Press, 1999.

Mitchell, Robert. "The Violence of Sympathy: Adam Smith on Resentment and Executions." Special Issue of *1650–1850: Ideas, Aesthetics and Inquiries in the Early Modern Era* 8 (2003): 321–41.

Molineux, Catherine. "False Gifts/Exotic Fictions: Epistemologies of Sovereignty and Assent in Aphra Behn's *Oroonoko*." *ELH* 80.2 (Summer 2013): 455–88.

Morgan, Philip D. "Encounters Between British and 'Indigenous' Peoples, c.1500–1800." In *Empire and Others: British Encounters with Indigenous Peoples, 1600–1850*, edited by Martin Daunton and Rick Halpern, 42–78. Philadelphia: University of Pennsylvania Press, 1999.

Morgan, Gwenda, and Peter Rushton. *Eighteenth-Century Criminal Transportation: The Formation of the Criminal Atlantic*. New York: Palgrave, 2004.

Moss, Laura, ed. *Is Canada Postcolonial: Unsettling Canadian Literature*. Waterloo: Wilfred Laurier University Press, 2003.

Muller, Kevin R. "From Palace to Longhouse: Portraits of the Four Indian Kings in a Transatlantic Context." *American Art* 22.3 (Fall 2008): 26–49.

Nelson, William. *New Jersey Biographical and Genealogical Notes*. Baltimore: Genealogical Publishing, 1973.

Nolan, J. Bennet. "Peter Williamson in America, A Colonial Odyssey." *Pennsylvania History* 31 (January 1964): 23–9.

Nussbaum, Felicity. *Torrid Zones: Maternity, Sexuality, and Empire in Eighteenth-century English Narratives.* Baltimore: Johns Hopkins University Press, 1995.

O'Brien, Paula. "Miller, James (1704–1744)." *Oxford Dictionary of National Biography.* Online ed. Oxford University Press, 2005.

O'Neill, Daniel. *Edmund Burke and the Conservative Logic of Empire.* Oakland: University of California Press, 2016.

O'Toole, Fintan. *White Savage: William Johnson and the Invention of America.* State University of New York Press, 2005.

Pagden, Anthony. *The Fall of Natural Man: The American Indian and the Origins of Comparative Ethnology.* New York: Cambridge University Press, 1982.

Pearce, Roy Harvey. *Savagism and Civilization: A Study of the Indian and the American Mind.* Baltimore: Johns Hopkins University Press, 1967.

– "The Significances of the Captivity Narrative." *American Literature*: 19.1 (March 1947): 1–20.

Pearce, Susan, and Kenneth Arnold. *The Collector's Voice.* Vol. 2: Early Voices. Farnham, UK: Ashgate, 2002.

Phillips, Ruth B. *Trading Identities: The Souvenir in Native North American Art from the Northeast, 1700–1900.* Montreal: McGill-Queen's University Press, 1998.

Phillips, Ruth B., and Dale Idiens. "'A Casket of Savage Curiosities': Eighteenth-Century Objects from North-Eastern North America in the Farquharson Collection." *Journal of the History of Collections* 6.1 (1994): 21–33.

Pincus, Steve. *1688: The First Modern Revolution.* New Haven: Yale University Press, 2009.

Pomedli, Michael M. "Eighteenth-Century Treaties: Amended Iroquois Condolence Rituals." *American Indian Quarterly* 19.3 (Summer 1995): 319–39.

Porter, Roy, ed. *Rewriting the Self: Histories from the Renaissance to the Present.* London: Routledge, 1997.

Pratt, Mary Louise. *Imperial Eyes: Travel Writing and Transculturation.* New York: Routledge, 1992.

Pratt, Stephanie. *American Indians in British Art, 1700–1840.* Norman: University of Oklahoma Press, 2005.

– "From Cannassatego to Outalissi: Making Sense of the Native American in Eighteenth-Century Culture." In *An Economy of Colour: Visual Culture and the Atlantic World, 1660–1830,* edited by Geoff Quilley and Kay Dian Kriz, 60–84. New York: Manchester University Press, 2003.

– "The Four Indian Kings." *Between Worlds: Voyagers to Britain 1700–1850*, 22–35. London: National Portrait Gallery, 2007.

– "Representatives and Representation: Southern Indians in Eighteenth-Century England." In *Native Americans and Anglo-American Culture, 1750–1850: The Indian Atlantic*, edited by Tim Fulford and Kevin Hutchings, 112–35. Cambridge: Cambridge University Press, 2009.

Preston, Thomas R. "Smollett Among the Indians." *Philological Quarterly* 61.3 (Summer 1982): 231–41.

Rae, John. *Life of Adam Smith*. London: Macmillan and Co., 1895.

Rasmussen, Birgit. *Queequeg's Coffin: Indigenous Literacies & Early American Literature*. Durham, NC: Duke University Press, 2012.

Richter, Daniel K. "'Some of Them … Would Always have a Minister with Them': Mohawk Protestantism, 1683–1719." *American Indian Quarterly* 16.1 (Fall 1992): 471–84.

– *Trade, Land, Power: The Struggle for Eastern North America*. Philadelphia: University of Pennsylvania Press, 2013.

Rigal, Laura. "Framing the Fabric: A Luddite Reading of *Penn's Treaty with the Indians*." *American Literary History* 12.3 (Autumn 2000): 557–84.

Roach, Joseph R. *Cities of the Dead: Circum-Atlantic Performance*. New York: Columbia University Press, 1996.

Rome, Alan S. *The English Embrace of the American Indians: Ideas of Humanity in Early America*. New York: Palgrave Macmillan, 2017.

Rosaldo, Renato. "Imperialist Nostalgia." *Representations* 26 (Spring 1989): 107–22.

Runnell, Kathryn. "Defoe and the Black Legend: The Spanish Stereotype in *A New Voyage Around the World*." *Rocky Mountain Review of Language and Literature* 52.2 (1998): 13–28.

Sabin, Joseph, Wilberforce Eames, and R.W.G. Vail. *A Dictionary of Books Relating to America, from its Discovery to the Present Time*. 19 vols. Amsterdam: N. Israel, 1961.

Sandberg, Brian. "Beyond Encounters: Religion, Ethnicity, and Violence in the Early Modern Atlantic World, 1492–1700." *Journal of World History* 17.1 (2006): 1–25.

Saunders, Charles. *The Horrid Cruelty of the Indians*. 1763. New York: Garland, 1975.

Sayre, Gordon M. *Les Sauvages Américains: Representations of Native Americans in French and English Colonial Literature*. Chapel Hill: University of North Carolina Press, 1997.

Schiavo, Jr, Anthony P., and Claudio R. Salvucci, eds. *Iroquois Wars I: Extracts from The Jesuit Relations and Primary Sources from 1535 to 1650*. Merchantville, NJ: Evolution Publishing & Manufacturing, 2003.

Schnapp, Alain. "Ancient Europe and Native Americans: A Comparative Reflection on the Roots of Antiquarianism." In *Collecting Across Cultures: Material Exchanges in the Early Modern Atlantic World*, edited by Daniela Bleichmar and Peter C. Mancall, 58–80. Philadelphia: University of Pennsylvania Press, 2011.

Shannon, Timothy J. "Dressing for Success on the Mohawk Frontier: Hendrick, William Johnson, and the Indian Fashion." *The William and Mary Quarterly* 53.1 (January 1996): 13–42.

– "King of the Indians: The Hard Fate and Curious Career of Peter Williamson." *The William and Mary Quarterly* 66.1 (January 2009): 3–44.

– "Queequeg's Tomahawk: A Cultural Biography, 1750–1900." *Ethnohistory* 52.3 (2005): 589–633.

Shoemaker, Nancy. *A Strange Likeness: Becoming Red and White in Eighteenth-Century North America.* Oxford: Oxford University Press, 2004.

Skelton, Douglas. *Indian Peter: The Extraordinary Life and Adventures of Peter Williamson.* Edinburgh: Mainstream, 2005.

Slotkin, Richard. *Regeneration Through Violence: The Mythology of the American Frontier, 1600–1860.* Middletown, CT: Wesleyan University Press, 1973.

Smith, Linda Tuhiwai. *Decolonizing Methodologies: Research and Indigenous Peoples.* New York: St Martin's Press, 1999.

Smith-Rosenberg, Carroll. *This Violent Empire: The Birth of an American National Identity.* Chapel Hill: University of North Carolina Press, 2010.

Snader, Joe. *Caught Between Worlds: British Captivity Narratives in Fact and Fiction.* Lexington, KY: University Press of Kentucky, 2000.

Sorensen, Lise. "Savages and Men of Feeling: North American Indians in Adam Smith's *The Theory of Moral Sentiments* and Henry Mackenzie's *The Man of the World*." In *Native Americans and Anglo-American Culture, 1750–1850: The Indian Atlantic*, edited by Tim Fulford and Kevin Hutchings, 74–93. Cambridge: Cambridge University Press, 2009.

Sorenssen, Janet. "Vulgar Tongues: Canting Dictionaries and the Language of the People in Eighteenth-Century Britain." *Eighteenth-Century Studies* 37.3 (Spring 2004): 435–54.

Spector, Robert Donald. "Smollett's Use of *Tsonnonthouan*." *Notes and Queries* 6 (1959): 112–13.

Spitta, Silvia. *Misplaced Objects: Migrating Collections and Recollections in Europe and the Americas.* Austin: University of Texas Press, 2009.

Steele, Ian K. *Betrayals: Fort William Henry and the "Massacre."* Oxford: Oxford University Press, 1990.

– *Setting All the Captives Free: Capture, Adjustment, and Recollection in Allegheny Country.* Montreal: McGill-Queen's University Press, 2013.

Stevens, Laura M. *The Poor Indians: British Missionaries, Native Americans, and Colonial Sensibility.* Philadelphia: University of Pennsylvania Press, 2004.

– "Transatlanticism Now." *American Literary History* 16.1 (Spring 2004): 93–102.

Stevenson, John Allen. *The Real History of Tom Jones.* New York: Palgrave Macmillan, 2005.

Stewart, Susan. *On Longing: Narratives of the Miniature, the Gigantic, the Souvenir, the Collection.* Durham, NC: Duke University Press, 1993.

Suleri, Sara. *The Rhetoric of English India.* Chicago: University of Chicago Press, 1992.

Sussman, Charlotte. *Consuming Anxieties: Consumer Protest, Gender, and British Slavery, 1713–1833.* Stanford: Stanford University Press, 2000.

– "Lismahago's Captivity: Transculturation in *Humphry Clinker.*" *ELH* 61.3 (1994): 597–618.

Swann, Marjorie. *Curiosities and Texts: The Culture of Collecting in Early Modern England.* Philadelphia: University of Philadelphia Press, 2001.

Sweet, Julie Anne. "Will the Real Tomochichi Please Come Forward?" *American Indian Quarterly* 32.2 (Spring 2008): 141–77.

Taylor, Alan. *The Divided Ground: Indians, Settlers, and the Northern Borderland of the American Revolution.* New York: Vintage Books, 2006.

Taylor, Charles. *Sources of the Self: The Making of the Modern Identity.* Cambridge, MA: Harvard University Press, 1989.

Thomas, Jennifer. "Compiling 'God's great book [of] universal nature': The Royal Society's Collecting Strategies." *Journal of the History of Collections* 2.1 (2011): 1–13.

Thompson, E.P. *The Making of the English Working Class.* New York: Pantheon Books, 1964.

Thrush, Coll. *Indigenous London: Native Travelers at the Heart of Empire.* The Henry Roe Cloud Series on American Indians and Modernity. New Haven: Yale University Press, 2016.

Tilton, Robert S. *Pocahontas: The Evolution of an American Narrative.* New York: Cambridge University Press, 1994.

Tobin, Beth Fowkes. *Picturing Imperial Power: Colonial Subjects in Eighteenth-Century British Painting.* Durham, NC: Duke University Press, 1999.

– "Wampum Belts and Tomahawks on an Irish Estate: Constructing an Imperial Identity in the Late Eighteenth Century." *Biography* 33.4 (Fall 2010): 679–713.

Todd, Angela, "Your Humble Servant Shows Himself: Don Saltero and Public Coffeehouse Space." *Journal of International Women's Studies* 6.2 (June 2005): 119–35.

Todorov, Tzvetan. *The Conquest of America: The Question of the Other*. New York: Harper & Row, 1984.

Toulouse, Teresa A. *The Captive's Position: Female Narrative, Male Identity, and Royal Authority in Colonial New England*. Philadelphia: University of Pennsylvania Press, 2007.

Turgeon, Laurier. "The Tale of the Kettle: Odyssey of an Intercultural Object." *Ethnohistory* 44.1 (Winter 1997): 1–29.

Vaughan, Alden T., *Transatlantic Encounters: American Indians in Britain, 1500–1776*. Cambridge: Cambridge University Press, 2006.

Vaughan, Alden T., and Edward W. Clark, eds. *Puritans among the Indians: Accounts of Captivity and Redemption, 1676–1724*. Cambridge, MA: Harvard University Press, 1981.

Visconsi, Elliott. "A Degenerate Race: English Barbarism in Aphra Behn's *Oroonoko* and *The Widow Ranter*." *ELH* 69.3 (Fall 2002): 673–701.

Vizenor, Gerald. *Manifest Manners: Postindian Warriors of Survivance*. Hanover, NH: Wesleyan University Press, 1994.

Wahrman, Dror. *The Making of the Modern Self: Identity and Culture in Eighteenth-Century England*. New Haven: Yale University Press, 2004.

Wallace, Tara Ghoshal. *Imperial Characters: Home and Periphery in Eighteenth-Century Literature*. Danvers, MA: Rosemont Publications, 2010.

Watt, Ian. *The Rise of the Novel; Studies in Defoe, Richardson, and Fielding*. Berkeley: University of California Press, 1957.

Weaver, Jace. *The Red Atlantic: American Indigenes and the Making of the Modern World, 1000–1927*. Chapel Hill: University of North Carolina Press, 2014.

Weinbrot, Howard D. *Menippean Satire Reconsidered: From Antiquity to the Eighteenth Century*. Baltimore: Johns Hopkins University Press, 2005.

Weston, Peter J. "The Noble Primitive as Bourgeois Subject." *Literature and History* 10.1 (1984): 59–71.

Wheeler, Roxanne. "The Complexion of Desire: Racial Ideology and Mid-Eighteenth-Century British Novels." *Eighteenth-Century Studies* 32.3 (1999): 309–32.

– *The Complexion of Race: Categories of Difference in Eighteenth-Century British Culture*. Philadelphia: University of Pennsylvania Press, 2000.

White, Hayden. *Tropics of Discourse: Essays in Cultural Criticism*. Baltimore: Johns Hopkins University Press, 1978.

White, Richard. *The Middle Ground: Indians, Empires, and Republics in the Great Lakes Region, 1650–1815*. Cambridge: Cambridge University Press, 1991.

Whitney, Lois. *Primitivism and the Idea of Progress in English Popular Literature of the Eighteenth Century*. 1934. New York: Octagon Books, 1965.

Wilson, Kathleen. "Empire, Gender, and Modernity in the Eighteenth Century." In *Gender and Empire*, edited by Philippa Levine, 14–45. Oxford: Oxford University Press, 2004.

– *The Island Race: Englishness, Empire and Gender in the Eighteenth Century*. London: Routledge, 2003.

Wintroub, Michael. "Civilizing the Savage and Making a King: The Royal Entry Festival of Henry II (Rouen, 1550)." *The Sixteenth Century Journal* 29.2 (Summer 1998): 465–94.

Woodfield, Ian. *English Musicians in the Age of Exploration*. Hillsdale, NY: Pendragan Press, 1995.

Woodward, Arthur. "The Metal Tomahawk: Its Evolution and Distribution in North America." *The Bulletin of the Fort Ticonderoga Museum* VII.3 (January 1946): 2–42.

Worms, Laurence. "Walker, Anthony (1726–1765)." *Oxford Dictionary of National Biography*. Oxford: Oxford UP, 2004; online ed., May 2006. Accessed 26 November 2010.

Wright, Ronald. *Stolen Contents: Five Hundred Years of Conquest and Resistance in the Americas*. New York: Houghton Mifflin, 2005.

Yaya, Isabel. "Wonders of America: The Curiosity Cabinet as a Site of Representation and Knowledge." *Journal of the History of Collections* 20.2 (2008): 173–88.

Zuroski Jenkins, Eugenia. *A Taste for China: English Subjectivity and the Prehistory of Orientalism*. New York: Oxford University Press, 2013.

Index